Inland Waterways of France

Volume 2 – Northeast and Southeast

David Edwards-May

Imray, Laurie, Norie & Wilson Ltd

Published by
Imray, Laurie, Norie & Wilson Ltd
Wych House, St Ives, Cambridgeshire PE27 5BT
England
www.imray.com
2021

All rights reserved. No part of this publication may be reproduced, transmitted or used in any form by any means – graphic, electronic or mechanical, including photocopying, recording, taping or information storage and retrieval systems or otherwise – without the prior permission of the publishers.

First published 1956
5th edition 1984
6th edition 1991
7th edition 2002
8th edition 2010
9th edition 2021 (published in three volumes)

© David Edwards-May 2021

David Edwards-May has asserted his right to be identified as the author of this work, including all unattributed photographs, in accordance with the Copyright, Designs and Patents Act 1988.

ISBN 978 178679 306 5

British Library Cataloguing in Publication Data.
A catalogue record for this book is available from the British Library.

CAUTION
While every care has been taken to ensure accuracy, neither the Publishers nor the Author will hold themselves responsible for errors, omissions or alterations in this publication. They will at all times be grateful to receive information which tends to the improvement of the work.

Printed in Croatia by Denona

Contents

PREFACE 1

INTRODUCTION 3

Part I - PLANNING A CRUISE 9

Part II - ROUTE DESCRIPTIONS AND MAPS 21

CHAPTER IV – NORTHEASTERN FRANCE 23

    37. Canal de la Meuse 24
    38. Canal des Ardennes 30
    39. Moselle 34
    40. Canal de la Marne au Rhin 40
    41. Canal de la Sarre and River Sarre 52
    42. Canal des Vosges 55
    43. Petite Saône 60
    44. Rhin (Rhine) 66
    45. River Ill and Canal du Rhône au Rhin (northern branch) 70
    46. Canal du Rhône au Rhin 76

CHAPTER IV – SOUTHEAST FRANCE 87

    47. Grande Saône 88
    48. River Seille 97
    49. Canal de Pont-de-Vaux 99
    50. Rhône 101
    51. Petit Rhône and Canal de Saint-Gilles 110
    52. Haut Rhône 112
    53a. Canal d'Arles à Fos 116
    53b. Liaison Rhône-Fos-Marseille 118

INDEX 12à

Companion volumes
Inland Waterways of France – Volume 1: North and Centre
Inland Waterways of France – Volume 3: South and West

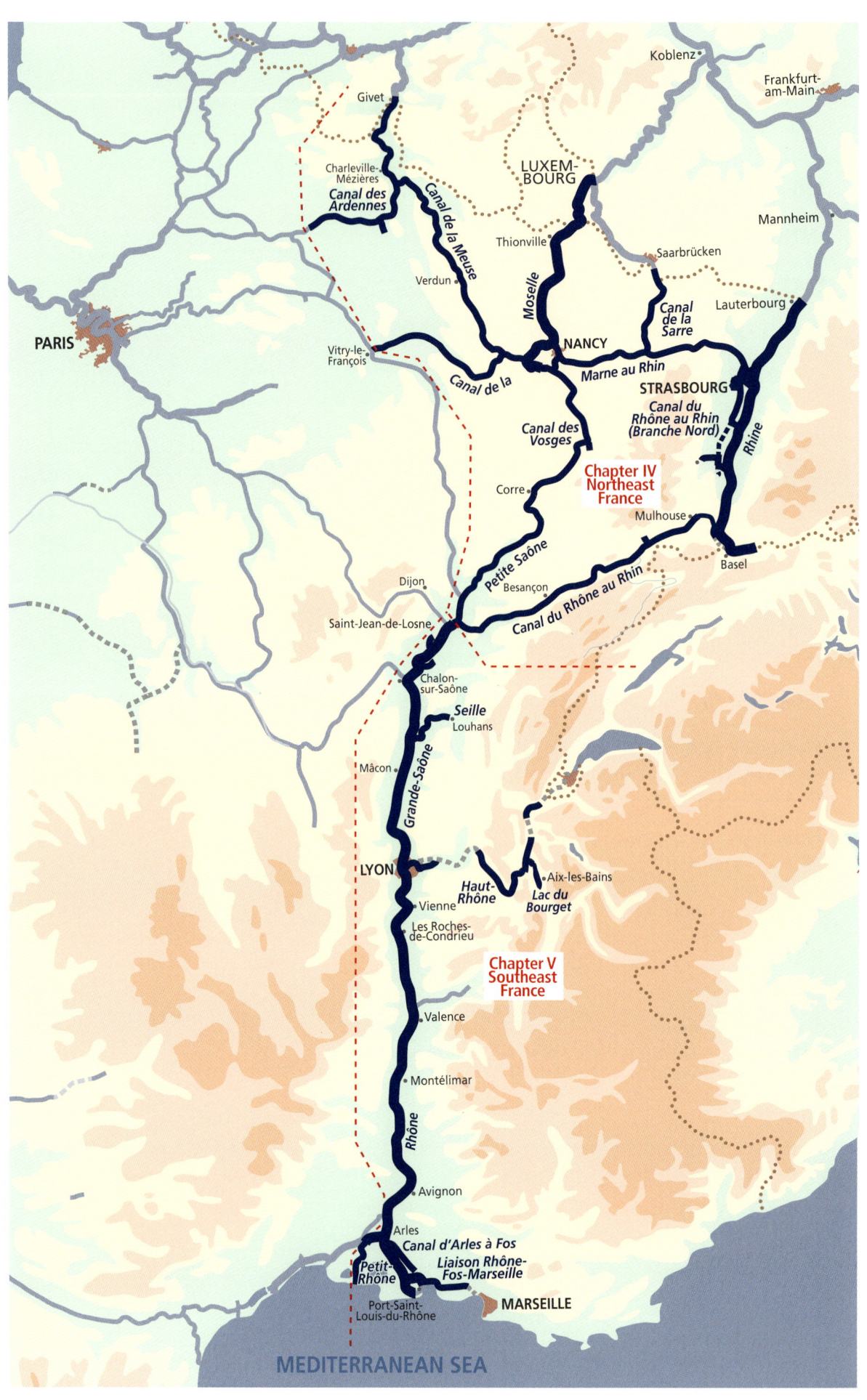

Preface

The ways of enjoying the uniquely diverse and appealing waterways of France are changing. In this digital age, we felt that it was important to publish products that would be of greatest practical use, not only to boaters but also to all the other waterway users who are increasingly attracted to the canal towpaths and river valleys. This work was first published two thirds of a century ago as a single volume presenting nearly 80 waterways in alphabetical order. However, boat ownership, cruising habits, leisure and lifestyle choices have changed significantly over the years, and the extent of useful information has expanded.

Consequently, the 9000 kilometres of navigable waterways in France are now covered by three volumes. Volume 1 covers Northern France down to the capital region Île-de-France, central France and Burgundy. This volume 2 presents the waterways from the northeast to the southeast, hence the classic cruising itineraries from Northern Europe to the Mediterranean Sea via the Rivers Meuse, Moselle, Sarre or Rhine, converging on the 'common trunk' of the Saône and Rhône. Volume 3 brings together all the other navigable waterways, from Southern France (the 'Midi') via the rivers flowing into the Atlantic Coast, to the remarkable network of canals and canalised rivers in Brittany.

Among the reasons for expanding into three volumes is the insertion of descriptive texts – and more images – into the itineraries, to do better justice to the varied places encountered along the waterways. The new texts break up the former 'distance tables'. These texts do not pretend to replace tourist guides for the places visited, but give some context and tips, relating either to the mooring facility itself or to the corresponding town or village.

For convenience and reference, the sequence of eight chapters is continued through the three volumes. This volume includes Chapter IV, Northeastern France, and Chapter V, Southeast France. Each volume has its separate index. We hope that all those who love exploring the French waterways, or who are planning future adventures, will find all three of the expanded, split publications both an inspiration to extend their own travels and practical to use while actually navigating on the system.

As author I am indebted to James Newcombe for his contributions and extensive feedback from users. His website, **french-waterways.com**, reproduces much of the contents of this work, and by agreement with Imray is the place to go for updates for any specific route or waterway.

Imray's editor Jane Russell was a forensic proof-reader whose corrections and suggestions have added significant value to the guide. Both Jane and Imray's managing director Lucy Wilson gave constant guidance and encouragement during the preparation of this work, and for that the author is truly grateful.

Voies Navigables de France has given the author meaningful support for this edition, as in the past, through its Development Department and the unit in charge of waterway tourism and services to users, with special thanks to Aurélie Millot, Nicolas Delaporte and Adrien Quivoron. VNF is to be credited for its efforts to develop 'green' navigation by providing battery charging stations on the waterways of the northeast: the Canal de la Sarre and Canal de la Marne au Rhin. With significant post-pandemic recovery funding by the French Government, agreed in 2021 with the Grand Est region, it is to be hoped that the rest of the system – both the VNF network and the waterways managed by the regions and départements – will be similarly equipped as soon as possible, gradually making navigation greener and quieter.

The author is also grateful to the many contributors of photographs as well as information updates and corrections since the last edition was produced.

I would like to thank here my family and friends who have accompanied me in my own travels on the waterways in the last 10 years, Padraic Neville, who cycled with me on the towpaths from Givet to Paris in 2017, and Thierry and Catherine Eschbach, owners of the 1600-tonne *Bucentaure*, for the memorable voyage on the Seine from Tancarville to the Port of Gennevilliers in February 2019.

Finally, my thanks to all boaters, *plaisanciers* and *Sportsschiffer* – and the surviving *mariniers* in their 220-tonne barges – for their confidence and continued reference to this work.

David Edwards-May, July 2021

For Émilie and Charlotte

Introduction

FRANCE IS THE WORLD'S number one holiday destination, and the country's waterways have become increasingly popular with tourists from across the world. River cruise ships ply all the high-capacity (*grand gabarit*) waterways, making up one fifth of the network of around 8500 km; hotel barges offer all-inclusive cultural and gastronomic cruises on the smaller canals; comfortable self-drive boats may be hired at nearly a hundred locations. Considering the value of all these products and the €2 billion of economic activity generated annually, there is understandably a keen awareness among decision-makers – in the French Government and in the various regions concerned – of the importance of maintaining the waterway infrastructure for all these operators, as well as for the commercial traffic, their prime vocation, and providing moorings and services to meet the constantly increasing demand. While hopefully of value also to these other waterway interests, this book – since its first edition in 1956 – has been addressing the particular needs of a user that has often received less attention than the commercial waterway tourism operators: the private boat owner. This is the user category that commands respect for having started waterway tourism in France all those years ago. The boats have changed, becoming larger and more comfortable for living aboard, and the cruising practices even more so, becoming slower and more sustainable, but it is striking how the enthusiasm of boat owners for France as a destination to enjoy through her waterways seems to endure all the possible causes for discouragement. And there have been a few such causes over the years.

When the previous edition of this work was produced, the national managing body *Voies Navigables de France*, set up in 1991, had recently been instructed by the Government to concentrate its efforts on the commercially viable routes, making up less than half of the national network. The canals of Burgundy had been handed over experimentally to Burgundy Region, a move that seemingly announced the dismemberment of the national network. In fairness to the policy-makers, the principle of transfer of management or even ownership simply takes one stage further the process of devolved administration that began with the concessions to the *départements*, starting with the Brittany canals and Anjou rivers in the 1960s, continuing with the Nivernais in 1971 and the Somme west of Péronne in 1992. However, there is a fundamental difference between these concessions and the situation in the period 2010-2013. In the above examples, local authorities voluntarily accepted to manage the waterways on behalf of the State for a fixed concession period, to keep them open. The Government allocated budgets to renovate structures as required, and made available State employees through the public works administration for each *département*. In short, there was plenty of sugar to help the medicine go down. In recent years, the State has been presenting to regional or local authorities what amounts to an ultimatum: 'take over this sensitive and vulnerable infrastructure, or we close it down'! The experimental management by Burgundy Region was stopped after two years, after it was found by the regional council to be unfeasible. This is the administrative echelon with the least resources, the most recently created (1983) and with neither the organisation nor the experience required to take on such responsibilities. This created a hiatus, and concern among all parties involved in boating and development of waterway tourism. In the absence of any agreement on transfer, all progress in resolving the difficulties inevitably arising on the network was blocked.

In 2013 another significant change was made, when VNF was made an administrative arm of the State, still empowered to collect revenue but no longer a purely commercial body (*établissement public d'intérêt industriel et commercial*, EPIC). The change was brought about largely by a typically French struggle with all the accompanying industrial action and drumbeating. The thousands of public servants on the Ministry's payroll, 'made available' to the commercial body since 1991, refused to give up their *fonctionnaire* status to be employed directly by VNF. The change of status to an *établissement public administratif* enabled a return to a more unified management.

The waterways (in any country, it should be added) are under permanent threats that are more real than the consequences of any administrative and policy decisions: deterioration of the structures, under the combined effects of age and aggression by extreme climate events. This has been the case for a number of canals in recent years. The deal proposed by the Government, through VNF, to the regions and *départements* crossed by little-used rural canals was already unattractive for many while the canals were operating. Imagine how much more difficult the negotiations became after structures failed or the canals silted up, making them impassable!

The French political culture takes brinkmanship to extremes. The worst possible outcome feels certain to occur. Then, at the eleventh hour, pragmatism kicks in and all is resolved! The processes are fascinating to observe, and I have had the privilege of being involved for more than 35 years, but for the foreign boaters whose plans may be thwarted by closure of part of their intended route, the short-term picture may seem bleak.

Fortunately, in 2021, several dramatic situations have been turned round and waterways restored, and with some local nuances the show goes on. I predict that there will be a heightened appreciation of French waterways and all they have to offer as the world comes out of the COVID-19 pandemic that has changed so much in our lives. More French boaters will hopefully join the ranks of the boaters from many other countries, especially the UK, Germany, the Netherlands, Belgium and the Scandinavia, and grow the numbers of boats cruising through most of the year. After the overview of recent developments on the smaller waterways, I will come back to the main VNF network of high-capacity waterways.

Regional and local waterways

After a series of closures of French waterways in recent years, it is heartening that two routes were reopened in 2021.

The **Canal de la Sambre à l'Oise** welcomed boats for the first time in 15 years on July 1, 2021, following a €23.5 million programme of works including the reconstruction of its two aqueducts, dating from 1836 and 1837, renovation of 25 locks on the Oise side of the summit level, and dredging to a depth of 1.60m for the passage of recreational boats. The locks were equipped for automatic operation, and a large volume of marsh pennywort (*hydrocotyle vulgaris*) had to be removed: 30 000 m² was cleared of the weed in 2020.

This success was obtained by vigorous local campaigning and lobbying, and underlined how the future of the waterways can only be guaranteed by bringing together the widest possible partnership. VNF, under pressure from the Ministry of Finance in Bercy, would have let the canal fall into ruin without substantial co-funding of the restoration project by the Hauts-de-France region and the *département* Aisne. The lobbying by local authorities was supported by the international boating community, including DBA The Barge Association and Inland Waterways International, whose members signed an on-line petition. This took the local stakeholders by surprise, and helped them to obtain the exceptional contribution from the Government, enabling VNF to commit to three quarters of the cost.

Local bodies including *Réussir notre Sambre* designed a tourism development strategy to maximise the benefits of the restored waterway. This includes rehabilitating lock cottages to give them new use, improving tourism infastructure and developing the canalside cycleway (*véloroute voie verte*). The partners agreed to share the annual operating costs, estimated at €2.3 million, for a period of 20 years, during which it is hoped that the itinerary will become a magnet and generate economic benefits for the seven districts and the region as a whole.

The **Canal des Ardennes** was closed for a shorter period – just three years – after a lock wall the collapsed at Neuville-Day during an extreme flood on a small stream, and was reopened to navigation on May 1st 2021. Here too, the canal would have been sacrificed by the number-crunchers in Bercy without a concerted effort by the region and Ardennes *département*. VNF signed a 'contract for the territory' with the Grand Est region in October 2020, injecting €43 million into waterway investments in the vast region over the next two years. To be eligible for part of this fund, the *département* Ardennes and the local districts (groups of communes) were required to submit a coherent tourism development plan, with services and activities that will attract tourists to the canal, both by boat and along an extension of the highly successful Trans-Ardennes cycle route, which runs 121 km from above Sedan to Givet. Again, the successful conclusion of this project demonstrates how real the risk of dismemberment of the network has been in recent years. Even before the flood damage occurred at Neuville-Day, this canal was on the list of little-used routes to be 'remaindered', to use the term coined by the UK Government in the late 1960s, when the equivalent axe was poised above many English canals. Up to 20% of VNF's waterways were under threat of being no longer operated, hence the new French word *dénavigation*, which for several years was on the lips of every civil servant involved in setting VNF's budget.

The **lower River Lot** was extended in April 2021 by the opening of the restored lock at Saint-Vite. This is the eighth lock from the Garonne at Nicole, and was rebuilt in a combined investment with construction of a new adjacent hydropower plant. The pandemic and restrictions on movement prevented us from using the opportunity to promote restoration of the remaining missing links upstream.

The first boat through Saint-Vite lock in April 2021

Studies are in progress for a travel-lift solution at Fumel dam, estimated at €500 000 for the lift itself, plus €3.5 million for road access, the actual ramps down into the river above and below the dam, and cutting an approach channel to the ramp from downstream. The project would be funded 50% by the *département* Lot-et-Garonne. A lock here would cost €16 million, which it is believed would have no chance of being approved in the short term. The *tour de table* securing investment in the waterway is more complex than in the two cases examined above. Despite the spectacular progress overall (three quarters of the total length restored and navigable), there are marked contrasts between the 'grand scheme' promoted at the interregional level and the agendas of each *département* involved. For several years the Lot *département* adopted a short-sighted policy, being content to reap the benefits

Introduction

of its 64 km long section with 14 locks opened in 1991. Downstream, Lot-et-Garonne theoretically had the advantage of being connected to the main network. This left Aveyron, upstream, in isolation. When local politicians succeeded in getting the *département* to apply for funding to start restoration at the upstream end of the 266 km waterway, this was opposed by the Lot council, its downstream neighbour! The latter was under pressure from its own local authorities to extend the navigable length, in particular on a new section around Puy-l'Évêque, and tried to divert the funds allocated to Aveyron on the grounds that navigation was not feasible upstream. Their arguments were rejected, and the first 11 km section of the river in Aveyron was opened in 2010. This inside story is only an anecdote, but it serves to underline the risks inherent in the current situation, with planning responsibilities inadequately defined and distributed. The *départements* are also continuing to refuse outright ownership of the waterway, which is maintained and operated by each of the three authorities under the legal regime of *authorisation*. The implications of the change in the river basin authority, from an *entente* to a *syndicat mixte*, are too complex and subtle to develop here; suffice it to say that the political force of the five *départements* of the Lot valley has diminished, while both the French Government and the European Commission have pulled the plug on further investments to complete the project started in 1987. *La lutte continue!*

The history of the **Roubaix Canal** restoration project is also revealing of the difficulty in securing the long-term future of canals for inland navigation. In September 2003, when the EU's Interreg secretariat suggested that the restoration project could be submitted for funding, the local partners were willing to go ahead, but the owner VNF was reluctant to commit itself in contradiction with national policy. Instructions from the ministry were to focus exclusively on the priority network. The mayor of Roubaix succeeded in persuading VNF to be lead partner of the Blue Links project, but VNF insisted that a new owner and operator had to be identified and in place within two years. The *Région* Nord-Pas de Calais refused, which left Lille Métropole as the only 'candidate'. Here the incentive of the EU funding and the cross-border nature of the project meant that the dynamic was maintained despite this difficulty. Eventually *Lille Métropole* agreed in October 2009 to take over canal operation and maintenance for an experimental period of two years starting in May 2010. Boaters and readers of this guide played no small part in this successful outcome, by turning up in significant numbers at the highly successful 'Blue Days' rally at the Union site in Roubaix on September 19-20, 2009. The onerous tasks of operating this essentially urban canal, with its 12 locks and 8 moving bridges, and water supply by back-pumping, has forced the Lille metropolitan council to the brink of a decision to close the canal to navigation, on several occasions in recent years.

The 'northern branch' of the **Canal du Rhône au Rhin** was to be reopened by 2010, establishing a direct connection for boats between Strasbourg and Colmar, but unlike the Roubaix Canal, this project was not completed. This itinerary, avoiding the Rhine, would be open to the hire boats operating in the region. The canal had already been closed, which made it impossible for VNF to operate the completed waterway, even temporarily; it could only be project engineer for the restoration works. These started in 2006, but a year later Alsace regional council interrupted the works. The decision was motivated partly by escalation of costs; the final bill was going to be double the €7 million originally budgeted. But the main reason was that operation and maintenance were going to be entirely at the local authorities' expense, without any contribution or staff available from the French Government, through VNF. The region's intention was then to explore how the half-restored canal could be made to work as an asset without being navigable. The regional council agreed to fund the works after Colmar led a vigorous campaign, securing the support of all riparian municipalities for a sensible compromise solution: Alsace would foot the bill for the works, but the local councils together would operate and maintain the canal. This sequence of events underlined several aspects of the situation throughout the network: first, the *région* was ill-equipped to take on the management of inland waterways; secondly, the economic benefits of waterway tourism are perceived more keenly at the local than at the regional level; consequently, local authority groupings are likely to be increasingly involved in future governance models. This project is now unlikely to be completed in the near future, also because one completely new lock is required to connect the old canal with the lowered pound above lock 75, where the connecting canal from the Rhine enters.

The sorry spectacle of lock 67 on the Canal du Rhône au Rhin in 2017, just north of Marckolsheim; The lock is fully restored while the canal itself remains impassable. Bank consolidation is required before the canal could be filled to its normal depth, but the Region Grand Est no longer wants to complete this project

The **Brittany canals** were complex, because there was an additional level of authority between the *région*, which now owns the system, and the *départements*. Public institutions were set up in the 1960s and 1970s to operate and maintain some waterways, while others continued to be managed directly. These bodies were rendered redundant after the *Région Bretagne* took over. Prospects are now good for the system, since the regional council has recognised their importance for tourism inland, and is continuing to make substantial investments in restoration and dredging. There remains a threat to integrity of the network because of an ongoing campaign to demolish the weirs on the canalised rivers. The main advocates of weir demolition on the Aulne and the Blavet are the angling community and their representative organisations, who want to encourage migrating fish species to return to these rivers. After careful study of the impacts of weir removal, the idea was abandoned as unfeasible. Regional ownership of the waterways has been instrumental in avoiding this scenario of demolition, but the 'return to nature' movement is constantly in ambush, which means that vigilance and education are also a constant challenge. On the other hand, the region is not pursuing the project to build a bypass at the 1923 Guerlédan dam on the **Canal de Nantes à Brest**. The possible solution shown in this book is to be considered as a 'local project'. Local politicians are indeed still pushing hard, and have suggested that the bypass could be completed by about 2025, where the region's reluctance could perhaps be compensated by EDF, owner of the structure. It was EDF's duty under their original concession to ensure the continuity of navigation. In the absence of an act of parliament relieving them of that obligation, it remains in force.

The partnership needed to keep a canal properly maintained and operating, as in the above examples, can never be a foregone conclusion. One VNF waterway that has regrettably been downgraded to canoeable status is the **Scarpe inférieure** between Douai and Saint-Amand-les-Eaux. This was another closure forced by a structural failure, the lift-bridge at Lallaing, in the early 2000s. This made the newly opened *port de plaisance* at Saint-Amand-les-Eaux a *cul-de-sac*. Making the port accessible at least from the downstream junction with the Escaut was indispensable, and a practical solution was found relatively quickly in this case. Operating staff were provided by the community of communes for the Porte du Hainaut district, and are assigned during the season to the lowest two locks on the river. Saint-Amand nevertheless sees little traffic, but the authorities refuse to spend the €15 million required to dredge the waterway and restore its locks and lift bridges. In the absence of local commitment equivalent to that for the Canal des Ardennes, for example, the Scarpe inférieure remains closed. VNF continues to monitor the waterway for hydraulic continuity, and carry out minimal maintenance to ensure efficient conveyance of flood flows, and may count the occasional canoe. This is a sad destiny for the once essential industrial waterway featuring in the novels of Émile Zola.

In other parts of the network, the *départements* have been pursuing their projects without regional support. This is the case of the *Région* Centre, which does not appear to have a strategy for its historic waterways. This may be because they form a disparate and disconnected network, but it is no less regrettable. The **canalised River Cher** suffered a serious setback when the upstream *département* Loir-et-Cher stopped all works on the construction of two new gated weirs, designed to replace dangerous needle weirs. As on the Canal du Rhône au Rhin south of Strasbourg, described above, the authority was alarmed by the escalating cost of the works. A further difficulty stemmed from the local interpretation of the EU's Water Framework Directive. Civil servants, prompted by anglers and environmentalists, saw the possibility of downgrading the river from a canalised or 'heavily modified' state to a natural water body, in other words free-flowing. The downstream *département* of Indre-et-Loire has been resisting this move, supported by the Association *Les Amis du Cher Canalisé*, but negotiations are complex. The State bodies which issue authorisations for works on rivers are insisting that all weirs, old or new, should not be raised until the end of the fish-spawning season on 1st July each year, which naturally calls into question the feasibility of the weir rebuilding programme. The current situation is an unsatisfactory stalemate.

The neighbouring *département* of Loiret has made remarkable progress in restoration of the **Canal d'Orléans**, although the difficulties of water supply to the central summit level section have to date prevented completion of this valuable project. This narrow canal is expected to be opened to electrically-powered craft only, but even that now appears to be a remote prospect.

Another case where spectacular progress was made in the period 2000-2010 is the **Upper Rhône**, which remains a State-owned waterway, theoretically in the priority network for development of navigation, despite having been abandoned more than 70 years ago! Two-lock bypasses were built at the hydropower plants built by CNR at Chautagne and Belley. The Upper Rhône, like the river Loire, serves to cool a nuclear power station, and that is the argument for maintaining the 'officially navigable' status, while navigation is an optional extra to be negotiated on a case-by-case basis. The Upper Rhône scheme faced opposition from environmentalists, whose main concern was to kill for ever any prospect of a Rhine-Rhône waterway by this route and through the Swiss lakes and the canalised river Aar to the Rhine. When the Upper Rhône project was studied in 1999-2000, the *Verts* wanted the locks to be built to smaller than Freycinet dimensions, precisely to prevent any commercial use of the waterway. Recreational boating, in their short-sighted view, could be tolerated as being intrinsically more compatible with protection of the environment. Fortunately this attempt to downgrade the project was resisted, and the new locks were built to Freycinet dimensions, like the earlier lock at La Feyssine in Lyon, built in the 1980s.

Despite the lack of navigable connection with the main system at Lyon, the new locks opened up a remarkable cruising area in the heart of the Alps, extending 75 km with five locks, and this is my local waterway, with the delightful canalside village of Chanaz on the natural Canal de Savières. Works are to start soon on construction of a new lock to bypass the hydropower plant at Brégnier-Cordon, which will add 30 km to this navigation.

Introduction

One of the most emblematic sites on the French waterways is the Briare aqueduct on the Canal latéral à la Loire, opened in 1896.
© SYLVAIN CAMBON

The **Upper Canal de la Somme** is another missing link in the network, which could receive funding as a spinoff from the Seine-Nord Europe Canal project, to restore the 16 km long canal with four locks through the small town of Ham. The canal became silted up and closed in 2006.

These are just a few examples of recent developments on the system. Many other stories could be told, of projects successfully completed or frustrated by political or funding difficulties, as may be experienced in any country. Overall, the situation in France is no more alarming than, say, in Germany or the UK. The risk of cuts in public spending, whether for investments or to subsidise bodies giving a public service, is universal. The main challenges are environmental: to ensure that water resources are not diverted from canal supply to other functions, and to prevent 'downgrading' of river navigations to free-flow conditions by the removal of weirs, as promoted by those who assume, often without foundation, that demolition of structures built 200 years ago will automatically make the rivers more appealing for shad, salmon and other migrators.

To conclude this overview of the smaller waterways, the fact that tourism is France's biggest export industry has justified enormous investments in waterway restoration schemes, adding hundreds of kilometres to the length of the waterway network. It is not unreasonable to predict that the institutional difficulties outlined here will eventually be resolved, as long as we users keep making our voices heard. The inevitable questioning of budget commitments at the State level, and the brinkmanship mentioned above, will doubtless lead to more scares in the future, adding to those caused by extreme climate events.

There will inevitably be some frustrations, as boaters encounter stoppages or cutbacks in service and have to change their plans accordingly. The most frequent incidents are likely to be restrictions on the use of locks across the summit level canals, even closure during extreme drought, but there can be no doubt that the waterways provide the key to enjoyment of many French regions, with all their diversity, their history and culture, their gastronomy and wines. Towns and villages alike have awoken to the vast potential, and are gradually developing boat moorings of varying configurations and size, from the landscaped quay or pontoons, generally referred to by the term *halte nautique*, to the fully-equipped boat harbour or *port de plaisance*. We use the French terms in this guide because they are are so conveniently descriptive. These facilities and the associated information, activities and services will help the boater to get the maximum enjoyment from the cruising experience.

Integrated network for water transport

It feels strange to be heralding impending change in this edition in almost the identical terms to those used in 2010, when I referred to the 'imminent start of works on the new Seine-Nord Europe Canal' but such is the reality of the French Government's seemingly chronic hesitations regarding the waterways and the future role of inland water transport. At least now, works on the first of four sections of the 107 km long canal between Compiègne and Aubencheul-au-Bac, are starting in 2022. Interconnecting the high-capacity (*grand gabarit*) waterways in the interests of Europe as a whole remains VNF's objective and *raison d'être*. A *société de projet* was created by Government decree in December 2016, and a parallel European Economic Interest Group for financial management including toll collection. Management of the project was transferred from the State to the region Hauts-de-France and its four *départements* in 2019. This is a strategic EU infrastructure project. The European Commission is convinced of the intrinsic value of this investment, along with others in the 'Connecting Europe Facility', justifying a 50% contribution to the total cost.

A careful process of studies and consultations had resulted in a consensus among all parties, massively in favour of the project. That was before the economic crisis, followed by the change of government in 2012. The projected cost, based on a public-private partnership, had by then increased from €4.2 to nearly €7 billion. A commission was set up to study possible savings. Its report was presented in late 2013, and suggested a route following the existing Canal du Nord for 8 km and eliminating one lock, lowering the summit level by 18.5 m. This modified route was formally adopted in 2018. The canal is divided into four distinct sections for the works and contracts, starting from the southern end. The first section along the river Oise should open in 2027, and the rest of the canal in 2028.

The link is projected to increase waterborne traffic on the Paris-Lille axis from 4 million to 13-15 million tonnes per year by 2030. Nearly all this traffic would be transferred from the A1 motorway, the busiest in France.

Implementation of the project should confirm a deep trend, which shows waterway projects as giving a greater overall return on investment than when analysis was based on freight transport alone. A major factor in gaining favour among all politicians was full consideration of the external costs of transport (including accidents, congestion and pollution), which economists and waterway lobbyists had been campaigning for since the 1960s. It was gratifying to see that the arguments were at last taken into consideration. The European Commission and Parliament have played a major role in this process, by pushing for proper accounting of these external costs, estimated at 8% of Europe's GDP.

Environmental concerns, particularly in the Somme valley, are met by routing the canal on the flank of the valley instead of along the bottom. The canal will have 5 locks, their depth ranging between 13 and 26 m, with a sixth lock (6 m rise) on the river Oise above Compiègne.

At least two other significant projects are going ahead. The first, now practically complete, is upgrading to Class Va of the **Canal du Rhône à Sète**, to improve the competitive position of the port of Sète; the second is upgrading to Class Vb of the **Upper River Seine** from Bray to Nogent.

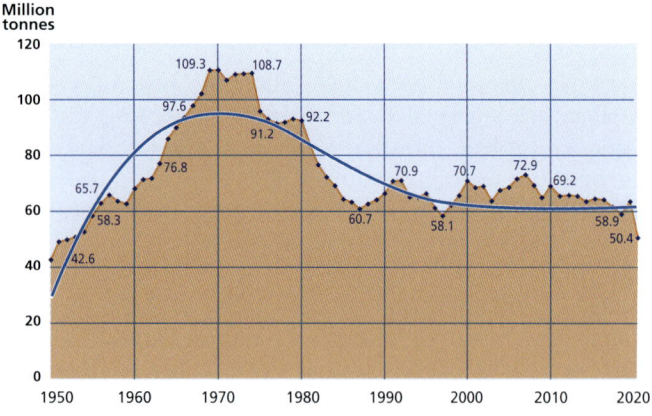

The graph for freight traffic on French waterways, including transit on the Rhine, shows a relative stagnation since the mid-1980s: approximately 65 million tonnes transported annually, for around 8.2 billion tonne-kilometres. The boost expected from the Canal Seine-Nord Europe is now on the horizon, but 2020 showed a significant decline on account of the pandemic.

When the entire Seine basin (a quarter of the French population and economy), already served by high-capacity waterways, is interconnected with the main European network, the mindset of politicians and industry will be radically transformed, and the climate could change for the other major project first conceived by the Roman General Vetus: the North Sea-Mediterranean link between the Moselle and the Saône. Discussions to revive this project started at the regional level a few years after the original project for the Rhine-Rhone waterway was abandoned by Environment Minister Dominique Voynet in 1997. It is premature to talk of a replacement project, because Alsace is not prepared to abandon its interest. Accordingly, the preliminary investigations of the potential for a new Saône-Moselle waterway include the possibility of a branch across the Vosges to link up with the high-capacity waterway in the Mulhouse area. This would roughly correspond to the historic Canal de Montbéliard à la Haute-Saône, which was never completed. The first timid move was made by the *Régions* Lorraine and Rhône-Alpes in 2004, when the question asked of consultants, with support from central Government and the other regions concerned (Bourgogne and Franche-Comté) was simply: is it worth studying the feasibility of a high-capacity waterway to link the Rhine and Rhône basins? The answer was yes, and the Ministry of Sustainable Development approved the subject for a national public debate which was supposed to be organised by VNF in 2012. Although the debate was cancelled, the broad vision of a French waterway system fully integrated in the European waterway network, used for bulk freight and combined transport, remains alive.

In the meantime, the bulk of VNF's investment programme concerns improvements to ageing infrastructure on the existing high-capacity network. New gated weirs have been built on the Oise and bridges are being rebuilt on the Liaison Dunkerque-Escaut to offer the new standard headroom of 7.00m, although some bottlenecks with bridges at 5.25m are likely to remain for at least 10 years.

The limited improvements made to the existing network have proved successful, contributing to a significant increase in overall traffic on the French waterways in recent years. As the graph shows, a 25% increase in tonnage transported was achieved by inland water transport between the low in 1997 and the pre-recession peak in 2007, and the industry has fared better than railway freight since then.

The owner-skippers of *péniches* carrying about 220 tonnes also continue to provide a useful service, but would like to see more maintenance of the canals they operate on. They are concerned that the current policy could gradually make commercial operation unfeasible on the smaller waterways.

On the bigger picture, the long-term trend suggests that the post-war peak of the early 1970s could be reached again by around 2030 or 2035, and the new Seine-Nord Europe Canal would clearly make a significant contribution to this growth.

Part I – Planning a cruise

9000 kilometres of cruising waterways

France has the most extensive waterway network in Europe, offering an extraordinary variety of scenery, tourist interest and cruising conditions. Water-borne transport remains the prime function over about a third of the network and remains a minority user over another quarter. That leaves almost half the above total maintained essentially for tourism and other functions not related to commercial navigation.

Recreation is accepted as one of the main justifications for maintaining the waterways, and considerable development has taken place accordingly. The French nomenclature of places to moor is uniquely practical and descriptive, so we have adopted it widely throughout the work: *port de plaisance* offers the full range of services to be expected of a marina, while *halte* denotes an overnight mooring, often with water and electricity, but not always, and especially not out of season. These facilities have sprung up at an astonishing rate throughout the system. Busy, high-capacity waterways make up more than a third of the 2500 kilometres covered in this volume: the Moselle, Rhine, Grande Saône and Rhône, but the commercial traffic is no obstacle to safe and pleasant cruising, provided certain precautions are taken. This having been said, it is obvious that readers without previous cruising experience should study the Cevni rules to be fully acquainted with all navigation signs and rules of the road. It is preferable to keep initially to the smaller waterways, if possible, where commercial traffic has ceased or is very slight.

Regulations – an overview
Notes by Tam and Di Murrell

(a) Registration documents
Formalities for boats entering France have been greatly simplified. Boat owners wishing to cruise in France, regardless of where and how they arrive, will need the boat's registration documents. Along with the other requirements set out on the following paragraphs, this will permit a stay without fiscal or other complications. The restriction on movements of UK citizens entering France, whose stay is now limited to 180 days, does not apply to their boats permanently moored in France.

Registration is a legal requirement. A boat takes its flag normally from either the nationality of the owner or the country of residence of the owner. Most countries have a simple register and a more complex one, which involves further checks, and tonnage and measurement surveys. In the UK, the Small Ships Register is the simple form of registration, and the Part 1 is the more involved register. Both have the same legal validity throughout the world, and they are both issued by the Registry of Shipping and Seamen in Cardiff (02920 747 333).

(b) VAT documentation
VAT paid in one EU country is recognised throughout the EU and import can be made for an indefinite period without complication. The only conclusive proof that a boat is 'VAT paid' is the original VAT certificate, which is issued to the original owner of a new boat and subsequently passed on to future owners. However, a variety of VAT exemptions apply to boats, and it is important for the traveller to become familiar with these rules prior to going abroad. For readers in the UK, the best place to get hold of this information is from the Revenue and Customs website, where various notices are available on line and can be downloaded. The address for Revenue and Customs is **http://customs.hmrc.gov.uk**. Particularly relevant is Notice 8 *Sailing your pleasure craft to and from the United Kingdom*. This summarises the main VAT rules, including the possibility of applying for exemption from VAT in the UK if the boat is to be permanently located in the EU under the 'Sailway' scheme. Then of course VAT will have to be paid in the destination country, as well as import duty. The site also explains the rules relating to temporary importation. Owners may bring their boat into the EU and use it for up to 18 months in a 2-year period without being liable for VAT.

HMC Notice 200 gives further details on temporary import, while notice 728 now applies only to boats moved from Northern Ireland to the EU, pending the drafting of the equivalent rules for the rest of the UK as a third state.

The general rule that remains applicable is that VAT is payable either in the country of purchase at that country's rate, or at the rate applicable in country of destination.

(c) Marine insurance
Insurance is compulsory on the inland waterways of Europe. In some cases it may be a requirement for the insurance documents to be translated. For further details refer to the relevant countries listed in the RYA's Foreign Cruising Guides, published jointly with The Cruising Association. These publications detail the regulations for European countries and list the documentary requirements of both the boat and the crew, including a section on inland waterways.

(d) Ship's radio licence
A radio telephone ship licence is required for every British ship with radio telephonic equipment installed, intended for public correspondence use. For British registered ships, this licence is available from the Radio Licensing Centre. The user should also have an operator's licence for the appliance.

(e) Helmsman's licence
Skippers of craft navigating inland need to hold a valid certificate of competence, and inland waterway regulations come into effect once a vessel is upstream of the seaward

limit of each estuary. The category of licence required is determined by the size of craft and the power of the engine. There is an exemption for boats less than 5m with no cabin and with a power factor T less than 1, calculated by the formula T = hp of the engine multiplied by 1.9, this sum then divided by the square of the boat's length. By this formula a 4.9 m long boat with a 12.5 hp engine just qualifies for exemption. The helmsman must be 16 or over.

(f) International Certificate of Competence

UN Resolution 40 introduced a Europe-wide helmsman's licence, known as an International Certificate of Competence (ICC). It is issued after a test of practical ability and knowledge of the 'rules of the road', and is available for cruising with a sail boat and/or a motor-driven one, with the test being taken on an appropriate craft. To gain an ICC with coastal endorsement requires a test of knowledge of the International Regulations for Preventing Collisions at Sea (COLREGS), and for an inland endorsement a test of the CEVNI rules, which govern inland boating. In the UK the ICC is issued by the Royal Yachting Association.

In 2011 the European Boating Association and DBA The Barge Association, along with the RYA, succeeded in getting an amendment to Resolution 40. Non-EU residents can be issued an ICC by countries which have accepted the Resolution. Residents/nationals of an EU country can only get theirs from the country where they live. A valuable study book for the ICC inland endorsement is the *RYA Book of European Waterways Regulations*. This book should be carried on board, but a copy of the CEVNI rules in the language of the country one is cruising is also worth having on board, as a courtesy towards the navigation authority.

Inland boating certificates issued by non-EU countries are not generally accepted, as the CEVNI rules are specific to the interconnected European inland waterways, and differ in significant ways from the COLREGS in use at sea. The study book for the ICC Inland endorsement is the RYA Book of *European Waterways Regulations*, which will also satisfy the requirement that a copy of the CEVNI rules is carried on board.

(g) French Certificates of Competence

French helmsman licences were reorganised in 2008. There are two categories of inland licence for recreational craft: a *Permis Plaisance* for craft between 5m and 20m, and an *Extension Grande Plaisance* for craft 20m and over. They can be held by persons of any nationality. The *Permis Plaisance* requires brief practical instruction on a small craft, and then a computerised multichoice test of knowledge of the CEVNI rules, in French. A person requiring the Extension Licence, whether for a larger craft or as a first step to a commercial licence for taking passengers on board, *must* first gain the small craft licence. There is then a minimum of nine further hours demonstrating ability to carry out common boating manoeuvres on an appropriate-sized vessel, plus instruction on various safety matters. The minimum age for holders of an Extension licence is 18.

A special temporary certificate called *Carte de Plaisance* is issued by the boat hire firms to all clients not in possession of one of the above, for cruising on waterways that are considered relatively safe. The hire firm is obliged to spend sufficient time with each client to explain the boat's operation and handling.

(h) Community Inland Navigation Certificate (ES-TRIN, formerly TRIWV))

This originates with the 2006 and ongoing UN Resolution No. 61. Various countries previously had their own rules for construction and equipping craft, and the ES-TRIN are intended to harmonise standards throughout the jurisdiction of the ECE, now including the Rhine. All craft over 20m on European inland waters must have a Certificate of Conformity, which will be issued by authorised bodies of any of the countries concerned (this does not have to be the country of registry).

(i) Boat licences – péage plaisance

Licences were introduced when Voies Navigables de France (VNF) was set up in 1991. The *péage* is payable by all boats for use of the waterways managed by VNF, per day of navigation, with or without passage through locks. Boats are divided into four categories, defined by length. (Regrettably, this penalises English narrow boats.) The table below gives the rates in € applicable in 2021 for each licence period: liberté or freedom, corresponding to the former annual licence, loisirs or monthly (30 days), 7 days and 1 day. The facsimile reproduced here shows the current vignette, which where the category, year and date of validity are clearly displayed.

The vignette is now easily purchased online – **vnf.fr/vnf/services/acheter-sa-vignette** – and printed at home, entering the boat owner's name and address, the boat's name and draught, length overall, the boat's registration number, or failing that, its serial number, the category of *vignette* required and the corresponding start date (for the *Loisirs*, 7-day and 1-day *vignettes*), a scan of the navigation permit, sea permit or French registration certificate, as well as proof of engine capacity. Payment is by debit or credit card. It is also possible to acquire the vignette at one of VNF's 31 designated customer service offices, which often correspond to the local offices listed in this guide.

VNF LICENCE RATES (VIGNETTE) 2021

Categories	I <8m	II 8<11m	III 11<14m	IV ≥14m
Liberté [1]	8.90 x L + 89.00	8.90 x L + 205.90	8.90 x L + 392.10	8.90 x L + 511.80
Loisirs [2]	7.80 x L + 28.60	7.80 x L + 41.60	7.80 x L + 54.40	7.80 x L + 69.50
7 days [3]	4.20 x L + 15.90	4.20 x L + 24.00	4.20 x L + 31.90	4.20 x L + 39.70
Per day [4]	3.20 x L + 11.70	3.20 x L + 17.60	3.20 x L + 23.10	3.20 x L + 28.70

1 Issued for the calendar year (1st January to 31st December)
2 Issued for 30 consecutive days
3 Issued for 7 consecutive days
4 Issued for any specified day

The amount is calculated according to the duration of navigation and the vessel's length. It is rounded up to the nearest decimal point. The calculation of the price of the vignette includes a variable part depending on the length of the boat (as indicated on the certificate of registration) and a fixed lump-sum part.
A discount of 17% is applied to the «Liberté» vignette only, if acquired before March 31.

The formalities indicated above are a small price to pay for the freedom enjoyed while cruising through the French waterways. Occasionally, generally at a lock, a boat owner will be asked for his ship's registration papers in order to furnish basic information; the boat's name, number and port of registry, and ownership details. He may also be asked to show his vignette.

The distinction between time spent navigating and time spent at a long-term mooring is important. The licence gives the right to moor free of charge for up to 48 hours anywhere on the network, or until asked to move on (a very rare occurrence, although charges are made at harbours leased to a public or private operator).

Long-term moorings are subject either to the charges applied by the harbour concessionary, or to a mooring lease or *autorisation d'occupation temporaire* (AOT) to be obtained from VNF.

Trailer sailing

Owners of trailed craft will find it much easier than in the past to launch on the French waterways. Facilities for boats have mushroomed, and the *ports de plaisance* are usually equipped with a slipway or crane suitable for most trailed boats. Hire firms also welcome private boats to make use of their facilities, except out of season or at weekends when they are busy turning round their own boats. Generally speaking, boat harbours with slipways are encountered more frequently on river navigations than on canals. Most facilities are indicated in the route descriptions, but reference may also be made to the individual waterway guides listed under *Guides and publications*.

If you are planning on trailer-sailing, the maximum authorised dimensions of vehicle and trailer without special permission and documentation are as follows: height, no restriction (but 4m is the practical maximum); overall width, 2.50m; overall vehicle length 12m, and overall trailer length, 12m. The vehicle/trailer combination should not exceed 18.5m. The RYA legal department publishes a booklet on trailer sailing.

Hire boats

A convenient way of discovering France through her waterways is to hire a comfortable cruiser (*houseboat* in French), ideally suited to inland navigation. There are about 100 hire bases operating on the French waterways, belonging to 50 separate companies, with a total of about 1800 boats. It is thus now possible to plan a week's cruise virtually anywhere on the network. Only the waterways between the Seine basin and north-eastern France remain poorly represented.

Listing all hire firms is a risky exercise, for changes occur from one season to the next, but it worth setting out all the details, for hire bases are such an important part of the French waterway scene. Bases are listed in alphabetical order by region. These include a number of relay bases which are operated mainly to allow clients to cruise one-way only. The possibility of one-way cruises is indicated.

There is no point in contacting the individual bases of the bigger firms for reservations, which are all centralised. These companies are listed under the first heading 'Central reservation offices'. Their web sites are not repeated under the individual entries.

Many of the smaller firms can offer high-quality boats at reasonable prices. Generally speaking, where lower prices can be obtained for a boat with the same number of berths, clients will get less for their money (older, smaller, less well-equipped and less comfortable boats).

Given the considerable choice of cruising areas, decide first which waterway and which region appeal to you most, and then consult the web sites or ask to be sent the brochures of the various firms operating in the area. Study carefully the characteristics of the boats and their equipment, and compare the dimensions of boats rather than taking for granted the spaciousness apparent in the wide-angle photographs.

Part I

Central reservation offices

Name	Tel	Website	Details
FPP Travel (Canalous)	03 85 53 76 70	fpp.travel	agency for a network of several small French operators
Le Boat	04 68 94 42 80	leboat.com	combines former Crown Blue Line and Connoisseur
Locaboat Holidays	03 86 91 72 72	locaboat.com	14 bases throughout France
Nicols Locations	02 41 56 46 56	nicols.com	8 bases throughout France, and agent for others

Northeastern France

Ardennes Nautisme	Pont-à-Bar	ardennes-nautisme.com	at the junction of the Meuse and Canal des Ardennes
Canal Evasion	Mittersheim	canal-evasion.fr	on the Canal de la Sarre
Canalous Plaisance	Languimberg	canalous-alsace.com	on the Canal de la Sarre
Canalous Plaisance	Waltenheim-sur-Zorn		Marne-Rhine, one-way to Languimberg
Kuhnle Tours	Niderviller	marina-niderviller.fr	Marne-Rhine, on the Vosges summit level
Le Boat	Hesse		Marne-Rhine, one-way to Boofzheim
Le Boat	Boofzheim		on the Canal du Rhône au Rhin (branche Nord)
Le Boat	Fontenoy-le-Château		Canal des Vosges, one-way to Gray (one week)
Locaboat Holidays	Pont-à-Bar		at the junction of the Meuse and Canal des Ardennes
Locaboat Holidays	Lutzelbourg		Marne-Rhine near Vosges summit (no one-way)
Meuse Nautic	Dun-sur-Meuse	valdunois.fr	Canal de la Meuse
Nicols Alsace	Saverne	nicols.com	Marne-Rhine, one-way to Harskirchen
Nicols Alsace	Harskirchen		at the junction of Marne-Rhine and Canal de la Sarre
Navig'France	Saverne	navigfrance.com	Marne-Rhine east of the summit level
Navig'France	Lagarde	navigfrance.com	Marne-Rhine on the Vosges summit level

Franche-Comté and Saône

Canalous Plaisance	Pontailler-sur-Saône		Saône, one-way to Louhans (1 week)
Canalous Plaisance	Louhans		Saône, one-way to Pontailler-sur-Saône (1 week)
Franche-Comté Nautic	Port-sur-Saône	fcnautic.com	Upper Saône, one-way cruises to Dole on the Doubs
Le Boat	Branges		Seille and one-way to Gray or Saint-Jean-de-Losne
Le Boat	Gray		on the upper Saône
Le Boat	Saint-Jean-de-Losne		Saône, one-way to Fontenay-le-Château
Locaboat Holidays	Scey-sur-Saône		Saône, one-way to Saint-Léger and Deluz
Locaboat Holidays	Deluz		Canal du Rhône au Rhin, one-way to Scey-sur-Saône
Locaboat Holidays	Mâcon		Saône
Nicols	Dole		Canal du Rhône au Rhin, one-way to Port-sur-Saône
Pavillon Saône	Tournus	house-boat.net	Bourgogne
Saône Plaisance	Louhans	saone-plaisance.com	at the end of the river Seille
Saône Plaisance	Seveux	saone-plaisance.com	on the Upper Saône

Canalous Plaisance hire boat (a Tarpon 42) in La Truchère lock on the river Seille

Planning a cruise

Navigable dimensions
The waterways of France in this volume (northeast to southeast) may be divided into three categories.

High-capacity (grand gabarit) waterways (Class V)
These are the Moselle, the Rhine, the and the Rhône, and part of the Petit-Rhône leading to the Canal du Rhône à Sète. Navigable dimensions obviously present no constraint for boats and barges on these waterways, which offer lock dimensions of at least 110m by 12m, a minimum navigable draught of 2.50m and a minimum air draught of 5m. These make up 900km of the 2500km covered in this volume.

'Freycinet' waterways (Class I)
Most of the waterways come into this category, offering standard dimensions established in 1879 by the Minister of Public Works Charles Louis de Saulces de Freycinet. Here too, the dimensions are ample for most boats, with minimum lock dimensions of 38.50m by 5.10m, minimum navigable draught of 1.80m and a minimum air draught of 3.40m (generally 3.50m). It must be noted, however, that the available depth on many canals is far short of the theoretical 2.20m, and that barges are increasingly forced to waste valuable energy ploughing their furrow through the thick layer of sediment that has deposited on the bed over the years. The remaining commercial carriers are even forced off the routes restored for recreational navigation, where the funding was agreed for dredging for a loading depth of 1.60m instead of the historic 1.80m. This reduced draught also of course excludes many recreational craft, especially yachts.

Smaller waterways (Class 0)
Here dimensions are more critical, especially for barges or deep-keeled yachts. Only two waterways in this volume come into this category:

Route	Length	Beam	Draught	Air Draught
Seille	30.40	5.20	1.50	3.90
Canal de Savières	18.00	4.00	1.60	3.50

The Canal de Savières is in any event part of an isolated waterway, the Upper Rhône, which it links to Lake Bourget.

Rules of the road
The rules of the road are relatively easy to comply with, and the ability to handle one's boat precisely and confidently is just as important as theoretical knowledge of the waterway code. The rules to be observed by boaters are documented thoroughly in the RYA *Book of European Waterway Regulations* by Tam Murrell, but some of the main points are summarised in the following paragraphs.

Priority to commercial traffic and other barges
Smaller boats must at all times leave room for barges to proceed on their course and to manoeuvre. Barges must never be forced by small boats to steer clear. Skippers of boats must constantly bear in mind this priority to working boats, including trip boats. They must also steer well clear of all craft under way, dredgers and other maintenance vessels, and any work sites on the waterways.

Meeting other craft (croisement)
Boats may pass each other only when the channel is wide enough, taking into account local circumstances and other traffic movements. Boats whose respective courses are such that there is no risk of collision must not alter their course or their speed in a manner likely to cause a risk of collision. Boats meeting must normally keep to the right (passing port to port). There is an exception to this rule (more important for barges than for small boats) on wider river navigations, where it is normal practice for boats heading upstream to keep to the inside of the channel in bends to take advantage of the slacker water, while boats heading downstream keep to the middle of the channel. This practice is covered by the international 'blue flag' rule, under which the upstream-bound barge wishing to keep to the left makes its intention clear by displaying a blue flag or panel on the right-hand side of the wheelhouse (or by night, a flashing white light). The barge heading downstream acknowledges by displaying its blue flag or flashing white light, and adopts the corresponding course. If the skipper of the first barge fears his intention has not been understood, he sounds two short blasts (to pass on the left), and this signal must be acknowledged. (Similarly, one short blast confirms the intention to pass normally on the right, and must be acknowledged.) Small craft are not bound to observe this rule, but being aware of it makes it that much easier to comply with the number one rule of priority to commercial craft.

On French river navigations, there are certain sections where all craft are forced by these conventional signs to cross over or keep to the 'wrong' side of the channel and pass oncoming boats starboard-to-starboard. Here too, the blue flag is normally displayed. At points where the course thus changes sides it is the boat heading downstream which has priority, the upstream-bound boat slowing down or stopping as necessary. Where there is insufficient width for two barges to pass abreast, this prohibition sign is often displayed. On encountering this sign, a boat must not proceed until the skipper has satisfied himself that the channel in the restricted section is not occupied. Barge skippers communicate by radio at such locations, using the ship-to-ship channel 10; boaters should proceed cautiously, sounding a long blast on their horn as appropriate. Generally speaking, it is the boat heading downstream which has priority over that heading upstream.

Overtaking (dépassement or trématage)
Overtaking normally takes place on the left. Only on wide river navigations may overtaking on the right be envisaged. The skipper of the overtaking boat must strictly indicate his intention by displaying a blue flag at the bow. If the overtaken vessel has to modify its course or speed to facilitate this manoeuvre, the overtaking one shall sound

two long blasts followed by one short one to signal he is overtaking to starboard, or two long blasts followed by two short ones for overtaking to port. Boaters must not accelerate momentarily for the exclusive purpose of passing another boat or barge, and should bear in mind that it is forbidden to overtake (a) whenever it is not certain that the manoeuvre can be effected safely, (b) within 500m from a lock and (c) wherever these prohibition signs  are displayed. Generally speaking, never try to overtake a barge on the 'Freycinet' canals unless invited to do so by the barge skipper, since this can be a dangerous manoeuvre. If no such invitation is forthcoming, and the boat skipper is certain that there is time to get far enough ahead of the barge before the next lock is reached not to cause any delay (in practice, this means that the next lock must be at least 2 or 3 kilometres away), he may signal his intention to overtake by sounding two long blasts and two short (to overtake normally to port). It is then permitted to overtake unless the barge skipper sounds one short blast, meaning that he would prefer to be overtaken to starboard, or five short blasts, meaning that he considers it unsafe or inappropriate to be overtaken at this point. However, only experienced navigators with loud horns should indulge in such dialogue; it is simpler, especially on a heavily-locked canal, to moor when the opportunity arises and let the barge get well ahead.

Turning (virement)
When a boat wishes to turn to head in the opposite direction, notice of the intention is to be given by one prolonged blast on the horn, followed by one short blast if swinging to the right and two short blasts if swinging to the left.

Navigation signs
The most common navigation signs are shown opposite.

Speed limits
The special regulations for each waterway (*règlement particulier de police de la navigation intérieure*) lay down speed limits, and the owner of any boat exceeding the authorised limit renders himself liable to prosecution. Throughout the smaller canal network the limit is 6km/h (3.7 miles/hour) for barges and pleasure boats displacing more than 20 tonnes, reduced to 4km/h for the passage of movable bridges and navigation at night (where allowed). The limit is eased to 8km/h and in some cases 10km/h for boats of less than 20 tonnes. One of the uses of the tables, with distances precise to within 100m, is to allow speed to be checked. In practice, however, speed in the smaller canals should constantly be adapted to local conditions, the basic rule being to ease off whenever the boat causes wash to break on the banks, as well as when passing moored boats and anglers, thus avoiding damage in the first case and unpleasantness in the second.

On canalised rivers, higher speeds are authorised in river sections than in lock-cuts or canal sections. For example, the limits are respectively 15km/h and 6km/h on the Marne, on the Saône above Auxonne and on the Yonne, while the maximum on the smaller river navigations is 10km/h.

On the large-scale waterways, much higher limits are applied, generally 15km/h in canals or lock-cuts and up to 35km/h in open river sections. Speeds higher still, up to 60km/h, are allowed on specified short reaches for the practice of water-skiing and small power boating only. It must be underlined that local restrictions may be applied on any waterway, and indicated by the conventional speed limit sign shown in the section on navigation signs.

Locks
Different recommendations must be given for negotiating locks according to the four main types of lock encountered on the network.

High-capacity (grand gabarit) waterways
The big locks on these waterways (as defined under navigable dimensions) are all controlled by lock-keepers, normally from a control tower located midway in the lock basin on one side or the other. The automatic lock filling or emptying sequences (and corresponding light displays for navigators) are subordinated to the lock-keepers' decisions, based on the observed or announced traffic situation. A boat navigating singly may thus be kept waiting for 20 minutes or longer if the lock is ready for a barge announced in the other direction. This is allowed for by the regulations, so do not be surprised if the double red light display persists for that time. In case of doubt, moor at one of the dolphins providing access to the bank and approach the lock-keeper to announce your arrival. Alternatively, a VHF radio call number is listed in the route descriptions for locks on these large-scale waterways, and lock-keepers may be called on VHF for an inquiry or to announce your arrival time. A single red or red and green lights side by side mean that the lock is being prepared. Wait until the double green light is displayed before entering the lock. If there are barges or other craft queueing at the lock, take your place in the queue, but in any event when the double green light shows, allow all barges to enter the lock first. When traffic is heavy, the lock-keeper will generally wave or use a loud-hailer to call boats into the spaces remaining in the lock chamber. Avoid coming close to a barge's stern until she has stopped in the chamber, in case there is an unexpected last-minute use of reverse at high revs causing pronounced turbulence for some distance behind the prop. The deepest locks have floating bollards or a series of bollards set in the wall vertically at intervals of one or two metres. These are referred to as 'step bollards' and require a certain amount of juggling with the bow and stern lines as the water level rises or falls. The recommended procedure here is to have two lines available or one lengthy line with an eye at each end at both bow and stern. This allows use of the 'one on - one off' method as you rise or fall. It is forbidden to make fast to the rungs of a ladder between two sets of bollards. It is sometimes more convenient to come alongside a barge (with the skipper's permission) and make fast to its bollards.

Automated locks on smaller waterways
To reduce operating costs on the smaller canals and canalised rivers (for example, the Canal de la Marne au Rhin, the Canal des Vosges and the Petite-Saône), a large number of locks have been equipped for fully automated

Planning a cruise

LIGHTS AT LOCKS

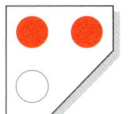    

Wait | Wait (lock in operation) | Wait, lock is being prepared | Enter the lock now | Lock not operational

OTHER LIGHTS

No entry to basin or channel indicated by white arrow

MANDATORY & WARNING SIGNS

No entry | No overtaking | No meeting or overtaking (i.e. single lane) | No mooring or anchoring | No anchoring | No mooring | No turning (winding) | Do not create wash | Motor boats forbidden

Proceed in direction indicated | Stop | Speed limit | Make a sound signal | Unspecified hazard | Major waterway ahead | Headroom limited | Width of passage or channel limited | Keep this distance from bank

Make radio contact with waterway staff* | Cross channel to pass boats starboard to starboard | Cross channel to pass boats port to port (normal) | Keep to port | Keep to starboard | Channel moves to port | Channel moves to starboard | No passage outside marked limits

* Note that channel 10 is the ship-to-ship channel on inland waterways throughout the continent.

OTHER SIGNS (RECOMMENDATORY OR INFORMATIVE)

Weir | Ferry | Chain ferry | Side turning | Tributary waterway | Priority waterway | Berthing permitted | Anchoring permitted | Making fast permitted | Turning

Recommended direction | Electricity cable | End of prohibition or restriction

SIGNS ON BRIDGES

Keep within limits (green) | Recommended channel (in both directions) | Passage only in direction indicated (other direction prohibited)

SOUNDS

- — Attention
- • I am moving (or holding) to starboard
- •• I am moving (or holding) to port
- ••• I am going astern
- •••• I am incapable of manoeuvring
- •••••• (6 very short) Imminent danger of collision
- — — — — (repeated) Distress signal
- — • I am turning to starboard
- — •• I am turning to port

Part I

*Don't forget to put on your lifejackets when passing locks on the high-capacity waterways! This is **Pacific** skipper Samuel in Dracé lock on the Saône.*

or semi-automatic operation. These locks, often grouped together and referred to as a *chaîne* or flight, are equipped with lights, with the same meanings as above: red = wait, red plus green = lock in preparation, and green = proceed into lock. A system of advanced detection registers the boat's arrival some distance before the lock. This system may be automatic (radar) or will involve using a remote control supplied by the lock-keeper at either end of the flight. Some canals still have the simple device of a pole suspended above the water, which needs to be given a quarter turn.

A flashing orange light near the detector, or the red plus green light display at the lock, means that the boat has been detected. When the green light is displayed, proceed slowly into the lock. Some locks have a chamber entry/exit detector, either a photoelectric sensor or on older locks a horizontal pole to be pushed forwards by your boat for at least 5 seconds. Once the boat is safely moored in the chamber, raise the blue rod situated on the edge of the lock, to start the automatic lock filling or emptying sequence. It will take a few seconds for the command to be registered. The red rod is be pulled in a case of emergency only. This not only stops the sequence, but shuts down the entire system, and requires intervention by waterway staff to set it up again. If it is an actual case of emergency requiring a rapid response you should also call on the interphone to advise someone of this, or your problem will simply be treated as a lock out of action, and an itinerant lock keeper will come to repair it in due course. At the end of the cycle, the gates open automatically. It is important to clear the chamber promptly. It should be noted that a group of boats locking together should pass the radar detector in close file. If the lock fails to start or fails in mid-sequence, use the telephone (interphone) outside the lock cabin.

Once in a flight it is important to maintain a constant speed between locks, and if it is decided to stop, if only for lunch, before the flight is completed, the lock-keepers must be notified of this intention. They are normally stationed at each end of the flight. In an emergency or in case of breakdown, they can be also be contacted by two-way telephone outside the small control cabinet beside each lock. If conditions are extremely difficult (strong wind or heavy rain, for example), the section lock-keeper will often be seen on the towpath on his scooter ascertaining that all is well.

Locks operated by lock-keepers

Staff cutbacks everywhere – on the VNF network and on the other waterways – combined with the cheap technology available for mechanal operation, whether automated or not, mean that there are now precious few locks on the 'Freycinet' network that are still operated by lock-keepers. It is not usually necessary to warn the lock-keeper of your arrival, but a short, polite beep on the horn may be required if there is no sign of any activity. Be sure not to do this during the lunch break, however! No action is necessary if other traffic is moored up waiting to lock through. In any event, it is advisable to make a complete stop 50m from the lock, to wait until the lock-keeper signals permission to enter, or until the gates are completely open. While waiting, if it is preferred not to moor up to the bank, care should be taken not to obstruct the passage of any boat which may emerge from the lock when the gates are opened. On entering the lock (at low speed), arrange for one of the crew to alight on the side opposite the lock-keeper, normally the towpath side, or whichever side he is not working. Having attended to the boat's lines it is customary to assist in working the lock (closing one of the gates when the boat has entered the lock, possibly working the gate paddles and opening the gate on the same side when the lock is ready). Some of the older locks on the Seine and Yonne have sloping sides, requiring particular caution, especially when descending. It is often possible and preferable to pass your mooring lines to the lock-keeper as you enter these particular locks. Be ready to bear off with boat-hooks, preferably one forward and one aft. Many of these sloping-sided locks have been upgraded in recent years, with a floating pontoon inside the chamber. This facility is suitable only for smaller vessels, unfortunately!

A recent development which is changing the practical arrangements for passing locks on considerable lengths of canal is the complete reorganisation of waterway personnel, the numbers of permanently posted lock-keepers being drastically reduced (by non-replaced departures or transfers to maintenance staff). Locks on designated sections are thus attended by mobile teams, which follow boats through successive locks, in some cases only two but perhaps as many as 20. This makes the boater a little less free to move as he pleases, for the team's movements obviously have to be programmed, and a spontaneous decision to stop between two locks will create confusion and perhaps even delay commercial traffic. Boaters are thus requested to cooperate by giving reasonable notice of their movements and stops.

Finally, it is worth noting that tipping the lock-keepers is not normal practice. Lock-keepers are State or local authority employees and are paid a fair salary for their job. On the other hand, they often do more than is strictly required of them, and in such cases the navigator should use his discretion and imagination in judging the best way of showing appreciation. Perhaps a cool drink on a hot day? Cash will obviously be appreciated if water is supplied from the lock-keeper's private tap, say €1.50 or €2, but water is generally provided by VNF at locks as part of the service paid for by the licence fee.

This 'bionic lock-keeper' at Corre, the first lock on the Canal des Vosges, dispenses the remote control for operation of locks on this canal. © OCÉAN-MANOR

Unmanned locks on the smaller waterways

'Do-it-yourself' lock operation has become the system on a number of waterways that are used only by tourist traffic. This is the case on the western section of Canal de Nantes à Brest, the Charente, the Seille and the Lot, for example. In all cases the lock operating gear is already installed, and a leaflet of instructions on lock operation is issued to navigators.

Observations by a seasoned canaller

The reflections by the late Robert Somerville that were included in previous editions of this work remain relevant today. The increasing popularity of the canals and rivers of France means an increased responsibility for all users, not just the long-term, perhaps retired, year-round navigator who will tend to know the ropes, the waterway etiquette, not to mention half of the entire family of seasoned canallers, but also the first-time family vacationer hiring a self-drive vessel for the first time, or perhaps the navigators passing through the system from or to the Mediterranean with their motor yacht or sailing boat for the one and only time.

Why have you been moored to that quay for three weeks? One should not expect to stay moored indefinitely to a public quay, usually where the services are superior and possibly free. A stay of two or three days is normally tolerated but by then it is time to move on and allow others to enjoy those same facilities, the sights and sounds that have kept you staying for as long as you have. Especially if others are being turned away daily! Have you considered breasting up? Perhaps the extended stay should be made in a privately-managed port. There are suitable facilities at or near most popular locations, and by paying the going rates you acquire the right to stay as long as you wish.

Why have you got your screwdriver out, to pry open the security door on the service panel? A charge of €2 for water is not excessive, nor is €3 for a nightly power hook-up. Once the services have been vandalised to save some small change, in all likelihood they will be unusable for the next user and probably will not be serviceable at all the following year.

Why are you moored in the middle of the quay? Snuggle up to the boat ahead of you or to one of the ends of the pontoon and leave some room for others who are certain to come along later. If the most recent arrival is having difficulty getting a line ashore and securing their vessel – take a minute or two to assist in securing the vessel – being careful not to trip over your own lines which may have been carelessly coiled on the pontoon!

Why are you cruising so fast? More importantly you're on holiday. Take a moment and have a look at your bow wave and behind at your wake! All canals and rivers have speed limits. They are designed to preserve the banks, respect the speed limit and the waterways' navigable depths will not be rapidly reduced as a result of collapsing banks.

Why is that other vessel owner yelling at you? Have you raced ahead to get to the next lock first? Have you overtaken in a dangerous location? Have you had too much to drink? There are 'rules of the road'; know what they are and follow them, but more importantly, respect your fellow boater!

On a completely different issue which I have found to be critical, canal guides make frequent reference to the concept of a *bassin* or canal basin. They come in various shapes and sizes and are normally found downstream of a lock, close to a small village or town, a loading quay or silo, or for no apparent reason in the middle of nowhere. In the past they were an important part of the commercial life on the canal and river system. They allowed *péniches* to turn around and proceed in the opposite direction to load or unload cargo or to return to a favoured port without having to travel great distances in the opposite direction to do so. Where situated in the middle of nowhere, their function was often to allow barges to moor while waiting for a new load. The biggest were given the more important title of *gare d'eau*.

Unfortunately, with the decline of commercial traffic these basins fell into varying degrees of disrepair. Many became silted up, overgrown with weed or worst of all served as a dumping ground for abandoned vessels or even cars. Consequently, a number have been staked off or have signs to indicate that entry is neither possible nor recommended. However, the majority have no indication of their suitability for turning or mooring.

This means that if it is contemplated to use a basin it is advisable to approach with extreme caution and expect the worst! Proceed slowly, bow first, ideally with a person up at the bow paying special attention to what is ahead. That stone quay just inside might look very inviting but in all likelihood there are no services and the risk of damage to your vessel is just not worth it. Look for a more suitable turning location or mooring a little further on.

Hours of navigation

It is as well when planning a cruise to realise that for all practical purposes there is no navigation after dark or, during the lighter months of the year, after 19:30. Locks are generally open between 06:30 and 19:30 in summer, and the working hours progressively shorten as the nights close in. However, now that many waterways are being handed over to regional councils or other local bodies, it is to be expected that operating hours will vary much more widely than in the past. Councils are known to be seeking to reduce the financial burden of operating costs, so boaters should expect some disappointments in the coming years. While it is possible to run between locks during the dark hours (the proper navigation lights being shown and the regulation reduction in speed being observed), there is little advantage for boats in doing so, except in an emergency.

Time of year

The season suitable for pleasure cruising extends from March to November, depending on how comfortable and well heated your boat is. The weather in France, being of the continental type, tends to be more settled than that of the British Isles, and long periods of high temperature are not infrequent in the summer. Before about the end of April, cold weather and night frosts may occur. Moreover, it is always colder on the water than on the land and, owing to the higher humidity, it feels colder. The weather is often fine in September and October, when the autumn colours make the scenery particularly beautiful. However, morning mists on the canals and rivers will often delay a planned early morning departure.

In the late autumn and winter, the intrepid navigator must be prepared for floods (from November to March, but often also in the spring months through to May) and also for icing (December to February). Bear in mind that some of the canals rise to a considerable height above sea level, and with the increase in altitude the fall in temperature is accentuated. Such severe conditions do not usually extend beyond the month of March.

Seasonal restrictions in the coming years will not be a question of climate, but of canal operating conditions, as indicated in the previous paragraph on hours of navigation. Some authorities will want to close their canals completely during the winter months, and some vigorous campaigning is likely to be required, before new waterway authorities will accept to pay for more staff time. The cause will be difficult to defend, since the resulting additional traffic will seem not to have been worth the effort.

Out-of-season cruising has become a genuine trend on the Canal du Midi, where it is seen by private boat-owners as the ideal way to enjoy the canal's charms without having to struggle with the large numbers of hire boats on the busiest sections of the canal.

Mast lowering

One important aspect of planning to enter the inland waterways, for sailing yachts, is mast lowering or stepping. This will benefit from some preparatory work. The marinas at Dunkerque, for example, whilst helpful and able to provide craneage, may not be as familiar with the techniques as the yard at Rouen. They cannot be relied on to know and do everything required. It might be advisable to talk to an experienced yard in your home country about the practicalities and the sequence: disconnecting electrics, the order in which shrouds and stays and their bottle screws should be loosened and released, how and where the lifting strop on the mast should be attached (to avoid the wrongly balanced mast tipping end over end), and how the mast should actually be lifted and laid down.

Planning a cruise

Feedback received from readers suggests that the most vital information is the location of quayside fuelling points and wastewater pump-outs. Hence the two maps on the following pages. The following through routes are relevant to users from northeast to southeast:

Givet to Lyon via Meuse and Canal des Vosges
 804km, 193 locks
This is the direct route to the south for navigators from the Netherlands and Belgium who enter the French waterway network from the Belgian Meuse at Givet.

Apach to Lyon via Moselle and Canal des Vosges
 638km, 133 locks
This route is used by many boat owners heading south from Germany, who avoid the difficult navigation conditions in the Rhine gorges by turning up the Moselle to enter the French waterways at Apach.

Strasbourg to Lyon via Canal du Rhône au Rhin
 552km, 126 locks
This is the route to the Mediterranean for boat owners who have braved the dangers of the Rhine to reach Strasbourg. For much of its length, the Canal du Rhône au Rhin follows the course of the river Doubs, which can be difficult in times of flood, but which offers spectacular scenery.

Lyon to Mediterranean (Port-St-Louis-du-Rhône)
 310km, 12 locks
This route continues the three preceding routes, running from Lyon to the Mediterranean (Gulf of Fos) at Port-Saint-Louis-du-Rhône. Navigation on the Rhône is usually without difficulty. This route also gives access to the Canal du Rhône à Sète and Canal du Midi by turning into the Petit Rhône a short distance above Arles.

Guides and publications

Much of the basic data for the route descriptions, particularly the kilometre distances or *points kilométriques*, was originally taken from the *Guide de la Navigation Intérieure*, a comprehensive two-volume guide published by Berger-Levrault in Paris in 1965. This continues to be my favourite reference work, at least where there has been no change in basic configuration of the waterways since that date. Imray's general map of the waterways of France, Belgium and the Netherlands, scale 1:1.500.000, produced by the author, is useful for cruise planning and for the overview it gives of the network in the three countries.

Planning a cruise

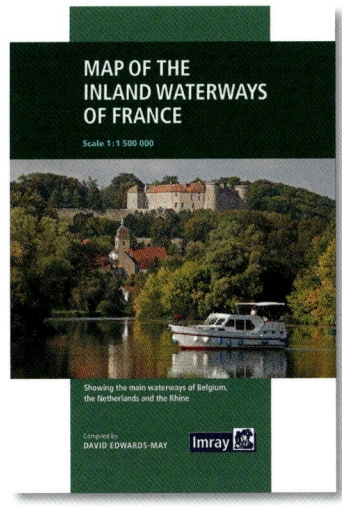
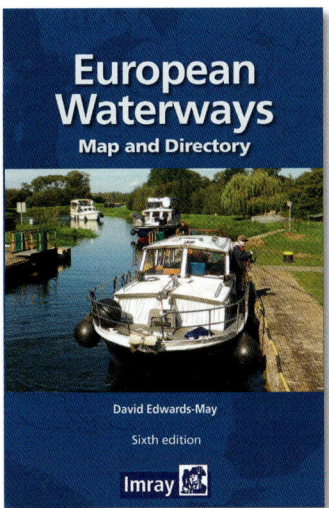

No. 3   Bourgogne/Franche-Comté
No. 4   Alsace/Lorraine
No. 9   Canal du Rhône au Rhin
No. 17 La Meuse
No. 18 Le Rhône
No. 22 Rhin
503, chemin Notre-Dame, 11400 Castelnaudary, France
+33 (0)4 68 23 51 35 **editionsdubreil.com**

Jane Cumberlidge has prepared a map broken down into regions in another Imray publication – *Waterway Routes Through France*. Éditions du Breil also offers a good French waterways map.

Another useful and popular map is the *European Waterways Map and Concise Directory* (sixth edition, 2021), compiled by the author and now also published by Imray (the previous editions were published by the author's publishing and consultancy firm Euromapping, then Transmanche Consultants). The map now becomes one of the 'family' of waterway publications. It covers the whole of Europe at scales of 1:3 800 000 (for the overview from Portugal and Ireland to the Caspian Sea) and 1:1 500 000 (for the main network from Dublin to Bratislava), and is accompanied by a 64-page directory with brief descriptions for each country.

A prime source of information is the online version of the present publication, included, by agreement with Imray, within the website **french-waterways.com**. The 'hands on' (or practical navigation) section of the website contains valuable guidance and recommendations, complementing those set out in this introduction, while the descriptions of each waterway or each chapter may be downloaded as pdfs, as well as compilations of through routes. We hope that boat owners will appreciate having the actual book at home or on board, despite the availability of much of its content in digital format! The site also sells the Imray, Éditions du Breil and Fluviacarte publications.

For a wealth of detailed information on navigable conditions, sites to visit, restaurants and practically everything else you might need to know while cruising, there is a choice of specialist guides. The most thoroughly researched and best-documented are those published by Éditions du Breil, the company founded by John Riddel in 1997.

Éditions du Breil

The maps in these guides are at 1:50 000 for canals and 1:25 000 for rivers, with the exception of the Saône (1:40 000).

Fluviacarte

Fluvial, the French monthly waterways magazine, publishes a useful *Guide du Plaisancier* every two years. It is like a condensed version of the present guide, and gives up-to-date information on nearly 700 mooring locations and more than 100 boatyards. Their *Fluviacarte* series includes the following guides covering waterways in the present volume:
No. 9   La Meuse et son canal
No. 10 La Saône de Corre à Lyon - La Seille
Marina Del Rey - Bât. A, 2 rue des Consuls - CS 30031, 34973 Lattes Cedex **fluvialnet.com**

The above guides have English and German texts alongside the French. They are available from specialised bookshops, from **imray.com** and from **french-waterways.com**. Inland Waterways International also has a useful online shop selling the main titles, but not the individual waterway guides: **inlandwaterwaysinternational.org**.

Other sources

The DBA website **barges.org** has a wide range of information for cruising on the continent, including a mooring guide and updates on current legislation, much of it available to non-members.

The Cruising Association **cruising.org.uk** also publishes *Cruising the Inland Waterways of France and Belgium*, compiled by Gordon Knight. This is an invaluable publication, formerly edited by Dr Roger Edgar. Now in its 25th edition, the 216-page guide is regularly updated via reports from members actively cruising the waterways. It supplements rather than replaces the above publications. Described as their 'Bible' by regular users and yacht skippers planning routes to and from the Mediterranean, the guide contains a wealth of information on cruising routes, cruising preparations, supplies, equipment, licences and documents, useful addresses, books and websites as well as listing around 250 mooring places throughout France and Belgium, with comments upon facilities (including where fuel may be obtained either alongside or within easy jerry can distance), depths, prices, closest shops and restaurants and nearby attractions.

For approaching the French waterway system from the coast (the Mediterranean Sea in this volume), the following publications are available:

Mediterranean France and Corsica Pilot
   Rod and Lucinda Heikell (Imray)
Cruising Almanac
   The Cruising Association (Imray)
Mediterranean Almanac
   Rod and Lucinda Heikell (Imray)
Votre Livre de Bord
   an almanac in French (with some English) available in two volumes: *Mediterranée* and *Mer du Nord Manche Atlantique* Bloc Marin

Part II – Route descriptions and maps

The route descriptions and accompanying maps and plans are designed to be of use both for planning and during the actual cruise. Distances are given precisely to within 100m, and possible mooring places are highlighted in bold type. The distance from the mooring to the centre of the locality is also indicated. This is not to be interpreted as a guarantee that mooring will be practicable at this point, but may be useful in emergency situations, as well as for all users of the towpath or riverside cycle itinerary. Junctions are readily identifiable by the use of a distinctive style with white text on a blue background. The route descriptions include sections that are not navigable, either because restoration is in progress or at least envisaged, or for continuity of the cycling itinerary, where feasible.

The abbreviations u/s and d/s are used for upstream and downstream, and r/b and l/b for right bank and left bank. These abbreviations are also used on canals, the downstream direction being implicit in relation to the summit level or parallel river. On summit levels or tidal waters, geographical directions are used instead, to avoid confusion.

Boat harbour entries (*ports de plaisance*) will be valuable for users of this guide, and have been researched in detail. Changes take place rapidly, however, so readers are invited to take the information as indicative only. 'Fuel' means that both diesel and petrol are available. The price indicated for visitor moorings is the average charge per night in season for a boat 10m in length. Prices will of course change over time. In most cases the local *taxe de séjour* will be charged, usually between 20 and 50 cents per person on board.

The index map shows the position of the waterway in the network, and the strip map, which is precise despite the relatively small scale, enables immediate identification of the boat's position in relation to the overall route, and to the towns and villages where it may be proposed to stop. Partial distances on these maps are shown between pin markers, with the number of locks in italics.

Most junctions and locations where alternative routes are possible are covered by detailed plans at a scale of approximately 1:15 000. These distinguish navigable and unnavigable water areas and give route indications, positions of moorings, main sites of interest and other useful information.

Details of the engineers responsible for each waterway – the local *unité territoriale* or *subdivision* – are given, and in case of specific enquiries or difficulties en route, they may be contacted. Otherwise the regional headquarters listed here will forward any queries to the appropriate office. For the waterways that are not managed by VNF, we have tried to be as explicit as possible, distinguishing the managing authority and the agency in charge of operation and maintenance.

VNF Regions

VNF Nord-Est
28 boulevard Albert 1er, C.O. 80062, 54036 NANCY
03 83 95 30 01   **dt.nordest@vnf.fr**

VNF Strasbourg
4 quai de Paris, CS 30367, 67010 STRASBOURG
03 67 07 92 15   **dt-strasbourg@vnf.fr**

VNF Rhône Saône
2 rue de la Quarantaine, 69321 LYON 05
04 72 56 59 00   **dt.rhonesaone@vnf.fr**

Head office
Voies Navigables de France
175 rue Ludovic Boutleux
B.P. 820, 62408 BÉTHUNE CEDEX
03 21 63 24 24

Paris office
156, rue du Faubourg Saint-Denis, 75010 PARIS
01 44 89 65 00

CHAPTER IV – NORTHEASTERN FRANCE

Routes south from Belgium, Luxembourg and Germany

This chapter covers the routes into and through the northeastern quarter of France, from Belgium (the River Meuse), Luxemburg (the River Moselle), Germany (rivers Sarre and Rhine) and Switzerland (the river Rhine in Basle). The rivers Rhine and Moselle are high-capacity waterways, but both offer ample opportunities to escape into *ports de plaisance* for the desired comforts and services. The Canal de la Meuse is the most beautiful itinerary into France, through the Ardennes gorge, while the Canal de la Sarre route is also a charming waterway. The Canal de la Marne au Rhin is the important east-west link across the entire region, now called 'Grand Est' and practically defined by this canal. The eastern section of this canal, crossing the Vosges, is one of the most popular cruising areas in France for hire boats, while efforts are also being made to increase barge carrying between Strasbourg and Nancy. This section includes the Arzviller inclined plane, which is one of the seven wonders of French waterways, although the author still prefers the superb flight of 17 disused locks that are bypassed by the 1968 structure. This flight of locks is now a towpath excursion only.

South of this east-west axis, three major canals cross the North Sea-Mediterranean watershed to converge on the River Saône. These are almost exclusively devoted to tourism, and are all delightful cruising waterways.

The Canal des Vosges and Canal du Rhône au Rhin are more popular routes, not least because they both use splendid navigable rivers for substantial lengths, the 'Petite' Saône, which the former joins at Corre, while the latter makes abundant use of the river Doubs over nearly two thirds of its length. This is also by far the most populated route, not only in the industrial centres of Mulhouse, Belfort, Montbéliard and Besançon, with its splendid citadel, tunnel and navigable river loop, but with sizeable villages and small towns dotted along the valley throughout. This is a route with considerable potential for retaining a *plaisancier* on their southward migration.

At the southern limit of this region is the famous hub of Saint-Jean-de-Losne, gateway to Burgundy and the waterways of central France (covered in Chapter III), if heading back north via Paris or Reims.

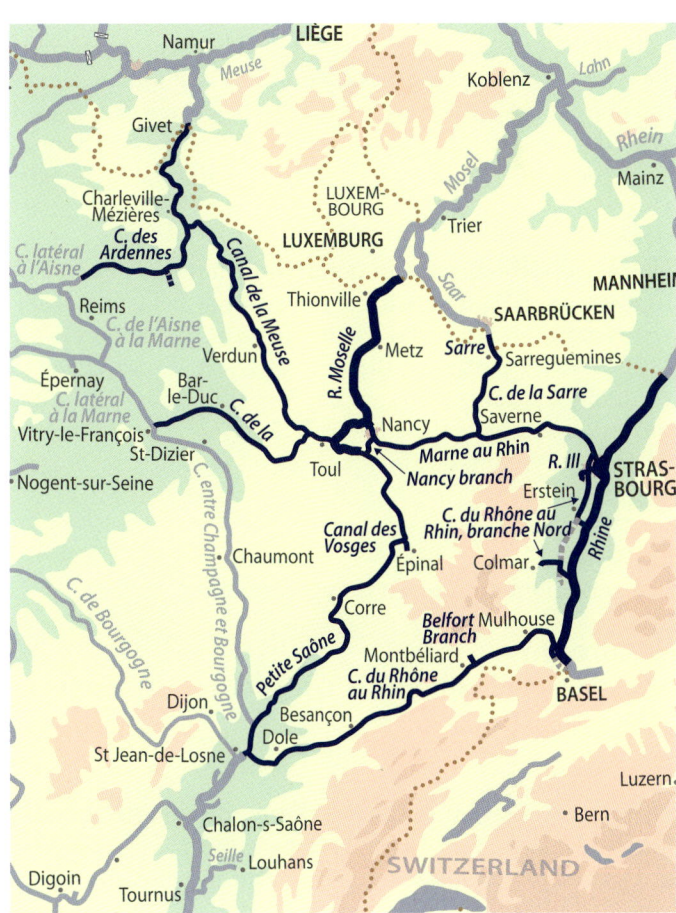

Boats will now be able to return to Le Chesne, on the summit level of the Canal des Ardennes, reopened in May 2021 after reconstruction of a lock destroyed by an exceptional flood on the long flight of 27 locks. VNF

IV – Northeastern France

37. Canal de la Meuse

THE MEUSE IS ONE OF THE GREAT NAVIGABLE RIVERS of Europe. It is navigable throughout most of its course in France and Belgium and bypassed by the Juliana Canal in the Netherlands province of Limburg, to continue with a few more locks and weirs, then as a free-flow navigation down to the Rhine delta. Canal de la Meuse is the name now given to the waterway which runs from the Belgian border (where it is a high-capacity Class Va waterway) to the Canal de la Marne au Rhin at Troussey, a distance of 272km. The river offers spectacular scenery where it cuts deep into the Ardennes hills downstream of Charleville-Mézières. Further south, from Sedan onwards, the broad valley offers beautiful unspoiled landscapes.

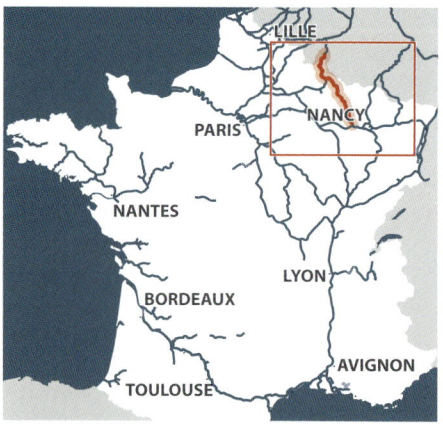

The river Meuse was canalised as the northern branch of the 'Canal de l'Est', a strategic link connecting the country's canals within the border after Alsace and Lorraine were occupied in 1871. The link was authorised by laws voted by the Assemblée Nationale in 1872 and 1874, and works began immediately. The canal was completed in 1880.

Navigation
A gently flowing river most of the time, the Meuse can flood quite dramatically. Boaters cruising in the spring should allow for the risk of being forced to remain in a port if navigation is interrupted. Navigation alternates between river sections and lock-cuts, and due attention should be paid to the cross-currents at weirs or where the canal joins the river. There are many well-equipped *ports de plaisance* and *haltes*. The waterway has not been entirely abandoned by commercial traffic, but *péniches* will rarely be encountered south of the junction with the Canal des Ardennes.

Locks
There are 59 locks, overcoming a difference in level of almost 150m. The first lock, close to the Belgian border, has a length of 100m and a width of 12m, giving access for high-capacity barges to the port of Givet. From Givet to Verdun, lock dimensions are 48.30m by 5.70m. The locks above Verdun have the standard 'Freycinet' dimensions of 38.50m by 5.20m. Most locks are equipped for automatic operation.

Draught
The maximum authorised draught is 1.80m throughout.

Headroom
The minimum headroom is 3.50m above normal water level.

Towpath
There is a towpath throughout, except through the tunnels. The TransArdennes cycle route uses the paved towpath throughout from Givet to Sedan, and is gradually being extended. A short section recently completed bypasses the Ham tunnel.

Tunnels
There are four tunnels, at Ham, 565m long, Revin, 224m long, Verdun, 45m long and Koeurs, 50m long. Ham tunnel has no towpath.

Authority
VNF Nord-Est
UTI Meuse-Ardennes
– 24 rue Oger, BP 155, 08600 Givet 03 24 42 10 02 (PK 0-79)
– 2 av. de Montcy Notre Dame, 08000 Charleville-Mézières 03 24 33 20 48 (PK 79-239)
– 1, rue de l'Ormicée, BP 523, 55012 Bar-le-Duc cedex 03 29 79 12 33 (PK 239-272)

Route description

PK 0.0	Belgian border, *junction with Belgian Meuse* (just upstream of Heer bridge)
PK 0.5	Lock 59 (Quatre Cheminées), beginning of 2.3km lock-cut, l/b
PK 2.2	Port of Givet, basins l/b
PK 2.7	Bridge (service road for access to weir)
PK 2.8	Flood gate and weir, navigation re-enters Meuse

Canal de la Meuse

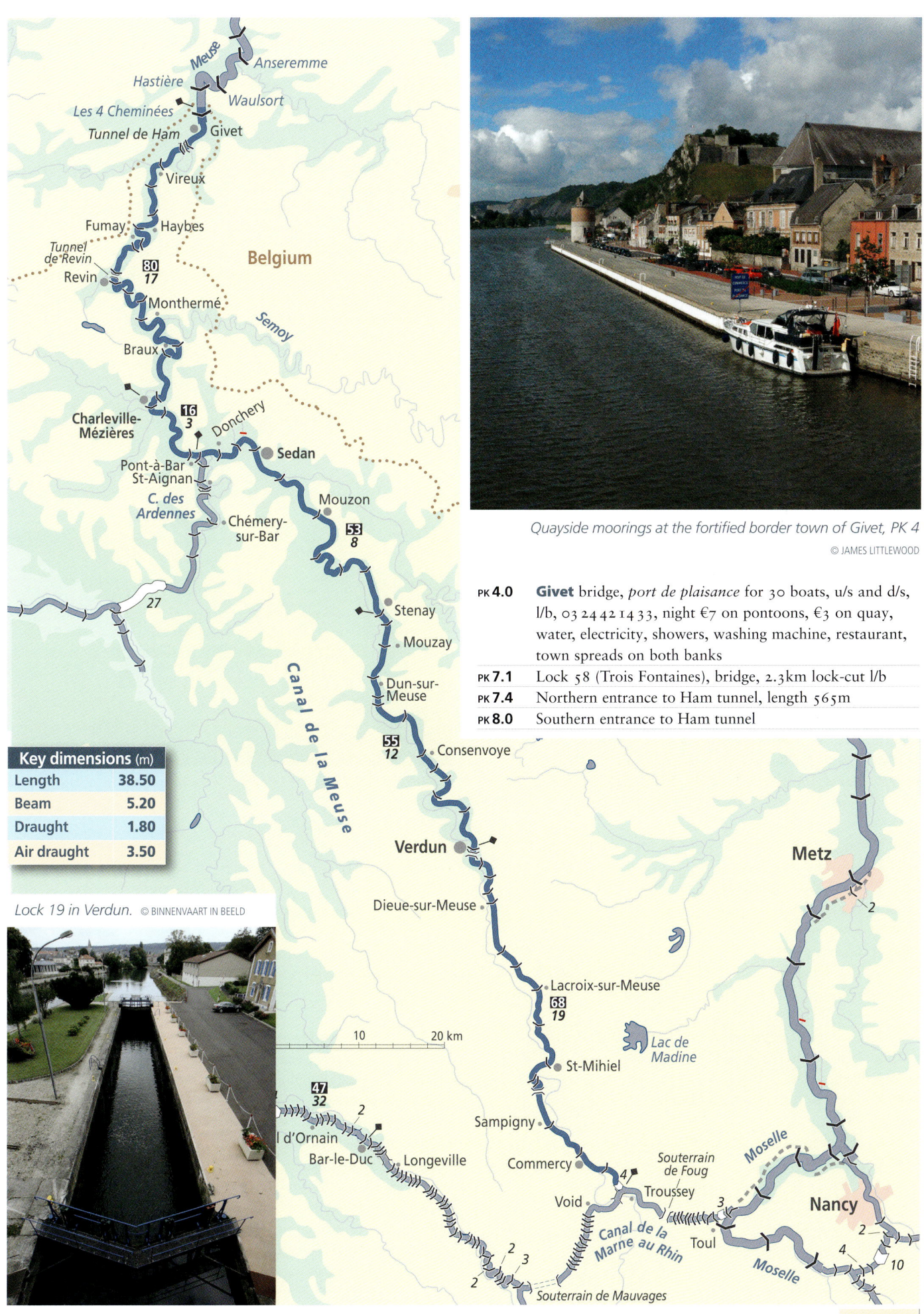

Quayside moorings at the fortified border town of Givet, PK 4
© JAMES LITTLEWOOD

PK 4.0	**Givet** bridge, *port de plaisance* for 30 boats, u/s and d/s, l/b, 03 24 42 14 33, night €7 on pontoons, €3 on quay, water, electricity, showers, washing machine, restaurant, town spreads on both banks
PK 7.1	Lock 58 (Trois Fontaines), bridge, 2.3km lock-cut l/b
PK 7.4	Northern entrance to Ham tunnel, length 565m
PK 8.0	Southern entrance to Ham tunnel

Key dimensions (m)	
Length	38.50
Beam	5.20
Draught	1.80
Air draught	3.50

Lock 19 in Verdun. © BINNENVAART IN BEELD

IV – Northeastern France

One of many idyllic moorings on the Meuse, at Vireux-Wallerand
© JAMES LITTLEWOOD

PK **8.4**	Lock 57 (Ham), bridge
PK **9.4**	Flood gate and weir, lift bridge, navigation re-enters Meuse, channel changes to r/b side, **Aubrives** l/b
PK **13.1**	Lock 56 (Mouyon) in 350m lock-cut, r/b
PK **14.3**	**Vireux-Wallerand** bridge, municipal *halte* for 11 boats d/s r/b, 03 24 40 59 54, night €5 including water, electricity €3/day, shower, slipway, village r/b
PK **17.1**	Lock 55 (Montigny), 1.9km lock-cut, r/b
PK **17.7**	Bridge (Jean Matine)
PK **18.9**	Weir, footbridge, navigation re-enters Meuse
PK **22.4**	Lock 54 (Fépin) in 380m lock-cut, r/b
PK **22.6**	Bridge (Fépin)
PK **22.8**	Flood gate and weir, navigation re-enters Meuse
PK **23.9**	Quay (Moraipré) r/b
PK **24.8**	**Haybes** bridge, municipal *halte* d/s r/b, 4 berths, night €5, water, electricity €3.20, showers €2, slipway, town r/b
PK **25.7**	Lock 53 (Vanne-Alcorps) in 610m lock-cut, r/b
PK **26.3**	Flood gate and weir, navigation re-enters Meuse
PK **27.4**	**Fumay** bridge, municipal *halte* u/s l/b, 06 30 65 25 79, 20 berths along quay, water, electricity €3.20, small town, channel changes to l/b side
PK **30.4**	Lock 52 (Roche d'Uf) in 130m lock-cut, l/b
PK **31.2**	Ferry for slate-works
PK **32.9**	Railway bridge, footbridge
PK **33.0**	Lock 51 (Saint-Joseph) in 300m lock-cut, l/b
PK **35.8**	Mooring at camp-site l/b
PK **39.1**	Lock 50 (**Revin**), VHF 20, automatic, in 420m lock-cut, r/b, municipal *halte* for 10 boats on Meuse u/s of lock-cut entrance, 06 07 05 74 01, night €12, water and electricity included, shower, slipway
PK **39.2**	Revin tunnel, length 224m, controlled by lights
PK **39.5**	Navigation re-enters Meuse, channel on r/b side
PK **40.4**	Bridge (Orzy)
PK **40.7**	Lock 49 (Orzy) in 300m lock-cut, r/b
PK **43.5**	Bridge
PK **44.8**	**Anchamps** quay l/b, small village
PK **45.0**	Railway bridge
PK **45.4**	Lock 48 (Dames de Meuse), automatic, in 2.1km lock-cut, r/b
PK **47.3**	Footbridge
PK **47.4**	End of lock-cut, navigation re-enters Meuse
PK **48.0**	Bridge (Laifour)
PK **48.5**	Railway bridge, quay u/s r/b, water
PK **49.0**	**Laifour** *halte* l/b (June-September), 15 boats, night €6.50, water, electricity €2.80, slipway
PK **50.0**	Lock 47 (Commune), automatic, in 350m lock-cut, r/b
PK **50.4**	Quay r/b (Laifour), mooring for 15 boats, 03 24 32 63 84, water, electricity
PK **51.8**	Quay r/b (Grande Commune)
PK **52.5**	Mairupt island, pass on r/b side
PK **53.7**	**Deville** quay l/b, village behind railway
PK **54.2**	Lock 46 (Deville), automatic, in 3km lock-cut, r/b
PK **57.1**	Flood gate, navigation re-enters Meuse
PK **58.5**	**Monthermé** bridge, mooring for 11 visiting boats u/s l/b, 03 24 35 10 12, night €7.50, water, electricity €2.80, showers €1.50 at *capitainerie*, pump-out, small town, channel changes to l/b side

A favourite stopping-place nestled in the superb loop of the Meuse and dominated by the Ardennes cliffs. Excellent moorings have been provided along the grassy bank upstream of the bridge (see photo). For the energetic, the climb to the top of the cliffs will be rewarded by the splendid views.

View from the cliffs to the long loop of the Meuse at Monthermé. © NITRO76

PK **59.0**	Industrial quay r/b
PK **59.8**	Quay (Saint-Rémy) r/b
PK **61.0**	Railway bridge
PK **61.6**	Private quay l/b, water and electricity
PK **62.4**	**Château-Regnault** bridge, mooring for 6 boats u/s r/b, 03 24 54 46 73, night €6.50, water, electricity €2.80, village overlooked by the Rocher des 4 Fils Aymon, **Bogny-sur-Meuse** on l/b
PK **63.8**	Lock 45 (Levrézy) in 250m lock-cut, l/b
PK **65.1**	**Braux** bridge, mooring d/s l/b, village l/b
PK **69.4**	**Joigny-sur-Meuse** bridge, *halte* on pontoon d/s r/b, night €6.50, water, electricity €2.80, village r/b
PK **70.1**	Lock 44 (Joigny) in 300m lock-cut, l/b, bridge
PK **72.7**	**Nouzonville** bridge, quay d/s r/b
PK **74.4**	Château de la Pierronnerie, l/b
PK **76.9**	Overhead power lines
PK **79.0**	Private quay r/b
PK **79.1**	Lock 43 (Montcy) in 400m lock-cut, r/b, bridge
PK **79.4**	Bridge (Montcy-Notre Dame), VNF office
PK **79.6**	End of lock-cut, continue on Meuse 1km downstream to *port de plaisance*, r/b, mooring for **Charleville-Mézières**, 50 berths, 03 24 33 23 60, night €12, water and electricity included, showers, slipway, restaurant, wifi

Canal de la Meuse

The biggest town on the waterway, offering all services and a number of attractions, including the spectacular Place Ducale in the centre.

PK 79.7	Railway bridge
PK 80.4	Private quays l/b
PK 81.0	Railway bridge
PK 81.2	Entrance to Mézières lock-cut, r/b
PK 81.3	Lock 42 (Mézières), VHF 20, automatic, water

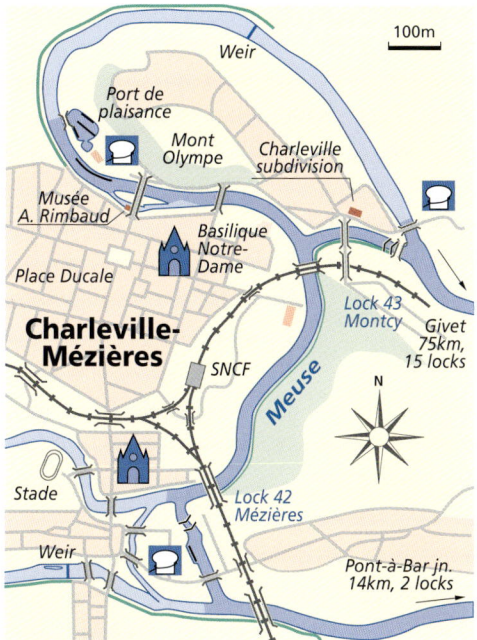

These moorings above Lock 42 at Charleville-Mézières – the biggest town on the canalised river Meuse – are tempting, but a longish walk from the centre. Boaters may prefer the marina on the by-passed river arm, turning right on entering the Meuse after lock 43. © PASCAL LEMAITRE/DOC VNF

PK 81.6	Bridge
PK 81.7	End of lock-cut, turn left into Meuse
PK 81.9	Railway bridge
PK 84.1	Quay (Roméry) r/b
PK 84.3	Lock 41 (Roméry), automatic, in 1.6km lock-cut, r/b
PK 84.9	Bridge
PK 85.9	End of lock-cut, bridge
PK 86.8	Motorway bridge (A34), bridge (Lumes)
PK 87.1	Railway bridge
PK 87.5	**Lumes** *halte* r/b, moorings for 6 boats, free, water, slipway, village 700m beyond railway
PK 88.4	Private quay r/b
PK 89.2	Meander cutoff (Ayvelles), l/b
PK 92.3	**Flize** disused railway bridge, private quay d/s l/b
PK 93.5	Nouvion bridge, town beyond railway, r/b
PK 94.8	Lock 40 (Dom-le-Mesnil), in 500m lock-cut, l/b
PK 96.3	**Junction with Canal des Ardennes** Pont-à-Bar, l/b
PK 97.3	Confluence of Bar, meander cut-off l/b
PK 99.6	Lock 39 (Donchery), automatic, in 900m lock-cut, l/b
PK 100.1	**Donchery** bridge, town r/b
PK 101.2	Overhead power lines
PK 102.9	Railway bridge, private quay d/s l/b
PK 103.3	Lock 38 (Villette), in 1.5km lock-cut, motorway bridge (A203)
PK 103.7	Bridge (Villette)
PK 104.1	Lights controlling lock access r/b
PK 104.6	Bridge (Glaire)
PK 104.9	End of lock-cut
PK 105.2	Private quay r/b (textile factory)
PK 106.6	Bridge (Pont Neuf)
PK 106.7	Entrance to Sedan lock-cut, l/b
PK 107.0	Lock 37 (Sedan), automatic, bridge, water
PK 107.4	**Sedan** *port de plaisance* r/b (managed by Campingcar-Park), 03 24 57 83 23, 10 boats, night €9.20, water and electricity included, pump-out, wifi, slipway, centre 1km
PK 107.5	End of lock-cut
PK 107.7	Bridge (Pont de la Gare), private quay u/s l/b
PK 108.8	Bridge (N43 Sedan bypass)
PK 110.2	Overhead power line
PK 111.9	Meander cut-off l/b
PK 112.3	Railway bridge
PK 112.7	Entrance to 5.4km lock-cut, l/b, Meuse navigable 700m u/s to quay (Bazeilles, Hôtel du Port)
PK 112.8	Lock 36 (Remilly-Aillicourt), automatic
PK 113.7	Bridge (Aillicourt), private quay upstream l/b
PK 115.1	**Remilly** bridge, quay upstream l/b, village behind railway
PK 116.5	Bridge (Petit Remilly)
PK 118.0	Flood gate, end of lock-cut
PK 119.7	Villers-devant-Mouzon l/b, ferry, meander cut-off r/b
PK 122.5	Lock 35 (Mouzon), 1.5km lock-cut, r/b
PK 123.1	Bridge (Fourberie)
PK 123.4	**Mouzon**, municipal *halte* l/b in narrow lock-cut, 12 boats, 03 24 27 71 18, night €8, water, electricity, shower, wifi, slipway

Lock-cut through the small town of Mouzon, PK 123. © BOYO

IV – Northeastern France

Attractive small medieval town with good moorings and a museum in the old Burgundy tower.

PK **123.6** Bridge
PK **123.8** Private footbridge, private quay u/s r/b, services
PK **124.0** End of lock-cut
PK **130.8** Lock 34 (Alma), 1.0km lock-cut, r/b
PK **131.7** End of lock-cut
PK **134.6** Létanne quay l/b, meander cutoff r/b
PK **137.4** Entrance to Pouilly lock-cut, l/b, towpath bridge over Meuse
PK **137.9** Lock 33 (**Pouilly**), bridge, water, village 300m r/b
PK **138.1** End of lock-cut
PK **140.3** Meander cut-off l/b
PK **141.8** Entrance to 6.4km canal section, **Inor** quay, village r/b
PK **142.2** Lock 32 (Inor), bridge
PK **143.7** Martincourt-sur-Meuse bridge, basin u/s r/b
PK **146.9** Bridge (Cervizy)
PK **148.1** Flood lock (Stenay), bridge, end of lock-cut
PK **148.5** **Stenay** municipal *port de plaisance* through bridge on river arm r/b, 03 29 80 62 59, mooring for 16 boats, night €9, water and electricity included, showers, pump-out, slipway
PK **148.8** Lock 31 (Stenay), bridge, water
PK **149.4** Bridge
PK **149.5** Weir l/b
PK **151.3** Entrance to 7.2km canal section, r/b
PK **152.1** Lock 30 (Mouzay), bridge
PK **152.6** **Mouzay** bridge, quay d/s r/b, village 700m
PK **153.0** Pipeline crossing

Boat heading upstream leaves the long lock-cut to rejoin the Meuse at Stenay, PK 148. © ACESAR55

PK **153.7** Bridge
PK **155.5** Lock 29 (Sep), bridge
PK **158.4** Flood gate (Sassey), bridge
PK **158.6** End of canal section, navigation re-enters Meuse
PK **160.5** Meander cut-off, r/b
PK **160.7** Site of a former railway bridge
PK **161.8** End of cut-off (distance measured on Meuse)
PK **161.9** Dun-sur-Meuse quay, village r/b
PK **162.3** Lock 28 (Dun), bridge
PK **162.6** **Dun-sur-Meuse** *port de plaisance* opposite weir, Meuse Nautic hire base, 03 29 80 64 22, 20 boats, night €9, water and electricity included, fuel (03 29 80 90 38), showers, pump-out, slipway, restaurant

PK **163.8** Entrance to 7.9km canal section, r/b
PK **164.0** Lock 27 (Warinvaux)
PK **165.7** Lock 26 (**Liny-devant-Dun**), bridge, village 700m r/b
PK **166.9** Quay r/b
PK **171.2** Flood lock (**Vilosne**), bridge, village r/b
PK **171.7** Weir l/b, end of canal section
PK **172.5** Entrance to 4.2km canal section, r/b
PK **172.7** Lock 25 (Planchette), r/b, bridge
PK **174.2** **Sivry-sur-Meuse** bridge, basin r/b, village 600m r/b
PK **174.7** Bridge
PK **176.7** Flood gate (Sivry-sur-Meuse), bridge, navigation re-enters Meuse
PK **179.0** Lock 24 (**Consenvoye**) in short lock-cut, r/b (lock chamber with sloping sides), bridge, municipal *halte* for 6 boats, free, water, village r/b
PK **181.1** Entrance to 20.8km canal section, r/b
PK **181.3** Lock 23 (Brabant), bridge
PK **183.8** Bridge
PK **184.4** Lock 22 (Samogneux), bridge
PK **186.5** Champneuville bridge, basin u/s r/b
PK **188.4** Lock 21 (Champ), bridge
PK **194.1** **Vacherauville** bridge, basin u/s r/b (silted up)
PK **195.7** **Bras-sur-Meuse** bridge, village r/b
PK **196.2** Lock 20 (Bras), bridge, water
PK **198.5** Quay for grain silo l/b, water, telephone
PK **199.5** Bridge
PK **200.2** Thierville-sur-Meuse bridge, quay d/s r/b
PK **201.5** Belleville-sur-Meuse basin, D964 along r/b
PK **201.9** Flood gate (Belleville), bridge, navigation re-enters Meuse
PK **202.0** Railway bridge
PK **202.6** Bridge (Galavande), quay u/s r/b
PK **203.3** **Verdun** bridge (Porte Chaussée), municipal *halte* u/s r/b, 10 quayside moorings and pontoon for 6 boats, free, water, electricity, slipway, town centre on l/b
PK **203.6** Bridge (Legay), in bend (danger), Meuse divides immediately upstream, take r/b arm
PK **203.8** Bridge (narrow, followed by bend)
PK **204.1** Quay r/b, close to ramparts
PK **204.4** Lock 19 (Verdun), VHF 20, water, VNF office
PK **204.4** Tunnel (length 45m) under ramparts
PK **204.8** Weir (Grand Gueulard) l/b, watch out for cross-current

Excellent pontoon moorings await boaters in Verdun, close to the town centre. © FRAN BABISS

Canal de la Meuse

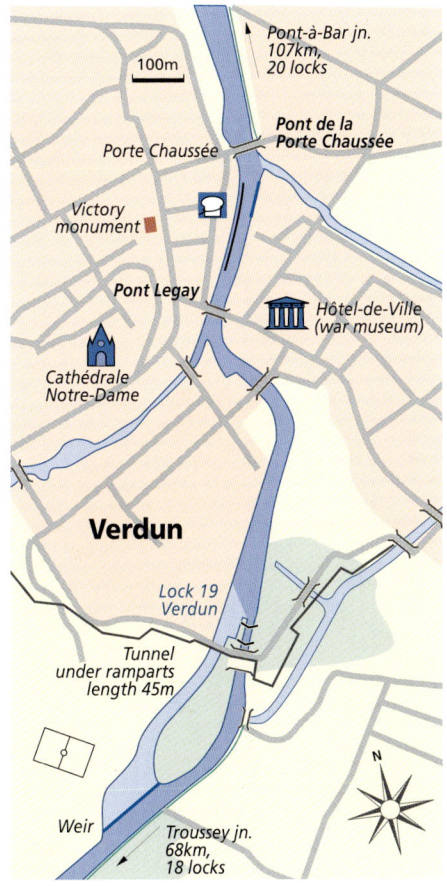

PK **205.1** Bridge, quay d/s l/b
PK **207.0** Entrance to 30km canal section, r/b
PK **207.4** Lock 18 (Belleray), bridge
PK **209.5** Bridge (Haudainville)
PK **210.4** Lock 17 (Haudainville), bridge
PK **211.6** Motorway bridge (A4)
PK **212.8** Basin l/b (silted up)
PK **213.7** Bridge
PK **214.8** Lock 16 (Dieue-Aval), bridge
PK **216.3** Bridge
PK **216.5** Lock 15 (**Dieue-sur-Meuse**), bridge, *halte* managed by VNF for 4-6 boats u/s r/b, 03 29 86 02 47, free (maximum 48 hours), water, village l/b
PK **217.6** Bridge
PK **219.3** Bridge
PK **220.7** Bridge
PK **221.1** **Génicourt-sur-Meuse** bridge, quay d/s r/b, village 700m r/b
PK **222.4** Bridge
PK **222.8** **Ambly-sur-Meuse** bridge, basin d/s r/b
PK **222.9** Lock 14 (Ambly)
PK **225.3** Bridge
PK **225.8** Lock 13 (Troyon), bridge
PK **226.8** Bridge
PK **227.9** Quay (Troyon) r/b, mooring for 6 boats
PK **229.7** Bridge
PK **230.7** **Lacroix-sur-Meuse** bridge, municipal *halte* u/s r/b, pontoons for 5-8 boats, free, water, electricity, village 400m
PK **231.2** Lock 12 (Lacroix), bridge, water
PK **232.0** Railway bridge (TGV Est)
PK **234.1** Lock 11 (**Rouvrois**), bridge, village r/b

PK **236.2** **Maizey** bridge, quay d/s l/b, basin r/b
PK **236.7** Flood gate, bridge
PK **237.9** Weir (Maizey), l/b, navigation re-enters Meuse
PK **239.0** Cliffs, r/b
PK **240.8** **Saint-Mihiel** bridge, municipal *halte* d/s r/b, pontoon for 5-6 boats, free, water, electricity April-October, town r/b
PK **241.5** Entrance to lock-cut, r/b
PK **241.6** Lock 10 (Saint-Mihiel), bridge, pontoon moorings for 7 boats u/s r/b, water, electricity, restaurant
PK **243.0** Flood gate, bridge
PK **243.2** Weir (Mont-Meuse) l/b, navigation re-enters Meuse
PK **244.4** Meander cut-off r/b
PK **246.3** Bridge (Koeur-la-Grande)
PK **246.5** Entrance to lock-cut, l/b
PK **247.0** Lock 9 (Koeur-la-Petite), bridge
PK **248.0** Lock 8 (Han), bridge
PK **248.8** Railway bridge (no visibility, sound horn)
PK **249.6** Kœur tunnel (length 50m) under D964 and railway

There are right-angle bends at each end of the tunnel, sound horn.

PK **251.4** Bridge
PK **252.2** **Sampigny** bridge, quay l/b, village l/b beyond railway
PK **254.9** Lock 7 (Vadonville), bridge
PK **256.3** **Lérouville** bridge, quay d/s r/b, village 800m l/b
PK **256.8** Bridge
PK **257.6** Railway bridges
PK **258.1** Flood lock, bridge, footbridge navigation re-enters Meuse
PK **259.2** Entrance to lock-cut, l/b
PK **260.6** Disused railway skew bridge
PK **260.8** Lock 6 (Commercy), bridge, industrial quay u/s l/b
PK **262.0** **Commercy** bridge, municipal *halte* u/s l/b, 03 29 91 33 16, pontoon for 5 boats, quayside moorings for 10 boats, free, water and electricity by token (€3 for 8 hours), small town 500m l/b, beyond railway
PK **263.1** Weir (*Barrage des Allemands*) r/b, navigation re-enters Meuse
PK **265.1** Entrance to canal section, r/b
PK **266.3** Lock 5 (**Euville**), bridge, municipal *halte* for 4 boats u/s r/b, water, electricity, restaurant, village 1km r/b
PK **268.4** **Vertuzey** bridge, quay u/s r/b, water, electricity
PK **270.3** Bridge and railway bridge
PK **270.4** Lock 4 (Sorcy), bridge, quay u/s r/b
PK **271.1** Lock 3 (Sorcy), bridge
PK **271.9** Lock 2 (Sorcy)
PK **272.4** Lock 1 (Troussey), VHF 20, water, footbridge, **junction with Canal de la Marne au Rhin** (PK 111.3)

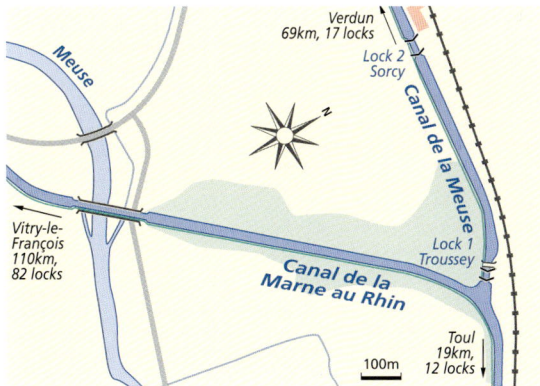

IV – Northeastern France

38. Canal des Ardennes

THE CANAL DES ARDENNES BRANCHES OFF from the canalised river Meuse (formerly the 'northern branch of the Canal de l'Est') at Pont-à-Bar, a short distance upstream from Charleville-Mézières. After crossing the watershed between the rivers Meuse and Aisne it drops down the Aisne valley to connect with the Canal latéral à l'Aisne at Vieux-lès-Asfeld. The distance from the Meuse to the Canal latéral à l'Aisne is 88km. Originally it was 5.5km longer, entering the Aisne further downstream, but this section was bypassed by the lateral canal in 1841. A 12km long branch leads from Semuy to the small town of Vouziers, further up the Aisne valley. Officially the canal is divided into two lengths, with distances counted separately on the watershed link, from Pont-à-Bar to Semuy, and on the canal following the Aisne valley, from Vouziers to Vieux-lès-Asfeld. It is thought more convenient here to carry the distance through from one end to the other, and to treat the section from Semuy to Vouziers as a branch, especially as it is heavily silted up and no longer navigable, even in light craft.

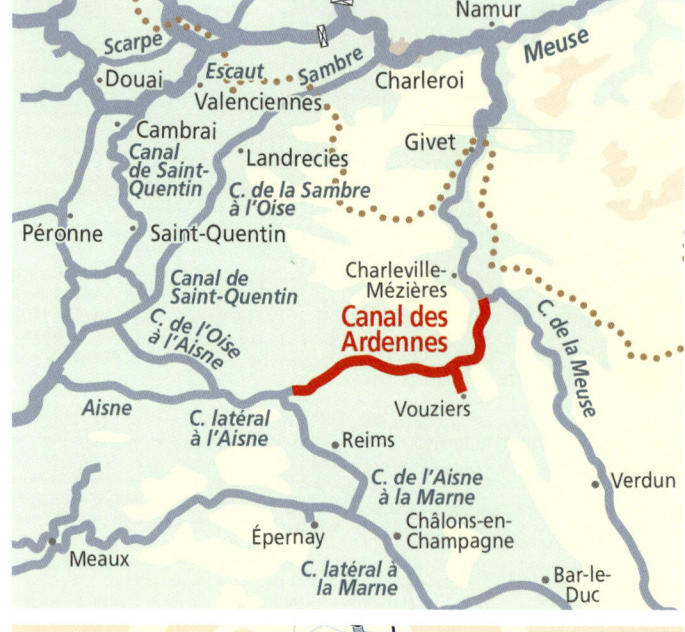

The canal was designed under the Revolution in the period 1793-1801 by the engineer Claude Deschamps, as a strategic connection between the rivers Aisne and Meuse. The designs were taken up in 1823 by the same engineer, and the canal opened in 1831. It was enlarged for 38m barges in 1846. Although it carries little commercial traffic, it remains in the national priority network. This designation does not apply to the Vouziers Branch, which is unfortunately threatened with closure. Boaters are encouraged to use this branch, also to help reduce weed growth during the summer months. The canal has a hire base at the Meuse end, but most clients stay on the Meuse. It is therefore mainly used by private boats in transit.

Navigation

The canal is pleasantly rural throughout its length, the main challenges being the flight of 27 locks at the western end of the summit level and the relative lack of *haltes* and villages to break up the journey. At Saint-Aignan there is a tunnel 197m in length, allowing one-way traffic only. The order of passage is that of arrival at the basin at the downstream

Key dimensions (m)	
Length	38.50
Beam	5.10
Draught	1.80
Air draught	3.50

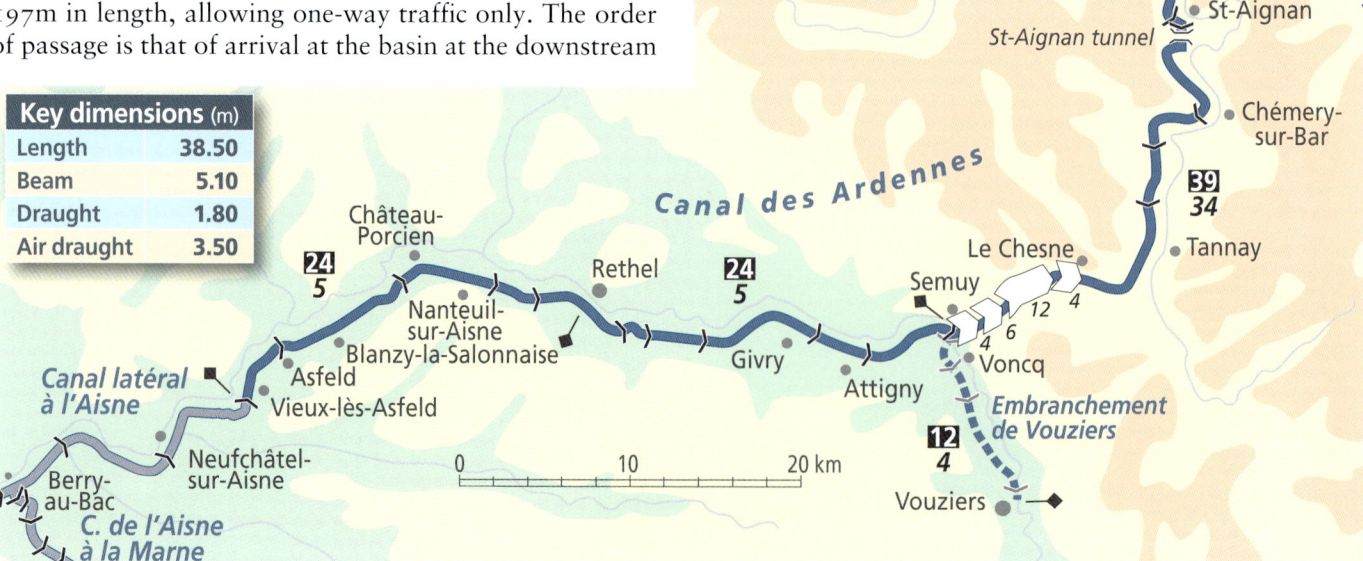

end of the tunnel, or at the mooring posts placed at the upstream end, at which points mooring is only authorised pending entry into the tunnel. There is no traffic control at this tunnel, hence the importance of carrying the usual lights, to be clearly visible to boats arriving at the opposite tunnel entrance.

Locks
There are 44 locks between Pont-à-Bar and Vieux-lès-Asfeld, of which 7 fall towards the Meuse and the remaining 37 towards the Aisne. There are 4 locks on the branch to Vouziers. All have standard dimensions of 38.50m by 5.20m. They are all automatic except for lock 27 (Rilly) on the Aisne side which is mechanised, and operated by a duty lock-keeper. Note that the sequence of operation of the flights of locks assumes that a boat entering the first lock will continue throughout the flight without interruption. This does not mean that boaters are not free to stop at will, but to avoid disrupting the operating cycle of the entire flight, it is essential in this case to advise the control centre of your intention (or walk back to the lock you have just left and use the telephone beside the control cabin). The four locks on the Vouziers branch are no longer operated and are in a sorry state.

Draught
The maximum authorised draught is 1.80m. This is still the official available depth on the Vouziers Branch, but weed growth is a serious problem on the branch, and makes progress almost impossible during the summer months.

Headroom
The maximum authorised air draught is 3.50m.

Towpath
There is a towpath throughout, but it has become almost impracticable from the Meuse to the summit level. A cycle path is projected throughout, and this will make the canal again fully accessible.

Authority
VNF Nord-Est
UTI Meuse-Ardennes
– 2 av. de Montcy Notre Dame - 08000 Charleville-Mézières 03 24 33 20 48   *uti.meuse-ardennes@vnf.fr* (PK 0-38)
VNF Bassin de la Seine
UTI Seine-Nord
– Quai Malmy, BP 5114 - 08303 Rethel 03 24 38 44 10 (PK 38-88 and Vouziers branch)

Route description

PK **0.0**	*Junction with Canal de la Meuse* (PK 96)
PK **0.1**	Lock 7 (Meuse), bridge
PK **0.9**	Lock 6 (Pont-à-Bar), bridge (D764), *port de plaisance* and Ardennes Nautisme hire base u/s r/b, 06 23 25 41 03, moorings for 55 boats, 3 visiting boats, night €12, *pontabarnautisme.fr*, water and electricity included, diesel, slipway, crane 20t, repairs, restaurant on barge
PK **3.0**	**Hannogne-Saint-Martin** bridge, village 500m l/b
PK **6.0**	Lock 5 (Saint-Aignan)
PK **6.1**	Lock 4 (**Saint-Aignan**), bridge, turning basin and quay d/s r/b, village 800m r/b

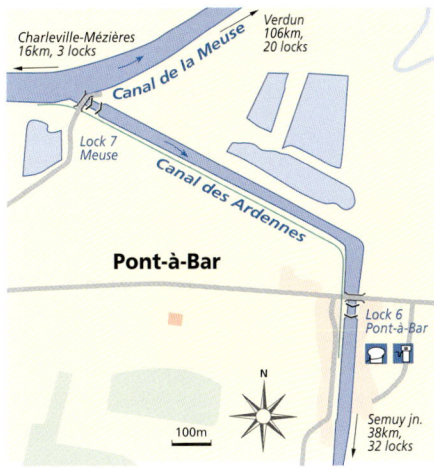

PK **6.3**	Saint-Aignan tunnel (length 196.50m)
PK **8.3**	**Omicourt** bridge, quay d/s l/b, small village l/b
PK **12.0**	Lock 3 (Malmy), bridge, quay u/s, r/b, **Chémery-sur-Bar** 1km r/b, café-tabac-restaurant
PK **13.0**	Turning basin l/b
PK **14.7**	Bridge (Morteau)
PK **15.8**	Ambly-sur-Bar bridge, quays u/s and d/s
PK **16.9**	Lock 2 (**Cassine**), bridge, small village l/b
PK **20.6**	Lock 1 (**Sauville**), start of summit level, bridge, village 1700m l/b
PK **20.8**	Aqueduct
PK **23.0**	**Tannay** bridge, village 1400m east
PK **24.8**	Bridge (Pont-Bar), quay

Quayside moorings at Le Chesne

IV – Northeastern France

PK 28.4 Skew bridge
PK 28.5 **Le Chesne** bridge, *halte* managed by VNF d/s r/b, 6 boats, free, water, electricity, turning basin, village l/b

A pleasant village and good *halte* to rest before the flight of 27 locks in 9 km. Water park in the nearby reservoir for the canal's water supply (Lac de Bairon).

Locks 1 and 2 on the Chesne flight, with an unusual sign inviting the 'downstream' boat to give priority to the oncoming boat. © SCHILLER70

PK 30.1 Lock 1 (Chesne), VHF 20, bridge, water, end of summit level
PK 30.3 Lock 2 (Chesne), turning basin d/s
PK 30.5 Lock 3 (Chesne), bridge
PK 30.8 Lock 4 (Chesne)
PK 30.9 Lock 5 (Montgon)
PK 31.3 Lock 6 (Montgon)
PK 31.5 Lock 7 (Montgon)

Looking from lock 7 towards lock 8 on the Montgon flight near the canal's summit level © BINNENVAART IN BEELD

PK 31.8 Lock 8 (Montgon)
PK 32.1 Lock 9 (Montgon)
PK 32.4 Lock 10 (Montgon)
PK 32.7 Lock 11 (Montgon), bridge, village 600m l/b
PK 33.0 Lock 12 (Montgon)
PK 33.1 Lock 13 (Montgon)
PK 33.4 Lock 14 (**Montgon**), bridge, village 500m l/b
PK 33.9 Lock 15 (Montgon)
PK 34.2 Lock 16 (Montgon)
PK 34.3 Lock 17 (Neuville-Day)
PK 34.7 Lock 18 (Neuville-Day)
PK 35.0 Lock 19 (Neuville-Day)
PK 35.3 **Neuville-Day** quay r/b, village 800m r/b
PK 35.4 Lock 20 (Neuville-Day), bridge
PK 35.8 Lock 21 (Neuville-Day)

This is the lock that had to be rebuilt after the flooding river Lametz caused its right-bank wall to collapse in 2019.

PK 36.5 Lock 22 (Neuville-Day), bridge
PK 37.2 Lock 23 (Semuy), bridge
PK 37.5 Lock 24 (Semuy)
PK 37.9 Lock 25 (Semuy)
PK 38.2 **Semuy** bridge, village r/b
PK 38.5 Lock 26 (Semuy), VHF 20
PK 38.6 Navigation enters river Aisne
PK 39.1 Navigation re-enters canal
PK 39.2 Lock 27 (Rilly), bridge, **junction with Vouziers branch** d/s of lock 4, disused, no navigation

The two locks at Rilly: in the foreground lock 27 on the through route, in the background the first lock of the currently disused Vouziers branch (see plan). © LUCAS JOIGNAUX

PK 40.0 Railway bridge (Sud des Ardennes tourist line)
PK 40.1 **Rilly-sur-Aisne** bridge, small village 300m l/b
PK 44.0 Lock 5 (Attigny), bridge, private quay u/s r/b
PK 44.9 **Attigny** bridge, municipal *halte* d/s l/b, free mooring for 14 boats, water, electricity, restaurant, village with shops and services l/b
PK 45.8 Private bridge (railway siding)
PK 47.2 Lock 6 (Givry), bridge, water
PK 48.2 **Givry** bridge, quay d/s r/b, small village l/b
PK 50.3 Private quay r/b
PK 52.9 **Ambly-Fleury** bridge, quay d/s r/b, village r/b
PK 55.0 Lock 7 (Seuil), bridge, small village 600m l/b
PK 57.7 Lock 8 (Thugny), bridge
PK 57.8 **Thugny-Trugny** quay r/b, village 600m r/b
PK 60.5 Lock 9 (Biermes), bridge
PK 60.7 **Biermes** quay r/b, village 800m l/b over bridge

Canal des Ardennes

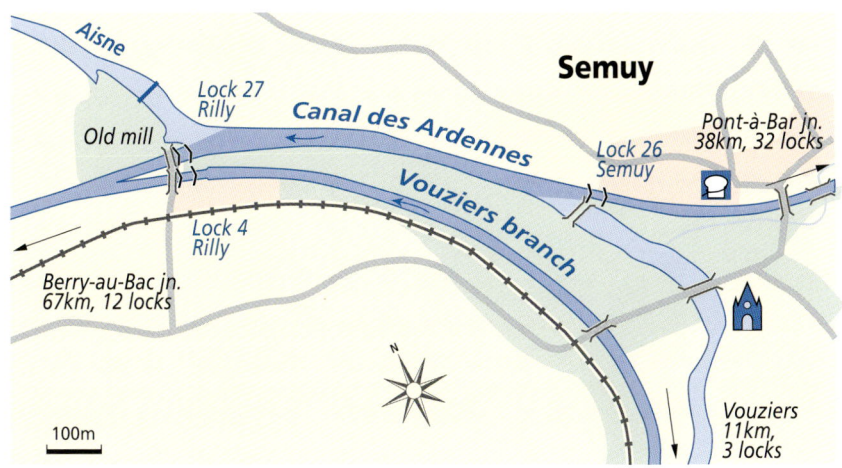

The 'watershed' canal from the Meuse to the Aisne ends here at Semuy, meeting what is effectively the Aisne lateral canal, which starts at the head of the Vouziers Branch. The second lock had to be built at this junction to keep the lateral canal separate from the river Aisne.

PK 61.2 Private quay l/b
PK 63.1 Turning basin r/b
PK 63.2 Railway bridge
PK 63.6 **Rethel** bridge, *halte* managed by tourist office for up to 10 boats on 100m long quay u/s r/b, water and electricity (8 connections), showers, town 800m r/b

A fair-sized town, and the only place on the canal where all kinds of provisions may be purchased. Attractive quayside moorings in the centre.

Mooring in Rethel, the town's modern church tower in the background. © CHRISTIAN RAU

PK 64.9 Motorway bridge (A34)
PK 65.0 Footbridge
PK 65.6 Lock 10 (Acy-Romance), bridge
PK 67.8 Lock 11 (Nanteuil), bridge
PK 68.2 **Nanteuil-sur-Aisne** quay and small village l/b
PK 70.8 Private quay r/b (Port-Arthur)
PK 73.0 **Château-Porcien** bridge, quay d/s r/b, village 500m r/b
PK 75.3 Lock 12 (Pargny), bridge
PK 78.3 Bridge (Blanzy)
PK 80.4 **Balham** bridge, quay u/s r/b, small village 400m r/b, Blanzy-la-Salonnaise 500m l/b
PK 83.4 Lock 13 (Asfeld), bridge, private quays u/s r/b
PK 85.1 Asfeld bridge, quay d/s r/b, village 700m l/b
PK 86.9 **Vieux-lès-Asfeld** bridge, quay u/s l/b, village 300m l/b
PK 87.9 Lock 14 (Vieux-lès-Asfeld), bridge
PK 88.0 *Junction with Canal latéral à l'Aisne*

Vouziers Branch

For information, currently unusable

PK 12.1 Lock 4 (Rilly), bridge, *junction with through route* (PK 39)
PK 11.3 Bridge (Rilly), quay d/s l/b, **Semuy** 400m r/b
PK 8.1 Lock 3 (**Voncq**), bridge, quay u/s l/b, village 1.5 km r/b
PK 4.7 Lock 2 (**Vrizy**), bridge
PK 3.4 Vrizy bridge, quay d/s l/b, village 700m l/b
PK 1.4 Bridge (Condé-les-Vouziers), quay d/s l/b
PK 0.5 Lock 1 (Vouziers), water, weir d/s r/b
PK 0.0 **Vouziers** bridge, head of navigation, quays d/s l/b, small town l/b

Small town with all services. The quay where barges formerly loaded grain from the silo is very high and for most boats would be an inconvenient place to moor.

IV – Northeastern France

39. Moselle

The Moselle is a modern waterway, made navigable to European Class Vb standard (for 1500-tonne barges and 3000-tonne push-tows) over a distance of 152 km in France from Neuves-Maisons near Nancy to the border with Luxembourg and Germany at Apach. The total length of the waterway to the confluence with the Rhine at Coblence is 394km.

The navigable Moselle connects with the Canal des Vosges at Neuves-Maisons (PK 394), the Canal de la Marne au Rhin, western section, at Toul (PK 369) and the Canal de la Marne au Rhin, eastern section at Nancy-Frouard (PK 346.5).

It should be noted that there are alternative routes for navigation at Toul (1.6km with one lock) and at Metz (10.5km, including the Canal de Jouy à Metz with its two locks, see plan). Distances in the right-hand column are those on the international waterway, counted from zero at Coblence.

The Becquey plan in 1830 provided for the Moselle to be canalised over its whole length in France. Works were conducted from Nancy towards Metz, where the Canal de Jouy à Metz had already been built. The 1870-71 war stopped the works, since Metz was thereafter in Germany. The existing locks were enlarged to the Freycinet dimensions in the late 19th century. After the return of Lorraine to France, the Canal des Mines de Fer de la Moselle was built to the Freycinet gauge (40.50m by 6m), but with extra width allowing for later enlargement. This canal was completed in 1932. In the meantime, the Moselle remained barely navigable through Luxemburg and Germany. When European economic construction began in the 1950s, canalisation of the whole river from Coblence to Metz, to 3m depth, was approved by the three riparian states in 1956, and works were completed in 1964. Locks were designed to receive two 1350-tonne barges (170m by 12m), and under pressure from France were extended by 6m to accommodate push-tows of two barges. The large-scale waterway was subsequently extended upstream, Nancy-Frouard being reached in 1972 (with locks 175m by 12m) and Neuves-Maisons in 1979 (locks 180m by 12m). This extension meant closing sections of the Canal de la Marne au Rhin and the Canal des Vosges. The available draught was increased to 2.80m in 2000.

Navigation
Like the Meuse, the Moselle is a tranquil river most of the time, but liable to impressive floods at any time during the spring, in particular. As on other large waterways, recreational craft may be asked to wait to share locks with commercial barges.

Locks
There are 16 locks between the German border and Neuves-Maisons. The first 10 to be built, from Apach up to Custines, have chambers 176 by 12m, with a sill depth of 3.50m. From Frouard upstream the locks were built slightly larger (185 by 12m, with a sill depth of 4m). The locks are electrically-operated and controlled by lights. Boat locks, 18.00m by 3.50m, were built at Apach and Kœnigsmacker, but these are no longer in use. At the four locks from Thionville to Metz-Nord there is a second lock chamber dating from the original canalisation, 40.50m by 6.00m, all restored in recent years and now generally to be used by pleasure traffic. The locks on the Canal de Jouy à Metz are no longer operated, and this canal is unfortunately only accessible from upstream for exceptional movements of residential barges.

Draught
Following a major programme of dredging works carried out under the aegis of the Moselle Commission by the authorities in all three countries, the maximum authorised draught has been increased to 3.00m from Coblence to Neuves-Maisons. The available draught on the Canal de Jouy à Metz is limited to 1.50m.

Headroom
The fixed bridges on the main waterway generally leave a minimum headroom of 6.00m above the highest navigable water level. The least headroom under the normal highest regulated level is 5.10m, while several bridges offer a headroom of less than 5m under the highest navigable water level. The lowest is the railway bridge below Fontenoy

Moselle

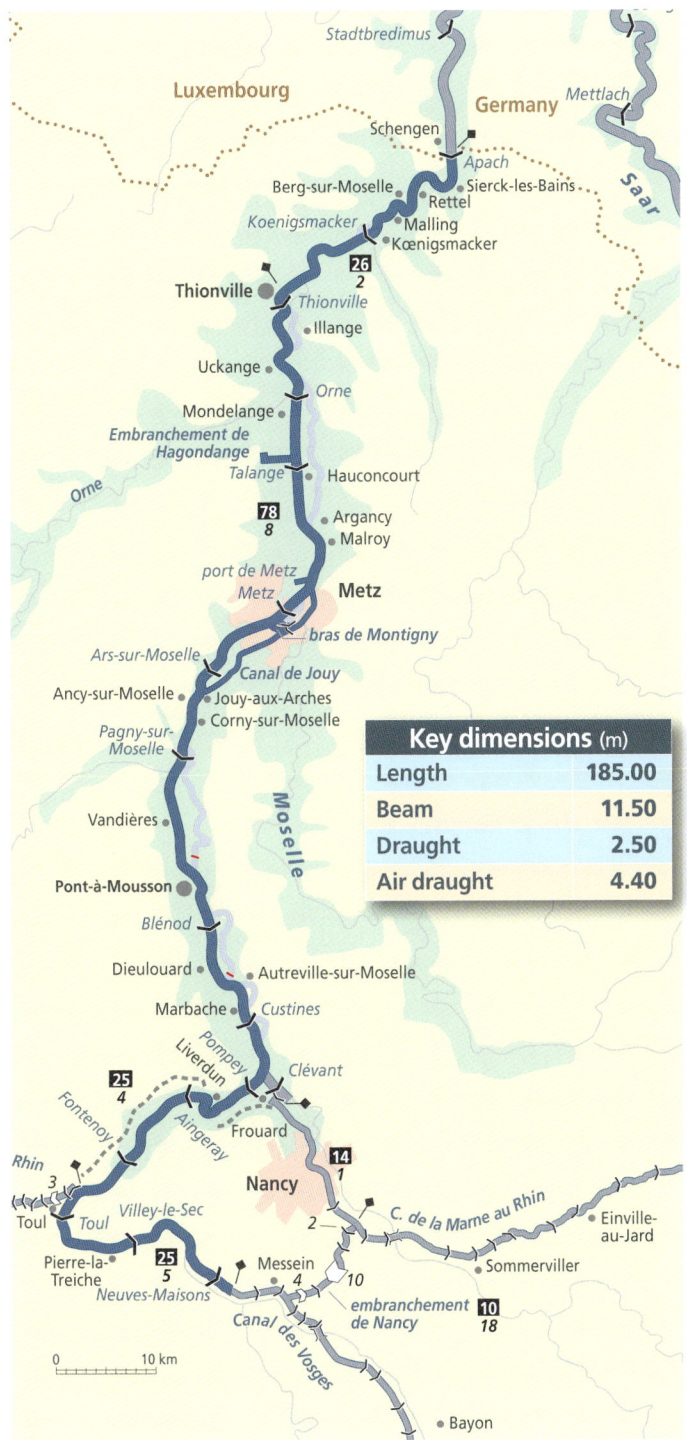

Route description

- PK 242.2 German (r/b) and Luxembourg (l/b) border (242.2km and 12 locks to Rhine at Koblenz)
- PK 242.4 Lock (Apach), VHF 20, lift 4.40m, r/b (all boats use the large lock)
- PK 243.3 **Apach** r/b, Luxembourg border l/b
- PK 245.5 **Sierck-les-Bains** r/b
- PK 246.8 Bridge (Sierck-les-Bains/Contz-les-Bains)
- PK 247.0 **Contz-les-Bains** l/b
- PK 249.5 **Rettel** r/b
- PK 252.5 **Berg-sur-Moselle** l/b
- PK 253.1 Meander cutoff r/b
- PK 254.0 **Malling** r/b
- PK 254.3 Bridge (Malling)
- PK 257.5 Entrance to diversion canal, **Kœnigsmacker** 700m r/b
- PK 258.2 Lock (Kœnigsmacker), VHF 20, lift 3.90m, bridge (boat lock out of order, all boats use large lock)
- PK 258.8 End of Kœnigsmacker diversion canal, **Cattenom** l/b
- PK 259.6 Overhead power lines
- PK 261.6 **Basse-Ham** *port de plaisance* r/b, 94 berths for boats up to 30m long, 06 35 82 37 28, night €13, electricity €1, water €1, pump-out, chandlery, slipway, *nautic-ham.fr*

New facility created by digging a cut through to gravel pits, attractive off-river mooring

Slipway and pontoons at the Basse-Ham boat harbour, PK 262

- PK 264.7 Arcelor Mittal factory r/b, overhead power lines
- PK 267.0 Railway bridge (Thionville-Nord)
- PK 268.0 Bridge (Pont des Alliés)
- PK 268.5 **Thionville** quay l/b, close to town centre

Historic town with many sites worth visiting.

- PK 268.9 End of diversion canal, boat club, 3 visitors' berths, 03 82 56 60 84, night €10, water, electricity, shower
- PK 269.2 Motorway (A31) and railway bridges
- PK 269.8 Lock (Thionville), VHF 20, lift 4.28m, parallel large and small chambers (small lock reopened 2021), bridge
- PK 270.0 Downstream limit of port
- PK 272.0 Upstream limit of port of Thionville-Illange, basins l/b
- PK 272.3 Flood gate (Uckange), footbridge
- PK 273.3 Entrance to Thionville diversion canal, l/b
- PK 273.7 Overhead power lines
- PK 274.1 Overhead pipeline crossing
- PK 275.2 **Uckange** bridge, town centre 1km l/b
- PK 275.9 Overhead Pipeline crossing
- PK 276.1 Motorway bridge (A31 Thionville-Nancy)
- PK 276.4 **Basse-Guénange** r/b

lock, giving a headroom of 4.30m under the HNWL), while several others give around 4.50m. This information may be useful for those who have a collapsible wheelhouse.

Authority
VNF Strasbourg, UTI Moselle
- 703 avenue du Colonel Péchot, BP 50326, 54201 Toul cedex 03 83 43 28 39 (PK 391-347)
- Écluse de l'Île d'Esch, CS 80243, 54701 Pont-à-Mousson Cedex 03 83 81 00 37 *agence-pam.uti-moselle.dt-nord-est@vnf.fr* (PK 314-347)
- 6 rue de Méric, CS 21052, 57036 Metz cedex 1 03 87 66 89 14 (PK 242-314)

IV – Northeastern France

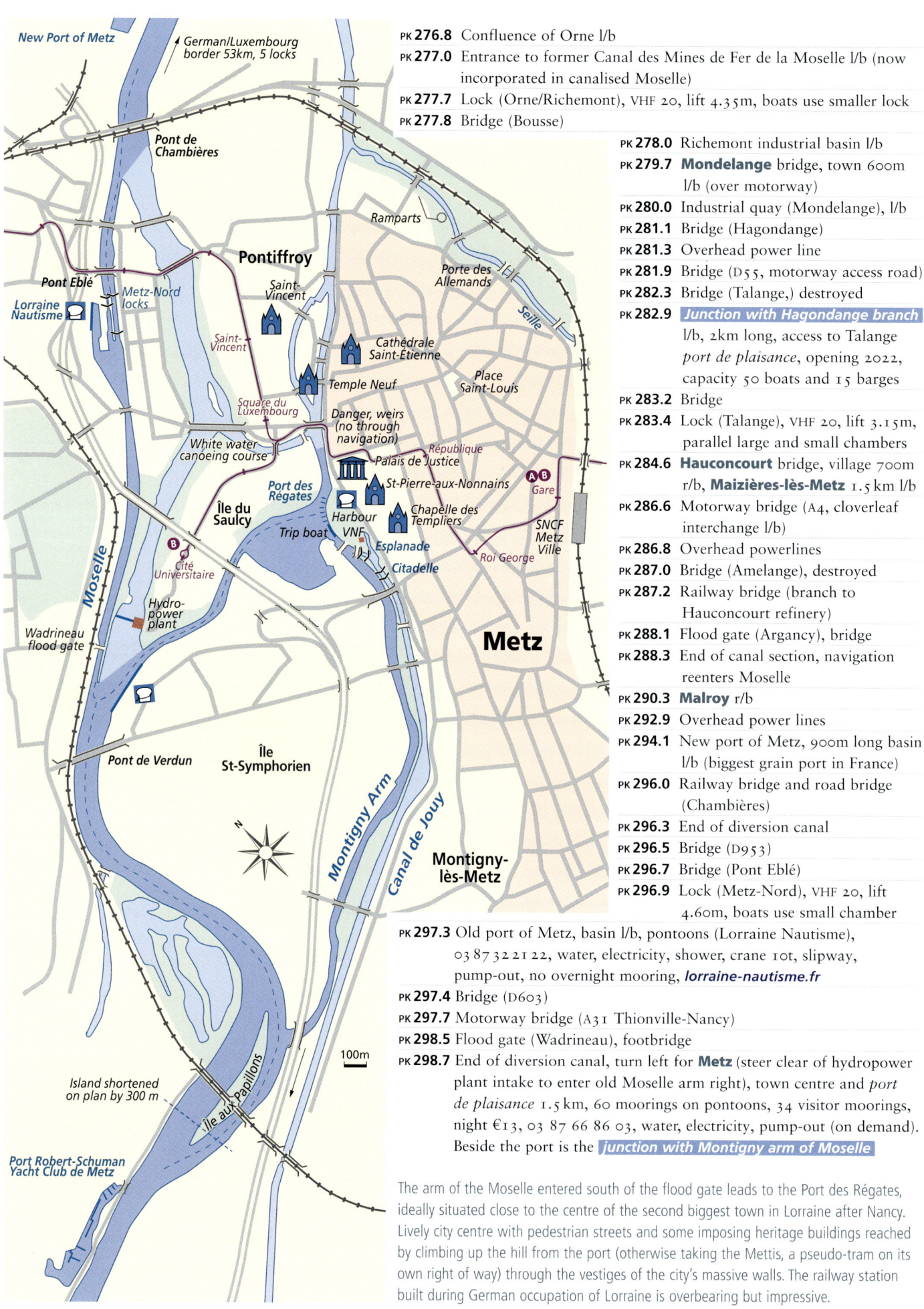

PK 276.8 Confluence of Orne l/b
PK 277.0 Entrance to former Canal des Mines de Fer de la Moselle l/b (now incorporated in canalised Moselle)
PK 277.7 Lock (Orne/Richemont), VHF 20, lift 4.35m, boats use smaller lock
PK 277.8 Bridge (Bousse)
PK 278.0 Richemont industrial basin l/b
PK 279.7 **Mondelange** bridge, town 600m l/b (over motorway)
PK 280.0 Industrial quay (Mondelange), l/b
PK 281.1 Bridge (Hagondange)
PK 281.3 Overhead power line
PK 281.9 Bridge (D55, motorway access road)
PK 282.3 Bridge (Talange,) destroyed
PK 282.9 Junction with Hagondange branch l/b, 2km long, access to Talange *port de plaisance*, opening 2022, capacity 50 boats and 15 barges
PK 283.2 Bridge
PK 283.4 Lock (Talange), VHF 20, lift 3.15m, parallel large and small chambers
PK 284.6 **Hauconcourt** bridge, village 700m r/b, **Maizières-lès-Metz** 1.5 km l/b
PK 286.6 Motorway bridge (A4, cloverleaf interchange l/b)
PK 286.8 Overhead powerlines
PK 287.0 Bridge (Amelange), destroyed
PK 287.2 Railway bridge (branch to Hauconcourt refinery)
PK 288.1 Flood gate (Argancy), bridge
PK 288.3 End of canal section, navigation reenters Moselle
PK 290.3 **Malroy** r/b
PK 292.9 Overhead power lines
PK 294.1 New port of Metz, 900m long basin l/b (biggest grain port in France)
PK 296.0 Railway bridge and road bridge (Chambières)
PK 296.3 End of diversion canal
PK 296.5 Bridge (D953)
PK 296.7 Bridge (Pont Eblé)
PK 296.9 Lock (Metz-Nord), VHF 20, lift 4.60m, boats use small chamber
PK 297.3 Old port of Metz, basin l/b, pontoons (Lorraine Nautisme), 03 87 32 21 22, water, electricity, shower, crane 10t, slipway, pump-out, no overnight mooring, *lorraine-nautisme.fr*
PK 297.4 Bridge (D603)
PK 297.7 Motorway bridge (A31 Thionville-Nancy)
PK 298.5 Flood gate (Wadrineau), footbridge
PK 298.7 End of diversion canal, turn left for **Metz** (steer clear of hydropower plant intake to enter old Moselle arm right), town centre and *port de plaisance* 1.5 km, 60 moorings on pontoons, 34 visitor moorings, night €13, 03 87 66 86 03, water, electricity, pump-out (on demand). Beside the port is the junction with Montigny arm of Moselle

The arm of the Moselle entered south of the flood gate leads to the Port des Régates, ideally situated close to the centre of the second biggest town in Lorraine after Nancy. Lively city centre with pedestrian streets and some imposing heritage buildings reached by climbing up the hill from the port (otherwise taking the Mettis, a pseudo-tram on its own right of way) through the vestiges of the city's massive walls. The railway station built during German occupation of Lorraine is overbearing but impressive.

Moselle

The port de plaisance (Port des Régates) with the imposing cathedral of Saint-Étienne. © N. GUIRKINGER

PK **299.0** Bridge (Pont de Verdun), **Longeville-lès-Metz** l/b
PK **299.5** Boat harbour in small arm l/b
PK **300.6** Junction with Montigny arm of Moselle r/b, access to Metz for boats (see plan opposite)
PK **301.0** Railway bridge
PK **301.5** Entrance to *port de plaisance* Robert-Schuman l/b (Yachting Club de Metz), 06 20 20 08 48, 15 visitors' berths, night €15, water included, electricity metered, wifi, shower, slipway, *yachting.club.metz@gmail.com*, **Scy-Chazelles** 1000m
PK **302.7 Moulins-lès-Metz** bridge, town 1 km l/b
PK **304.3** End of diversion canal
PK **304.7** Entrance to Vaux diversion canal, l/b
PK **305.8** Railway bridge
PK **306.1** End of diversion canal
PK **306.7** Lock (Ars-sur-Moselle), VHF 20, lift 4.00m
PK **307.1 Ars-sur-Moselle** bridge, town centre 800m l/b (beyond railway)
PK **308.6** Entrance to Ars diversion canal, l/b, and junction with Canal de Jouy à Metz, r/b (alternative route to Metz no longer navigable at present)
PK **309.3 Ancy-sur-Moselle** l/b, beyond railway and main road
PK **311.0** Entrance to **Corny-sur-Moselle** basin and municipal *halte* at campsite r/b, 07 67 59 05 55, pontoon for 5 visitor moorings, night €10, water and electricity included, shower at camp site, wifi (charged), slipway
PK **312.4** Bridge (Corny-sur-Moselle)
PK **312.6** Junction with former canal section (disused), l/b
PK **317.4** End of Pagny/Pont-à-Mousson diversion canal
PK **318.1** Lock (Pagny-sur-Moselle), VHF 20, lift 8.50m, bridge
PK **318.5 Pagny-sur-Moselle** basin, possible informal mooring l/b, town centre 700m l/b
PK **320.5** Overhead power lines
PK **320.7** Railway viaduct (Moselle, TGV Est)
PK **321.4** Bridge (Chécohée-Vandières)
PK **321.8 Vandières** public quay l/b, village with shops behind railway line
PK **322.8** Overhead power lines
PK **323.7** Bridge (Norroy)
PK **325.4** Flood gate (Pont-à-Mousson), bridge, access to grain loading quay l/b
PK **325.6** New entrance to Pagny/Pont-à-Mousson diversion canal, l/b
PK **325.7** Bridge (D910B, Pont-à-Mousson bypass)

PK **327.0** Upstream entrance to former canal section, l/b
PK **327.6** Bridge (Pont-à-Mousson)

Good mooring on the left bank downstream of the bridge. The concrete quay faces the imposing skyline of the old town, with the old abbey (Abbaye des Prémontrés) and Saint-Martin church just downstream. All services in the small town.

PK **328.0 Pont-à-Mousson** basin and municipal port de plaisance r/b, 99 berths on pontoons, 12 visitor berths, 03 83 83 53 52, night €12.50, water and electricity included, showers, pump-out, slipway
PK **328.2** Junction with former diversion canal (disused) l/b, possible mooring for Pont-à-Mousson in first 200m
PK **330.8** Entrance to diversion canal l/b
PK **331.6** Lock (Blénod/Pont-à-Mousson), VHF 20, lift 5.65m, bridge
PK **332.3** Road and railway bridge (access to Blénod power station r/b)
PK **333.3** Overhead power lines
PK **334.1 Dieulouard** bridge, small town centre 900m l/b
PK **335.3** Private quay (Atton) r/b
PK **336.1** Flood gate (Liégeot), footbridge
PK **336.5** End of Blénod-Liégeot diversion canal, navigation re-enters river Moselle
PK **336.9** Overhead power lines
PK **338.5** Motorway bridge (viaduc d'Autreville, A31)
PK **339.3** Overhead power line
PK **339.5** Entrance to diversion canal l/b, access via Moselle to **Millery** district *halte* r/b, 1200m, 30m pontoon, free (maximum 5 days), water, electricity, wifi, slipway
PK **340.5** Overhead power lines
PK **340.9** Bridge
PK **341.0** End of Belleville diversion canal, navigation re-enters river Moselle
PK **341.5** Motorway bridge (A31 Metz-Nancy)
PK **342.0 Marbache**, l/b
PK **343.0** End of diversion canal
PK **343.7** Lock (Custines), VHF 20, lift 3.85m, footbridge
PK **344.6** Bridge (Custines 1 km)
PK **344.8** Railway bridge (Nomeny branch line)
PK **344.9** Loading quay r/b
PK **345.2** Road and railway bridge (Pompey steel works)
PK **345.4** Entrance to Pompey/Custines diversion canal, l/b
PK **345.6** Bridge
PK **346.5** Junction with branch to port of Nancy-Frouard and Canal de la Marne au Rhin, east branch, r/b
PK **346.7** Railway bridge (lowest under normal high water level)
PK **346.9 Pompey** l/b, **Frouard** r/b, bridge (D657), district *halte* u/s l/b for 4 boats, 03 83 49 81 81, free (maximum 5 days), water, electricity, wifi, *tourisme@bassinpompey.fr*
PK **347.8** Lock (Pompey-Frouard), VHF 20, lift 2.70m, in 1 km diversion l/b
PK **351.7** Railway bridge
PK **351.9** Former Liverdun aqueduct of Canal de la Marne au Rhin (destroyed)
PK **352.1 Liverdun** bridge, small town 600m l/b
PK **352.9** Castle (Château de la Flye) r/b
PK **353.6** Railway bridge
PK **354.2** Access to moorings for Liverdun l/b, slipway

IV – Northeastern France

PK 355.7 Lock (Aingeray), VHF 20, lift 7.30m, in 700m diversion r/b, bridge
PK 360.9 End of Villey-Saint-Étienne/Valcourt diversion canal
PK 363.3 Bridge (Fontenoy)
PK 363.8 Railway bridge (least headroom under the highest navigable water level, 4.30m)
PK 364.0 Lock (Fontenoy), VHF 20, lift 4.40m, bridge
PK 366.5 Bridge (Gondreville)
PK 369.1 Bridge (D904)
PK 369.5 Junction with Canal de la Marne au Rhin, western section, l/b (350m link canal with one lock)
PK 369.6 Bridge (Toul)
PK 370.4 Railway bridge
PK 370.9 Bridge (D400, avenue Maréchal Foch)
PK 371.0 **Toul** lock, VHF 20, lift 4.40m, parallel lock in former Canal de l'Est, southern branch (see plan right), footbridge, town with all shops l/b
PK 372.5 Bridge
PK 372.6 Motorway bridge (A31)
PK 373.0 Entrance to diversion canal (Villey-Saint-Étienne/Valcourt), middle channel, Moselle on the right, former Canal de l'Est on the left, to be taken by boats
PK 376.1 **Pierre-la-Treiche** bridge, village 300m
PK 379.3 Lock (Villey-le-Sec), VHF 20, lift 7.20m, in 1200m diversion, l/b, bridge
PK 384.3 Former lock 50 (Sexey-les-Forges) l/b, destroyed
PK 386.8 **Maron** bridge, village r/b
PK 387.3 End of Maron/Neuves-Maisons diversion canal
PK 388.8 Turning basin
PK 389.6 Footbridge
PK 391.9 **Neuves-Maisons** bridge, town centre 1km r/b, Pont-Saint-Vincent 400m l/b
PK 392.2 Railway bridge
PK 392.4 Lock (**Neuves-Maisons**), VHF 20, lift 7.10m, bridge
PK 392.6 Neuves-Maisons steel works, private basin r/b
PK 393.1 Pipeline crossing
PK 394.0 Junction with Canal des Vosges, d/s of lock 47, turning basin

Frouard branch

PK 346.5 Junction with Moselle (PK 346.5)
PK 347.5 Lock (Clévant), VHF 20, one large and one small chamber, bridge
PK 348.0 **Nancy-Frouard** industrial port, basin 400m long, sharp right-hand bend under railway bridge
PK 348.1 Lock
PK 348.2 Junction with Canal de la Marne au Rhin (PK 154)

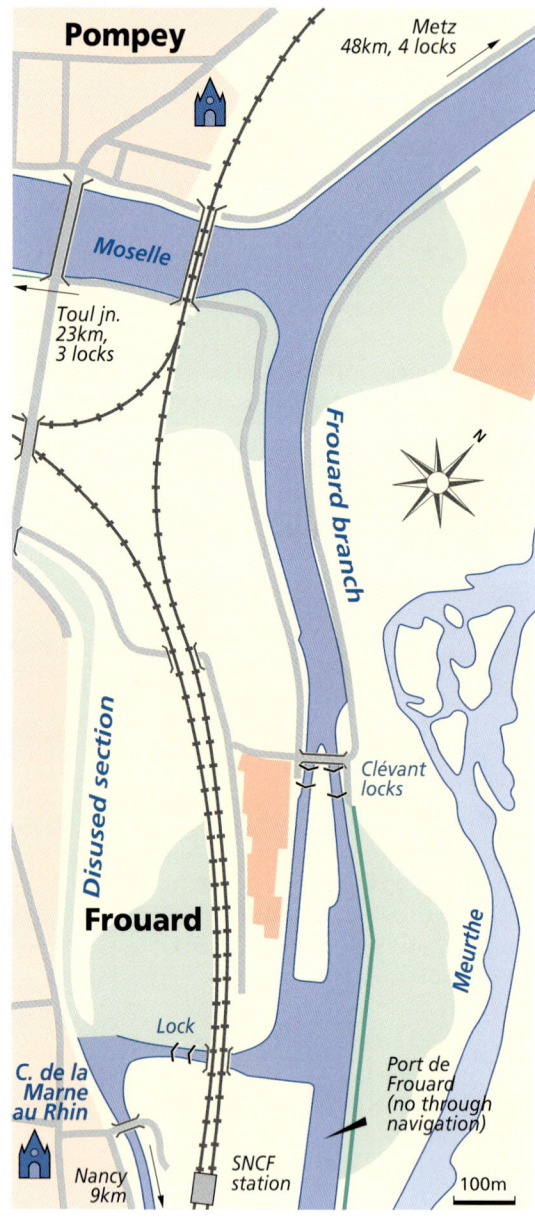

Moselle

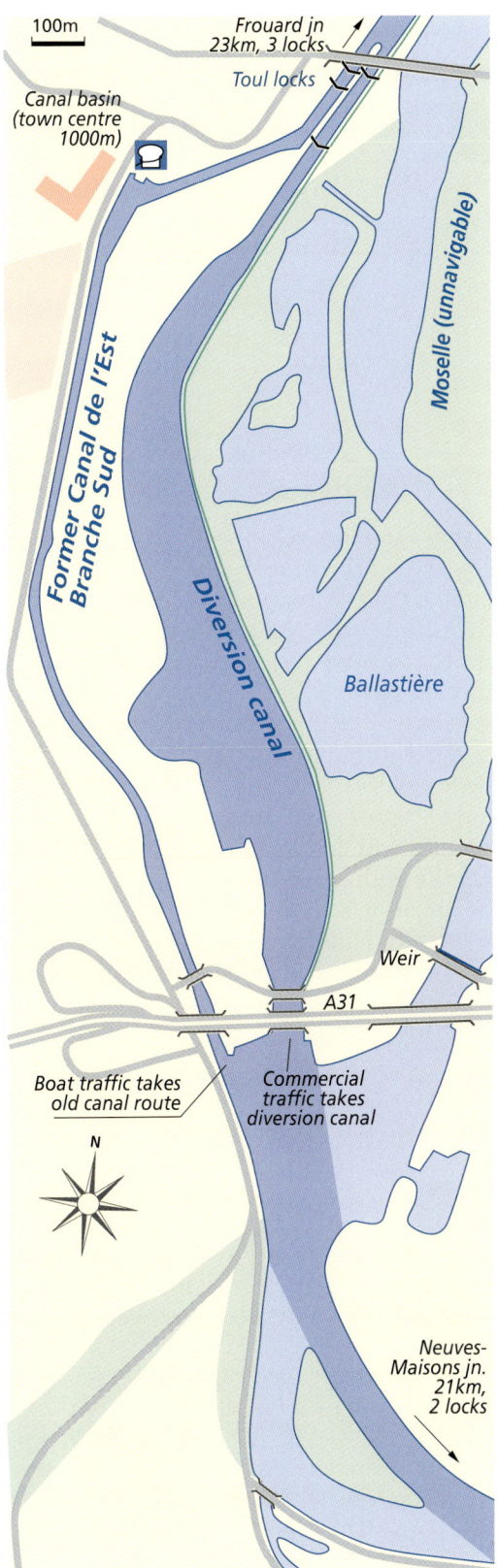

Canal de Jouy à Metz

This side canal, including the navigable arm of the river Moselle that leads to it, is given as an alternative through route, although in practice only the first 1.7km to Metz is normally navigable. The canal locks are operated exceptionally for local boats only.

PK 0.0	*Entrance from main channel of river Moselle* (PK 298.7), u/s boats turn sharp left on leaving the Metz lock-cut)
PK 0.6	Wadrineau dam and hydropower plant l/b
PK 1.2	Motorway bridge (A31)
PK 1.7	River widens to form Bassin des Régates, **Metz** town centre and moorings r/b, 03 87 62 28 97, 45 berths, night €10, water, electricity, shower, pump-out, navigation continues left upstream in navigable arm of Moselle
PK 1.8	Entrance to canal, bridge

The canal is accessible only to local craft by reservation. The description is continued for reference (and because of its potential).

The disused Canal de Jouy à Metz, just waiting to be restored to through navigation; the main obstacle is the need to man the two locks in Metz. © CAP TEMPÊTE

PK 1.9	Lock (Esplanade), bridge
PK 2.0	Lock (Citadelle)
PK 2.1	Bridge (motorway spur, avenue Joffre)
PK 7.3	Motorway bridge (A31)
PK 7.0	Bridge (Tournebride)
PK 6.1	Bridge (D157b, motorway spur)
PK 4.9	Bridge (Station Hydraulique)
PK 4.8	Railway bridge (8m passage)
PK 3.6	Bridge (rue des Couvents), **Montigny-les-Metz** 700m r/b
PK 2.9	Former industrial basin (La Vacquinière) r/b
PK 2.4	Bridge (rue Saint-Symphorien)
PK 2.2	Bridge (chemin du Port)
PK 8.2	Bridge
PK 8.3	Skew railway bridge, 9m wide passage
PK 8.9	Bridge
PK 9.0	Flood spillway l/b, former lock (Polka), open
PK 9.3	Factory r/b
PK 10.2	Bridge
PK 10.4	Flood gate, bridge
PK 10.5	*Junction with Moselle* (PK 308.6), Jouy dam on Moselle l/b

40. Canal de la Marne au Rhin

THE CANAL DE LA MARNE AU RHIN was completed in 1855 as a vital link between Paris and Alsace and Germany. It presents diverse landscapes, but is consistently delightful along its full length. The length from Niderviller (PK245) to Saverne (PK269) contains all that is best on the French waterways: the softly rounded countryside of Lorraine, then steep-sided wooded valleys, picturesque Alsatian villages, plus two tunnels and the unique Arzviller inclined plane. The canal passes through the historic towns of Bar-le-Duc, Toul and Nancy, and finishes in style just beyond the European Parliament in Strasbourg.

This was the longest canal in France (313km) until 1979, when a 23km section along the Moselle valley was closed following completion of the Moselle canalisation works between Frouard and Neuves-Maisons. The current route, from the junction with the Canal entre Champagne et Bourgogne and the Canal latéral à la Marne at Vitry-le-François to the port of Strasbourg on the Rhine, is now made up as follows:

a) Canal de la Marne au Rhin, western section (PK 0-131), connecting with the Canal de la Meuse at Troussey (PK 111), and including a short branch to Houdelaincourt (PK 85)

b) Navigable river Moselle from Toul to Frouard (a distance of 25km, slightly longer than by the original canal)

c) Eastern section from Frouard to Strasbourg (PK 154-313); this section makes connections with the Nancy branch of the Canal des Vosges at Laneuveville-devant-Nancy (PK 169) and with the Canal de la Sarre at Gondrexange (PK 228).

The western section in particular is very peaceful, and in VNF's current long-term plan is a low priority. The eastern section is seen as having potential to carry more freight, as well as being very pretty and justifiably popular, with several hire boat bases.

The canal has two summit levels, the Mauvages summit (altitude 281m) between the Marne and the Meuse, and the Vosges summit (267m) between the Meurthe and the Rhine. The first includes the Mauvages tunnel, 4877m in length, while the second has two tunnels within a short distance at its eastern end, Niderwiller (475m) and Arzviller (2307m). There is a fourth tunnel at Foug (867m), cutting through the low watershed between the Meuse and Moselle valleys.

There was another tunnel 388m long at Liverdun, on the section now bypassed by the navigable river Moselle.

Boats proceed through all tunnels under their own power, when the green light is shown. On entering Foug tunnel from the western end there is a pole to be pushed forwards for 5 to 10 seconds, to inform the tunnel-keeper at lock 14.

Navigation

The information here covers the canal only. See under *Moselle* the different conditions that apply on that broad river used by Rhine barges (25km link between the eastern and western sections).

This canal was built concurrently with the railway line, from 1839 to 1855, and on a parallel course. The locks were built to dimensions half way between the Becquey and Freycinet standards (34.50m by 5.20m, and depth of 1.80m). German occupation of Alsace in 1871 then also prompted construction of the Canal de l'Est (now the Canal des Vosges) south from Nancy to connect with the River Saône. The canal was deepened twice, first to 2.20m (for 1.80m draught) at the end of the 19th century, then to 2.50m (for 2.20m draught) in the 1960s, but only east of Nancy. At the same time, the terminal locks leading to the summit level were replaced, west of the Vosges, by the deepest Freycinet lock (Réchicourt), and towards Alsace by the inclined plane of Saint-Louis-Arzviller, a unique feat of engineering, overcoming a 44.55m difference in level.

Canal de la Marne au Rhin

The western section from Vitry-le-François to Toul, showing the former route taken over by the Moselle. For the eastern section map see p.49.

Key dimensions (m)	
Length	38.70
Beam	5.10
Draught	1.80
Air draught	3.60

Locks

There are in all 152 locks, plus the inclined plane of Arzviller/Saint-Louis (PK 255) opened in 1969. The western section has 97 locks, of which 70 rise from the Marne and 27 drop down to the river Moselle. The locks are 38.70m long and 5.13m wide, except for the new lock connecting with the Moselle at Toul, 40m by 6m. The eastern section now has only 55 locks (instead of 78). There are 21 from Nancy up to the summit level. The last, at Réchicourt, is a deep lock (15.70m) replacing the flight of six locks on the original canal. East of the summit level and Arzviller tunnel, a new cut clinging to the side of the Zorn valley leads to the inclined plane, which replaces a flight of 17 locks. These are disused, although there are plans to restore the first four down to an attractive basin surrounded by pine trees.

From the point where the downstream approach canal rejoins the old line there are 34 locks down to Strasbourg.

The minimum dimensions are the same as on the western section, although the inclined plane and the new lock at Saverne were built to the slightly greater width of 5.50m.

Locks are automatic ('magic eye' sensor) from PK 0 to PK 30 (lock 55). Before this lock is reached, the mobile lock-keeper will have supplied you with a remote control unit to be used throughout the rest of the canal. From PK 68 to PK 103 (Toul) the system automatically prepares the next in the series as one leaves the current lock.

Mobile phone numbers for the duty lock supervisors are 06 81 06 81 22 for Bar-le-Duc (locks 70-18), 06 88 18 03 12 for Void (locks 17-27A) and 06 83 84 26 43 for Einville (locks 26-2 Réchicourt). The automatic locks in the Strasbourg region are managed in four separate flights: 18-24, 25-36, 37-46 and 47-51, with mobile lock-keepers in the VNF vans often to be seen driving along the towpath. They can be called up on the intercom available at each lock if needed.

The Nancy branch has 18 locks.

Headroom

The maximum authorised air draught is 3.60m. Lift bridges are closed at lunchtime from 1200 to 1230.

Tunnels

There is a 5km tunnel at PK86-PK92 Mauvages, a 0.75km tunnel at PK121 Foug, a 0.5km tunnel at PK248 Niderviller and a 2.3km tunnel at PK249-PK251 Arzviller.

Draught

The maximum authorised draught is 1.80m on the western section and 2.20m on the eastern section. Since there is still some commercial traffic, these values can be considered as reasonably reliable.

Speed

Speed is limited to 6km/h throughout the canal, and 3km/h when passing moored boats.

Towpath

There is a good towpath throughout.

Authority

VNF Nord-Est
– UTI Canal de la Marne au Rhin Ouest
  1 rue de l'Ormicée, BP 523, 55012 Bar-le-Duc cedex
  03 29 79 12 33 (PK 0-129)
– UTI Canal de la Marne au Rhin Est – Branche de Nancy
  52 rue Charles de Foucauld, 54000 Nancy 03 83 17 41 20 (PK 155-222 and Nancy branch)

VNF Strasbourg
– UTI Canal de la Marne au Rhin
  12 rue de l'Orangerie, 67703 Saverne Cedex 03 88 91 80 83 (PK 222-313)

IV – Northeastern France

Route description

Western section, Marne to Moselle

Vitry is a pleasant enough small town (rebuilt following wholesale destruction in WWII) and has facilities such as supermarkets and a large 'brico' (DIY store). The 'harbour' lies on a bend 1km west of PK 0, opposite a large *péniche* repair yard. It is very small and shallow. However, it is possible to moor up outside, alongside the canal itself, although the quay is not large. The first section of the canal between Vitry and Bignicourt is fairly straight and featureless, although quiet and rural.

PK 0.0	Vitry-le-François basin, **Vitry-le-François** basin, **junction with Canal entre Champagne et Bourgogne** town centre 500m
PK 0.2	Commercial quay l/b
PK 0.6	Bridge (Vassues)
PK 0.9	**Junction with Canal latéral à la Marne** (new cut), r/b
PK 1.7	Bridge (N4)
PK 1.9	Bridge (Saint-Jacques)
PK 3.3	Lock 70 (Saint-Étienne), VHF 20, water, bridge, quay u/s l/b
PK 5.1	Lock 69 (Adecourt), bridge
PK 5.8	**Plichancourt** bridge, quay and turning basin d/s
PK 6.6	Bridge (Caure)
PK 7.6	Brusson quay l/b, village 300m
PK 7.9	Lock 68 (Brusson), access lights l/b, very tight corner, bridge (D995), aqueduct upstream
PK 9.4	**Ponthion** bridge, small village 300m r/b
PK 10.0	Lock 67 (Ponthion), bridge, quay and turning basin d/s
PK 12.4	Le Buisson bridge, village l/b
PK 13.6	Bridge (Pré-le-Doyen)
PK 14.4	**Bignicourt-sur-Saulx** quay l/b d/s, no services

Pleasant mooring in a rural setting, overlooked by the splendid neoclassical château in the Palladian style.

The imposing neoclassical château at Bignicourt, PK 14, makes an elegant backdrop to a peaceful mooring. © AURELIEN POITOUT

PK 14.6	Lock 66 (Bignicourt), bridge
PK 16.3	Étrepy quay l/b, village and castle 300m l/b
PK 16.6	Lock 65 (Étrepy), bridge, aqueduct upstream
PK 18.7	Lock 64 (Pargny-sur-Saulx), bridge, water
PK 18.8	**Pargny-sur-Saulx** basin and quay for 5 boats l/b, 06 49 47 94 49, night €6.50, water, electricity, restaurant, village 600m l/b

Good mooring with services.

Quay at Pargny-sur-Saulx © MICHAEL PAPENBURG

PK 19.1	Lock 63 (Pargny-sur-Saulx aqueduct), aqueduct upstream
PK 20.9	Bridge (Ajot)
PK 21.7	Lock 62 (Ajot)
PK 23.0	Lock 61 (Chaîne), bridge
PK 24.5	Lock 60 (Sermaize-les-Bains), bridge
PK 24.6	**Sermaize-les-Bains** basin, quay l/b, no services, small town 600m l/b
PK 24.7	Pipeline crossing
PK 24.9	Bridge (Remennecourt)
PK 25.2	Railway bridge, quay u/s l/b, caution, heavily silted
PK 25.7	Lock 59 (Remennecourt), bridge
PK 27.4	Lock 58 (Chevol), bridge
PK 28.1	**Contrisson** basin, quay l/b, village 400m
PK 28.4	Lock 57 (Contrisson), bridge
PK 29.1	Lock 56 (Braux), bridge, quay d/s l/b
PK 29.6	Railway bridge
PK 30.0	Lock 55 (Haie Herlin)
PK 30.6	Lock 54 (Damzelle), private quays u/s and d/s
PK 31.1	Lock 53 (Notre-Dame-de-Grâce), cement works, quay u/s l/b
PK 31.7	Lock 52 (Revigny), bridge, water
PK 31.8	**Revigny** quay l/b, water, small town 1.5km r/b
PK 32.0	Overhead power lines
PK 32.8	Lock 51 (Bois l'Écuyer), bridge

Canal de la Marne au Rhin

PK 33.8	Lock 50 (Petit-Fraicul)
PK 34.6	Lock 49 (Grand-Fraicul)
PK 35.3	**Neuville-sur-Ornain** quay l/b, no services, village 1km
PK 35.6	Lock 48 (Neuville-sur-Ornain), bridge
PK 36.7	Lock 47 (Doeuil), private quay u/s l/b
PK 38.5	Lock 46 (Mussey), lift bridge, water, basin u/s, Val d'Ornain l/b
PK 39.2	Lock 45 (Chacolée)
PK 40.3	Lock 44 (Varney), bridge, quay d/s l/b
PK 41.2	Lock 43 (Rembercourt), quay u/s r/b, restaurant
PK 43.1	**Fains-Véel** quay for 3 boats l/b, 03 29 77 19 52, water, electricity, village 500m
PK 43.3	Lock 42 (Fains-les-Sources), lift bridge, lights r/b
PK 44.5	Skew railway bridge and road bridge (D994)
PK 44.5	Lock 41 (Grand-Pré)
PK 45.0	Lock 40 (Pont-Canal de Chanteraines), aqueduct u/s

Lock 40 and aqueduct over the Ornain, PK 45 © EUROCANALS

PK 46.2	Bridge
PK 46.3	Lock 39 (Bar-le-Duc), bridge, water, waiting bollards u/s l/b
PK 46.8	Bridge (Triby)
PK 47.0	**Bar-le-Duc** municipal *halte* for 10 boats l/b, night €10, water, electricity, slipway, turning basin, town l/b over railway

Historic pretty small town, for many hundreds of years it was virtually an independent state and only became formally part of France in 1776. Birthplace of the bicycle. Quayside and finger pontoon moorings with services, near the railway station.

The well-serviced moorings at Bar-le-Duc, PK 47

PK 47.5	Lift bridge (Marbot), quays u/s, no services
PK 47.9	Lock 38 (Marbot), lift bridge (Cimetière)
PK 48.6	Lock 37 (Popey)
PK 49.2	Railway bridge and main road bridge (N135), delicate passage, proceed with caution
PK 49.9	Lock 36 (Savonnières)
PK 50.5	Lock 35 (Longeville), bridge, aqueduct u/s
PK 51.5	Longeville basin, village 800m
PK 51.7	Lock 34 (Grande-Chalaide), bridge
PK 52.2	Bridge (Petite-Chalaide), Longeville r/b
PK 53.3	Lock 33 (Maheux)
PK 54.1	Lock 32 (Tannois), bridge
PK 54.4	**Tannois** quay l/b, heavily silted, no services, village 300m
PK 54.6	Lock 31 (Silmont), bridge
PK 55.6	Lock 30 (Guerpont)
PK 56.3	Lock 29 (Bohanne), bridge
PK 56.9	Lock 28 (Tronville), bridge
PK 57.9	**Tronville** bridge, quays r/b, no services, turning basin, village 300m
PK 58.9	Lock 27 (Chessard), bridge
PK 59.5	Lock 26 (Nançois-le-Petit)
PK 60.2	Lock 25 (Velaines), bridge, water
PK 60.5	**Velaines** bridge, quay d/s l/b, village over railway
PK 61.6	Lock 24 (Maulan), bridge
PK 62.2	Lock 23 (Villeroncourt), bridge
PK 62.3	Motorway bridge (N4 Ligny-en-Barrois bypass)
PK 62.5	**Ligny-en-Barrois** basin r/b, quay for 10 boats, night €10, campsite 06 74 39 57 56, water and electricity included, shower, slipway, restaurant, town centre 500m

Small *port de plaisance* beside a campsite, reportedly shallow.

PK 62.7	Lock 22 (Ligny-en-Barrois), bridge, water
PK 63.3	Bridge (Herval)
PK 64.1	Lock 21 (Gainval)
PK 64.8	Lock 20 (Grèves)
PK 65.3	Givrauval quay l/b, no services, village 200m

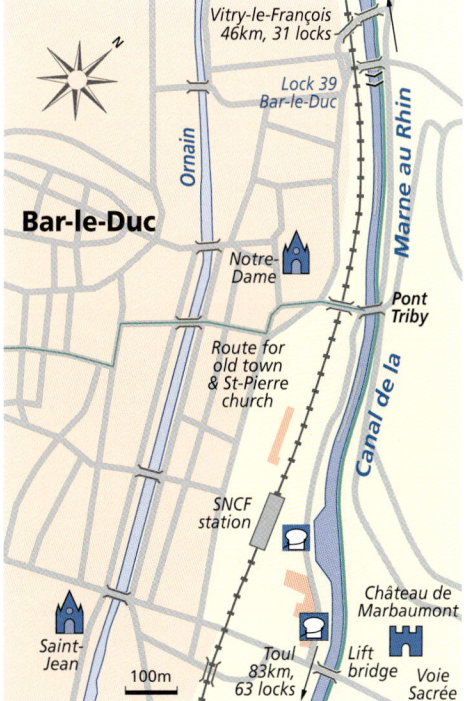

IV – Northeastern France

PK **65.6** Lock 19 (Givrauval), bridge
PK **66.9** Lock 18 (Longeaux)
PK **67.4** **Longeaux** bridge, quay u/s l/b, no services
PK **68.0** Menaucourt basin l/b
PK **68.2** Main road bridge (Patouillat) and railway bridge

N.B. Locks 17 (Menaucourt) to 1 (Demange) are equipped for automatic operation with radar detection, for easier transit maintain constant speed between locks.

PK **68.5** Lock 17 (Menaucourt), aqueduct u/s
PK **69.2** Lock 16 (Nantois), bridge
PK **70.4** Lock 15 (Naix-aux-Forges), bridge, quay u/s l/b, no services
PK **71.1** Lock 14 (Pont-canal de la Barboure), aqueduct u/s
PK **72.6** **Saint-Amand-sur-Ornain** bridge, quay d/s l/b
PK **73.1** Lock 13 (Saint-Amand)
PK **74.2** Lock 12 (Charmasson)
PK **75.5** Lock 11 (**Tréveray**), VHF 20, bridge, water, village 500m
PK **75.7** Turning basin and quay l/b, no services
PK **76.1** Lock 10 (Charbonnières)
PK **77.0** Lock 9 (Petite-Forge), private quay u/s l/b
PK **77.9** Lock 8 (Laneuville-Saint-Joire)
PK **78.4** **Saint-Joire** bridge, quay d/s r/b, village 500m
PK **79.0** Lock 7 (Saint-Joire)
PK **80.2** Lock 6 (Boeval)
PK **80.8** Lock 5 (Abbaye d'Evaux)
PK **82.2** Lock 4 (Montfort)
PK **83.2** Lock 3 (Bois-Molu)
PK **83.9** Lock 2 (Demange-aux-Eaux)
PK **84.1** Bridge (Croix-des-Morts)
PK **84.6** **Demange-aux-Eaux** quay for 4 boats r/b, free, water, village 700m over bridge

Good mooring close to the junction with the Houdelaincourt branch

PK **84.8** Lock 1 (Demange), bridge, water, beginning of Mauvages summit level
PK **85.1** Junction with Houdelaincourt Branch l/b, turning basin.
PK **85.3** Bridge
PK **86.6** Mauvages tunnel, western entrance, depth 4.80m, height 3.30m on sides, 5.20m at apex

Wait for the green light for the morning or afternoon passage. Passage takes approximately one hour.

Entering Mauvages tunnel eastbound, PK 91. © MICHAEL PAPENBURG

PK **91.5** Mauvages tunnel, eastern entrance, waiting quay, bollards

N.B. Locks 1 to 12 are equipped for automatic operation, with radar detection.

PK **92.3** Mauvages bridge, village 500m
PK **94.0** Lock 1 (Mauvages), end of Mauvages summit level
PK **94.6** Lock 2 (Villeroy), bridge
PK **95.3** Lock 3 (Chalède)
PK **95.9** Lock 4 (Grand-Charme), bridge
PK **96.8** Lock 5 (Saint-Esprit)
PK **97.6** Lock 6 (Corvée)
PK **97.9** **Sauvoy** bridge, small village 300m r/b

Birthplace of Nicholas-Joseph Cugnot, inventor of the first self-propelled mechanised vehicle in 1769

PK **98.2** Lock 7 (Sauvoy)
PK **98.6** Quay r/b (Sauvoy)
PK **98.8** Lock 8 (Varonnes), bridge
PK **100.0** Lock 9 (Biguiottes)
PK **100.9** Lock 10 (Haut-Bois), bridge
PK **101.7** Lock 11 (Vacon), bridge
PK **102.5** Lock 12 (Void), VHF 20, water
PK **103.9** **Void** quay, 50m, free, water €3/hour, electricity €3 for 8 hours, slipway, footbridge, village l/b
PK **104.0** Void bridge
PK **107.1** Main road bridge (Croix-le-Pêcheur), N4
PK **109.4** Bridges (Naviot)
PK **110.3** Troussey aqueduct (over Meuse)
PK **111.3** Junction with Canal de la Meuse, l/b

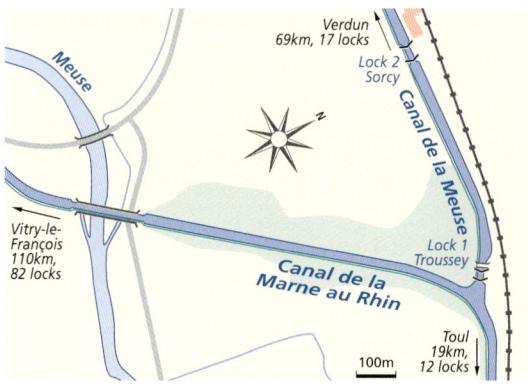

PK **115.9** **Pagny-sur-Meuse** bridge, municipal *halte* for 6-8 boats d/s r/b, 03 29 90 63 73, water, village 200m

Good pontoon mooring with services, but a sleepy village

PK **117.5** Railway bridge
PK **118.0** Cement works and quays, north bank
PK **119.9** Bridge (Lay-Saint-Rémy), basin, quay u/s l/b, water
PK **120.4** Bridge (Ugny), beginning of Lay-Saint-Rémy cutting
PK **120.6** Foug tunnel, western entrance
PK **121.5** Foug tunnel, eastern entrance

Plenty of width and headroom in this tunnel, controlled by lights. Mooring on the small island (remnants of the former lock) on the east side of the tunnel.

Canal de la Marne au Rhin

PK **121.6** Basin (Foug), mooring for 8 boats, no services
PK **121.9** Locks 14 and 14bis (twin chambers), deep chamber, VHF 20, caution, lights indicate which lock chamber to enter

Although permanently manned, it may be necessary to call the lock-keeper.

PK **122.6** Lock 15, bridge, water
PK **122.8** Industrial quay, l/b, mooring permitted
PK **123.3** Lock 16, water
PK **124.0** Lock 17
PK **124.3** Industrial quay, l/b
PK **124.7** Lock 18, bridge
PK **125.4** Lock 19
PK **125.7** Railway bridges
PK **126.1** Lock 20, bridge
PK **126.8** Lock 21
PK **127.4** Lock 22, bridge
PK **127.5** Railway bridge
PK **128.2** Lock 23
PK **128.9** Lock 24
PK **129.7** Lock 25, bridge, water
PK **129.8** **Toul** quay (Port de France), basin r/b with pontoon moorings for 60 boats, maximum 20m, 06 65 09 22 04, night €9, water, electricity, showers, pump-out, slipway, VNF office l/b, railway station and town centre 500m

Attractive port between the two locks. Toul is a substantial old fortified town with all facilities. Good train station with links to Paris, Nancy, Strasbourg, and down the Moselle valley to Luxemburg and Germany.

PK **129.9** Bridge (Génie)
PK **129.9** Lock 26, VHF 20
PK **130.5** Bridge (Caponnière, part of Toul's fortifications), Saint-Mansuy quay d/s r/b
PK **130.7** Railway bridge
PK **130.7** Saint-Mansuy lift bridge
PK **131.2** Lock 27, VHF 20, bridge, TSNI Marine boatyard d/s r/b, turning basin, 18 berths, 07 82 07 42 37, night €7, water, electricity, showers, slipway, services for larger vessels t.s.n.i@free.fr

TSNI is a respected boat repair and maintenance facilitiy, mooring (sometimes crowded) and offers secure overwintering. It is a small port but with a friendly, informal atmosphere. Shops are not too far away, and the town has good supermarkets and a brico store.

The popular port de plaisance *in Toul*, PK 130   PIERRE GLEIZES

PK **131.4** Entrance to new link to navigable river Moselle, r/b
PK **131.6** Lock 27bis, bridge
PK **131.7** *Junction with navigable river Moselle*

This junction marks the entrance to the *boucle de Nancy* or Nancy loop. See the map next page for the choice of itinerary, and the corresponding pages under the river Moselle and the Canal des Vosges. The description of the northern Moselle link is duplicated below for convenience, as the most practical route. This joins the eastern section of the Canal de la Marne au Rhin after 24.7 km and 5 locks, of which 3 on the Moselle, the other 2 on the Frouard branch.

IV – Northeastern France

Vauban-style extension to Toul's fortifications: the 'Pont de la Caponnière', PK 130 © EUROCANALS

PK **346.9** **Pompey** l/b, **Frouard** r/b, bridge (D657), pontoon u/s l/b for 4 boats, 03 83 24 27 32, night €9.47, water, electricity, shower
PK **346.7** Railway bridge
PK **346.5** Entrance to river Meurthe and branch to port of Nancy-Frouard r/b

Frouard branch

PK **0.0** Junction with Moselle (PK 346.5)
PK **1.0** Lock (Clévant), VHF 20, one large and one small chamber, bridge
PK **1.5** **Nancy-Frouard** industrial port, basin 400m long, sharp right-hand bend under railway bridge
PK **1.6** Lock
PK **1.7** Junction with Canal de la Marne au Rhin

Branch off Canal de la Marne au Rhin

Houdelaincourt Branch

PK **0.0** Junction with through route
PK **0.8** Bridge
PK **3.2** **Houdelaincourt** basin, grain-loading quay (disused)

Moselle link, northern route

PK **369.5** Canal de la Marne au Rhin, western section, enters Moselle, l/b
PK **369.1** Bridge (D904)
PK **366.5** Bridge (Gondreville)
PK **364.0** Lock (Fontenoy), VHF 20, lift 4.40m, bridge
PK **363.8** Railway bridge
PK **363.3** Bridge (Fontenoy)
PK **360.9** End of Villey-Saint-Étienne/Valcourt diversion canal
PK **355.7** Lock (Aingeray), VHF 20, lift 7.30m, in 700m diversion canal r/b, bridge
PK **354.2** Access to moorings for Liverdun l/b, slipway
PK **353.6** Railway bridge
PK **352.9** Castle (Château de la Flye) r/b
PK **352.1** **Liverdun** bridge, small town 600m l/b
PK **351.9** Former Liverdun aqueduct of Canal de la Marne au Rhin (destroyed)
PK **351.7** Railway bridge
PK **347.8** Lock (Pompey-Frouard), VHF 20, lift 2.70m, in 1 km diversion l/b

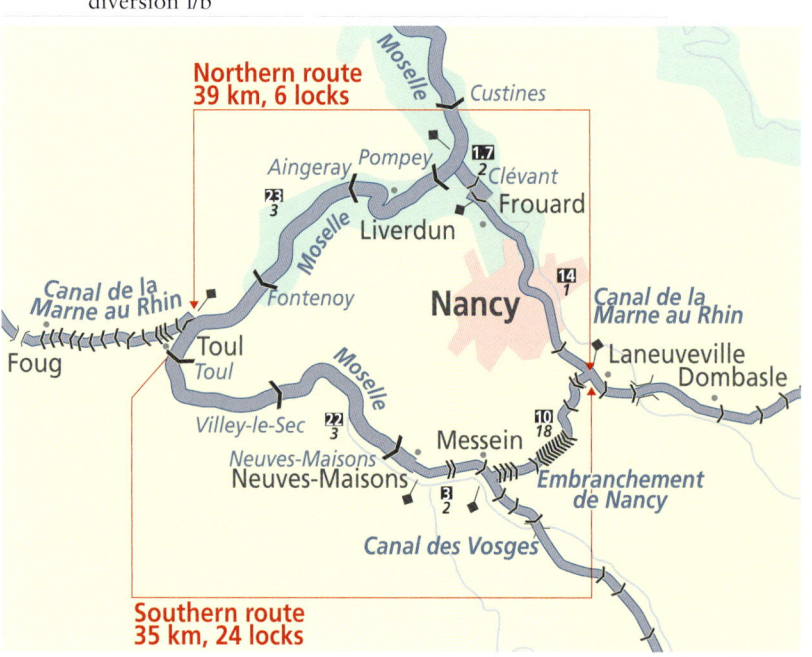

Canal de la Marne au Rhin

Eastern section
from the Moselle to the Rhin

PK **154.6** *Junction with navigable river Moselle, Frouard Branch*, port of Nancy-Frouard (canal not navigable north and west from this point), 12 berths, water, 03 83 81 00 37

PK **154.7** Bridge (access to Frouard railway station), quay

PK **156.1** Motorway bridge (A31)

PK **157.8** **Champigneulles** bridge (Pont de la Gare), basin, pontoon moorings for 8 boats d/s l/b, 03 83 34 23 00, free (maximum 5 days), water, electricity, wifi, town centre 200m l/b

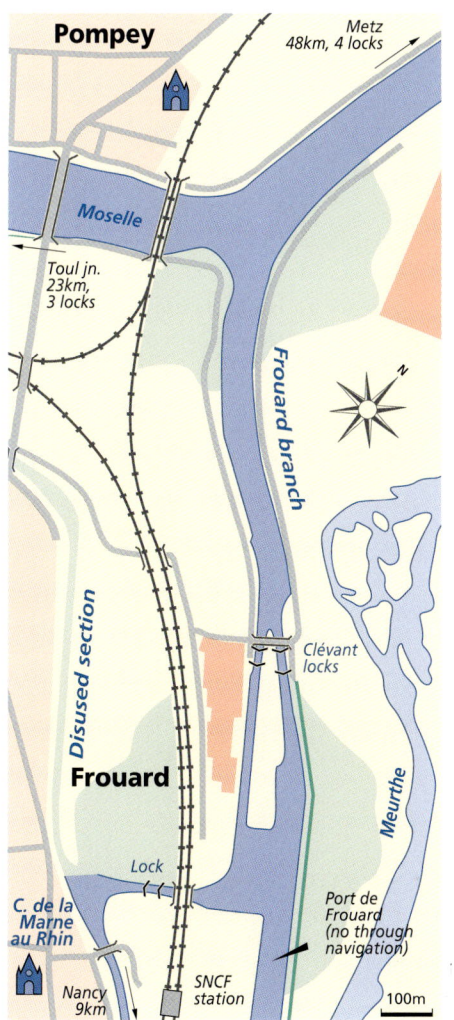

PK **158.6** Skew railway bridge

PK **160.3** Industrial quays d/s l/b

PK **160.5** Maxéville bridge

PK **161.1** Quay (Saint-Sébastien) l/b, water

PK **161.8** Bridge (Trois-Maisons)

PK **162.3** **Malzéville** lift bridge and footbridge, quay u/s l/b, water and Service Navigation subdivision

PK **162.6** Pipeline crossing

PK **162.8** Bridge (Gaz de la Sarre)

PK **163.1** Footbridge (Pépinière), quays u/s r/b

PK **163.5** Lift bridge (Sainte-Catherine) and footbridge

PK **163.6** Basin (Saint-Catherine), mooring for *péniches*, water and electricity, city

PK **163.7** Bridge (Pont Saint-Georges, tramway line T1)

PK **163.8** **Nancy** *port de plaisance* in basin l/b, 40 berths, 03 83 37 63 70, night €15, fuel, water and electricity (metered), showers (token €1.55), slipway, pump-out, wifi, restaurant, *capitainerie* and tourist office at the bridge *portdeplaisance@nancy.fr*

Port de plaisance Bassin Saint-Georges, services. Nancy was the French centre of Art Nouveau. Place Stanislas is reckoned the finest town square in France.

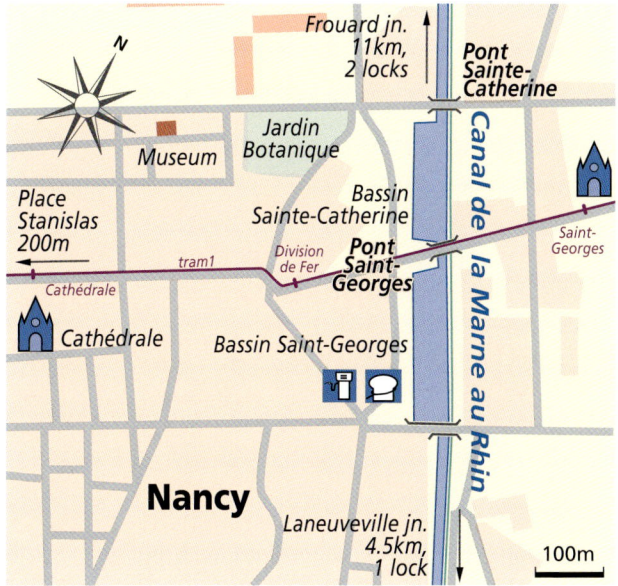

PK **163.9** Bridge (Tiercelins), quays u/s r/b, no services

47

IV – Northeastern France

Quayside mooring beside the footbridge (Passerelle de la Pépinière) PK 163, in Nancy © HENK WEVERS

PK **164.3** Pipeline crossing
PK **164.5** Bridge (avenue Charles E. Collignon)
PK **164.6** Covered footbridge (hospital)
PK **164.7** Tomblaine bridge
PK **164.8** Disused railway bridge, industrial quays and basin u/s
PK **165.6** Bridge
PK **165.8** Road bridge (D674, boulevard du Millénaire)
PK **165.9** Footbridge
PK **166.4** Lock 26/26a, bridge, basin d/s
PK **166.5** **Jarville-la-Malgrange** quays, no services, town l/b
PK **167.3** Bridge
PK **167.7** Pipeline crossings
PK **168.5** Laneuveville-devant-Nancy basin, junction with Canal des Vosges, Nancy branch, l/b

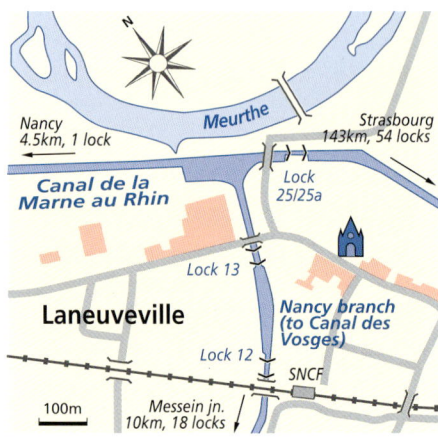

The Nancy Branch belongs to the Canal des Vosges. See under Section 42.

Eastern section continued
PK **168.6** Bridge
PK **168.7** Lock 25/25a, water
PK **169.5** Bridge (Noue)
PK **171.9** Lock 24/24a, bridge, water, industrial quay d/s r/b, basin u/s l/b, no services
PK **172.1** Private viaduct (pipeline crossing)
PK **172.5** Saint-Phlin aqueduct (over Meurthe)
PK **175.6** Chemical factory, quays and conveyor bridges
PK **175.8** **Varangéville** bridge, quays u/s, town r/b

PK **176.2** Footbridge, basin u/s l/b
PK **177.0** Lock 23/23a, water, bridge, industrial quays u/s
PK **177.7** conveyor bridge
PK **177.9** Private bridge (Solvay works)
PK **178.0** conveyor
PK **178.1** Private bridge (Solvay works)
PK **178.6** **Dombasle** bridge, basin d/s, proceed with caution, mooring towards upstream end (siltation), water and electricity, town with all services 400m l/b

Mooring pontoons, near France's biggest salt production works.

PK **179.2** Lock 22, water
PK **180.5** Sommerviller bridge, quay u/s l/b with services, village 500m l/b

N.B. Locks 21 (Sommerviller) to 7 (Réchicourt) are equipped for automatic operation with radar detection

PK **181.1** Lock 21, bridge, salt works u/s r/b
PK **182.6** Lock 20, bridge
PK **183.4** **Crévic** bridge, bankside mooring, village l/b
PK **187.0** Maixe bridge, quay and village u/s r/b
PK **187.5** Lock 19, bridge
PK **189.3** Salt works, quay r/b
PK **189.9** Lock 18, VHF 18, bridge
PK **190.7** **Einville-au-Jard** basin l/b, municipal *halte* for 16 boats, free (maximum 48 hours), water and electricity by tokens for €2.50, showers, village 300m
PK **191.1** Bridge, private quay u/s r/b
PK **191.4** Bridge (D914)
PK **193.4** Bridge
PK **194.7** **Bauzemont** basin, quay and small village r/b
PK **194.9** Lock 17, bridge
PK **195.2** Bridge
PK **197.3** Hénaménil bridge, quay d/s l/b, village 500m l/b
PK **198.7** Lock 16, bridge
PK **199.9** **Parroy** municipal *halte* for 12 boats d/s r/b, night €5, 06 41 38 64 60, water €2.50/300 litres), electricity €2.50 for 4 hours, showers, village 1 km r/b

Attractive mooring, bollards on stone quay backed by grassy bank beside a campsite. The site opens out onto a wide pool formed when the land was flooded between the original sinuous course of the canal and the straight cut opened out in the 1960s.

PK **200.0** Bridge
PK **201.1** Bridge (Parroy)
PK **203.0** Lock 15, bridge
PK **203.2** Mouacourt basin l/b, small village 300m l/b
PK **205.7** **Xures** bridge, basin d/s, Navig'France hire base, quay for 22 boats, 03 87 86 65 01, night €10, water, electricity, showers, village r/b
PK **206.1** Lock 14, bridge
PK **207.8** Lock 13, bridge
PK **209.2** **Lagarde** bridge, basin u/s r/b, Navig'France hire base, 40 berths, 03 87 86 65 01, night €12, diesel, water, electricity, showers €2, crane 9t, slipway, repairs, restaurant
PK **209.5** Small quay with boatyard, water
PK **209.7** Lock 12, bridge, water

Canal de la Marne au Rhin

PK **213.0** Lock 11, bridge
PK **215.1** Lock 10, bridge
PK **215.9** **Port-Sainte-Marie** bridge, mooring in basin d/s r/b, managed by Navig'France, 26 berths, 03 87 86 65 01, night €12, water and electricity included, diesel, village 1km l/b
PK **217.0** Lock 9, bridge, water
PK **218.6** Lock 8, disused railway bridge, basin u/s r/b
PK **219.4** Lock 7, bridge, basin (Saint-Blaise) d/s, quay r/b
PK **219.8** Beginning of new cut l/b (bypassing flight of 6 locks, r/b)
PK **222.1** Lock 2 (Réchicourt), bridge, beginning of summit level

This deep lock (16m rise) takes half an hour to complete one half-cycle, so there may be a long wait here, which may be used to visit the disused flight of six locks that this deep lock replaced in the 1960s. Travelling east, the summit level extends for 33km to Arzviller.

PK **222.4** Former access to flight of 6 locks r/b
PK **222.5** Old lock (open, narrow passage)
PK **223.1** Bridge (Col des Français) over cutting
PK **224.2** Stop gate
PK **225.3** Turning basin, possible quiet lakeside mooring
PK **227.6** Junction with Canal de la Sarre

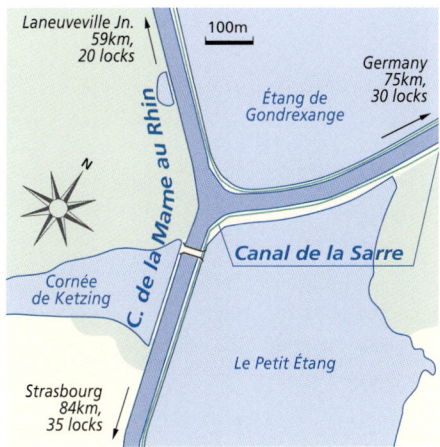

A short detour along the Canal de la Sarre leads to the Port du Houillon, with services. See under Section 41.

PK **227.7** Footbridge
PK **229.5** Gondrexange bridge, stop gate, village 200m
PK **230.2** Bridge (Prés)
PK **230.3** Skew railway bridge
PK **232.0** Bridge (Hertzing)
PK **232.4** New road bridge (N4)
PK **232.5** Bridge, basin d/s r/b
PK **233.0** Cement factory, conveyor bridge and pipeline crossing, private quay r/b
PK **233.2** **Héming** bridge (Pont de Lorquin), quays d/s r/b, village 400m r/b
PK **233.8** Towpath bridge
PK **236.0** **Xouaxange** bridge over narrow cutting, one-way traffic, *halte* for 4-5 boats d/s l/b, free, water, electricity, restaurant, small village r/b
PK **237.9** Destroyed bridge, narrow passage
PK **238.8** Laforge aqueduct (length 45m)
PK **239.7** Bridge (Germain)

PK **240.3** **Hesse** basin and Le Boat hire base r/b, 59 berths, 5 visitor berths, 03 87 03 61 74, night €20, water and electricity included, diesel, showers, crane 10t, restaurant, village 300m

Another long-established *port de plaisance* and hire base, with a huge boat shed. All functional rather than pretty. One of the canal's feeders enters the basin on the opposite side of the basin.

Xouaxange basin and moorings, PK 236 © EUROCANALS

PK **240.6** Bridge (Le Village), basins with quays both sides
PK **240.8** Skew railway bridge (disused)
PK **241.0** Bridge (Charmenack) over Hesse cutting, 465m long
PK **243.1** Bridge (Neuhof)
PK **243.6** Destroyed bridge, narrow passage
PK **243.7** Schneckenbusch bridge, mooring l/b, small village
PK **244.3** Bridge (Brouderdorff)
PK **244.9** Bridge (Buhl)
PK **245.5** **Niderviller-Neubruch** bridge, quay for 15 boats, Kuhnle Tours hire base, night €14, 03 87 24 92 00, diesel, water €3, electricity €3, showers, crane 25t, repairs, wifi, restaurant, village 1km, *niderviller@kuhnletours.fr*

Kuhnle Tours hire base in Niderviller-Neubruch, PK 245 © M. DUDLE-AMMANN

PK **246.0** Bridge (Hombesch)
PK **247.0** Bridge (Niderviller-Altmuhle), *port de plaisance* u/s, 20 berths, 03 87 24 92 00, night €10, water €1/100 litres, electricity €4/day, shower, slipway, restaurant

The 'public' *port de plaisance* for Niderviller. Visitor moorings to sheet piling quay on the south side of the basin.

PK **248.0** Niderviller tunnel, western entrance

IV – Northeastern France

The Arzviller inclined plane, opened in 1969 for 250-tonne barges, has become a major tourist attraction. © NORDLICHT

One-way only, controlled by lights. Tunnel length 475m.

PK **248.5** Niderviller tunnel, eastern entrance
PK **249.0** Basin (quays to tie up and wait for passage if necessary)
PK **249.3** Arzviller tunnel, western entrance

One-way only, controlled by lights. Tunnel length 2307m. Depth 2.70m, height 4.50m on sides, 5.10m to apex.

PK **251.6** Arzviller tunnel, eastern entrance
PK **251.8** Arzviller basin
PK **251.9** Entrance to new canal section, r/b, bypassing flight of 17 locks (if using towpath, follow the old flight)
PK **252.0** Saint-Louis bridge, village 1km r/b
PK **254.7** Saint-Louis-Arzviller inclined plane, VHF 18, basin u/s with waiting quay r/b as required

One of the major features of the French canal system, opened in 1969 to replace 17 locks which took eight hours to negotiate. Boats travel up and down the slope (height 44.5m) very smoothly in a 41m long water-filled steel caisson. A mini-*port de plaisance* is planned in the lower basin.

PK **255.3** Bridge
PK **255.6** New cut rejoins original line of canal below lock 17, l/b
PK **256.0** Lock 18, water
PK **256.1** Railway viaduct (Hofmuhle), turning basin d/s
PK **256.7** Lock 19, bridge

N.B: Locks 18 to 30-31 are a regulated flight with automated operation, activated by lights.

PK **257.5** Lock 20, water
PK **258.1** Locaboat hire base in basin r/b, caution: very tight bend, 5 berths, 03 87 25 70 15, night €20, water and electricity included, showers, repairs, restaurant
PK **258.5** Lock 21, bridge, water
PK **258.7** **Lutzelbourg** quay and l/b, picturesque village
PK **258.9** *Port de plaisance*, 03 87 25 30 19, water €2, electricity €2, shower €1, restaurant

Very pretty village, quayside mooring, services

PK **259.1** Lock 22, bridge, water
PK **260.3** Lock 23
PK **261.1** Lock 24
PK **262.2** Lock 25
PK **263.0** Lock 26, lift bridge, mooring possible d/s r/b
PK **264.3** Lock 27, footbridge
PK **264.9** Lock 28, bankside mooring possible d/s l/b

Dramatic scenery with ruined castles on cliff tops.

PK **266.1** Lock 29, bridge (D132)
PK **266.3** Railway viaduct (Haut-Barr), quay u/s l/b, no services
PK **268.4** Footbridge
PK **268.5** Bridge (D1004)
PK **268.6** Deep lock 30/31, VHF 18, bridge, end of regulated flight
PK **269.0** **Saverne** basin, Nicols hire base and moorings l/b, 40 berths, 03 88 71 88 81, night €15, water, electricity, shower, pump-out, slipway, restaurant, limited moorings r/b, town centre r/b

Extensive *port de plaisance*, services. A typically Alsatian, small town. Half timbered, painted or carved, houses and the immense red sandstone summer palace of Cardinal Louis de Rohan.

PK **269.5** Bridge (Orangerie)

N.B: Locks 32 to 36 are a regulated flight with automated operation..

PK **270.1** Lock 32, railway bridge u/s
PK **271.0** Lock 33, bridge
PK **272.0** New road bridge (D1404)
PK **272.2** Lock 34, bridge
PK **272.5** Lock 35
PK **273.7** Lock 36, bridge, end of regulated flight
PK **273.8** **Steinbourg** bridge, new *halte* d/s r/b, water, electricity, e-charging, village 800m l/b

Splendid new halte *at Steinbourg*

PK **277.1** **Dettwiller** bridge, quay u/s r/b, no services, village 1km l/b
PK **277.6** Lock 37, beginning of regulated flight to lock 41
PK **278.0** Bridge (D112)
PK **278.9** Lock 38
PK **279.3** Bridge
PK **279.8** Lock 39
PK **280.1** **Lupstein** bridge, bankside mooring, village 500m r/b
PK **281.4** Lock 40, bridge, Wilwisheim 700m l/b
PK **281.8** Bridge

Canal de la Marne au Rhin

PK 283.2 Bridge
PK 283.6 Lock 41, bridge, end of regulated flight
PK 286.2 **Hochfelden** bridge, quay d/s l/b, village 1 km l/b
PK 288.0 Lock 42, bridge, quay (Mutzenhouse) d/s r/b
PK 288.8 **Schwindratzheim** bridge, village 800m l/b
PK 289.1 Lock 43
PK 290.7 **Waltenheim** bridge, municipal *halte* d/s r/b, 8 berths, free, water €2 per 15 minutes, electricity €4 per 8 hours, wifi, village 200m r/b
PK 291.0 Lock 44, bridge
PK 292.1 Lock 45
PK 293.0 Bridge
PK 294.0 Lock 46, bridge, end of regulated flight, restaurant d/s l/b
PK 296.8 Bridge (D30), quay d/s r/b, no services, **Brumath** 2.5km l/b
PK 297.5 Bridge (D60)
PK 300.3 **Eckwersheim** bridge, village 1200m r/b
PK 300.6 Lock 47
PK 301.7 Lock 48, VHF 18
PK 302.0 **Vendenheim** swing bridge, village 500m r/b
PK 302.2 Railway bridge
PK 302.4 Bridge (D263), quay (Vendenheim) d/s r/b, no services
PK 303.9 Bridge
PK 304.5 Motorway bridge (A4)
PK 305.0 Bridge (D63, motorway access road)
PK 305.2 Bridge
PK 305.7 Lock 49, bridge, **Reichstett** 800m l/b
PK 306.9 **Souffelweyersheim** municipal *halte* r/b, pontoon for 8 boats, night €12, water €2 per 15 minutes, electricity €4 per 8 hours, wifi, village 800m r/b

Port de plaisance with basic services in a pleasant location on the outskirts of Strasbourg. Excellent public transport links into Strasbourg. The municipality has been rewarded several times for its floral displays.

PK 307.0 Lock 50, bridge
PK 307.9 Railway bridge
PK 308.0 Bridge (D468)
PK 308.7 **Hoenheim** bridge, village r/b (Strasbourg suburb)
PK 309.5 **Bischheim** bridge, quay u/s r/b, town centre 300m r/b
PK 309.9 Bridge (rue de la Zorn)
PK 310.2 **Schiltigheim** bridge (tramway line B), quay d/s r/b, town centre 800m r/b
PK 310.6 Lock 51, footbridge
PK 310.7 River Aar crosses on the level (not navigable)
PK 311.1 Bridge (tramway line E)
PK 311.2 Bridge (Wacken), **Strasbourg** *halte*, two landing stages 25m managed by VNF, 03 88 45 84 00, 4 boats, limited to 48 hours, water and electricity (payable by credit card)

Ideal mooring for visiting the European Parliament building. Tram stop on the bridge.

PK 311.3 Lock 52 (stop lock), bridge
PK 311.6 Junction with river Ill, turn right for access to centre of **Strasbourg** and northern section of Canal du Rhône au Rhin
PK 311.9 Bridge (Rose Blanche)
PK 312.6 Bridge (Porte du Canal)
PK 313.0 Canal terminates in Bassin des Remparts (basin in the port of Strasbourg), Junction with River Rhine 1.2km through northern locks of the port of Strasbourg, 03 88 21 74 74, water, electricity, slipway

For Strasbourg, continue through the Bassin des Remparts to moor at Europe Boat Trading, which offers moorings, fuel, chandlery, repairs and maintenance (lift-out) at quai des Belges: **europe-boat-trading.fr** 06 07 21 82 45. The river Ill flows through the centre of the historic city and is navigable through to the quay at the junction with the Canal des Faux Remparts, even beyond but use of this route is strongly discouraged so as not to interfere with the incessant movements of the passenger boats. Hence the recommendation to take a skippered boat trip to appreciate the city. There are connecting locks into the Rhine to the north-east and the south-east. The northern branch of the Canal du Rhône au Rhin begins south-west of Strasbourg and heads 31km south, parallel with the river, to Boofzheim and then into the Rhine/Grand Canal d'Alsace. See Section 45.

For a broader view of the waterways through Strasbourg, see Section 45: River Ill and Canal du Rhône au Rhin (northern branch).

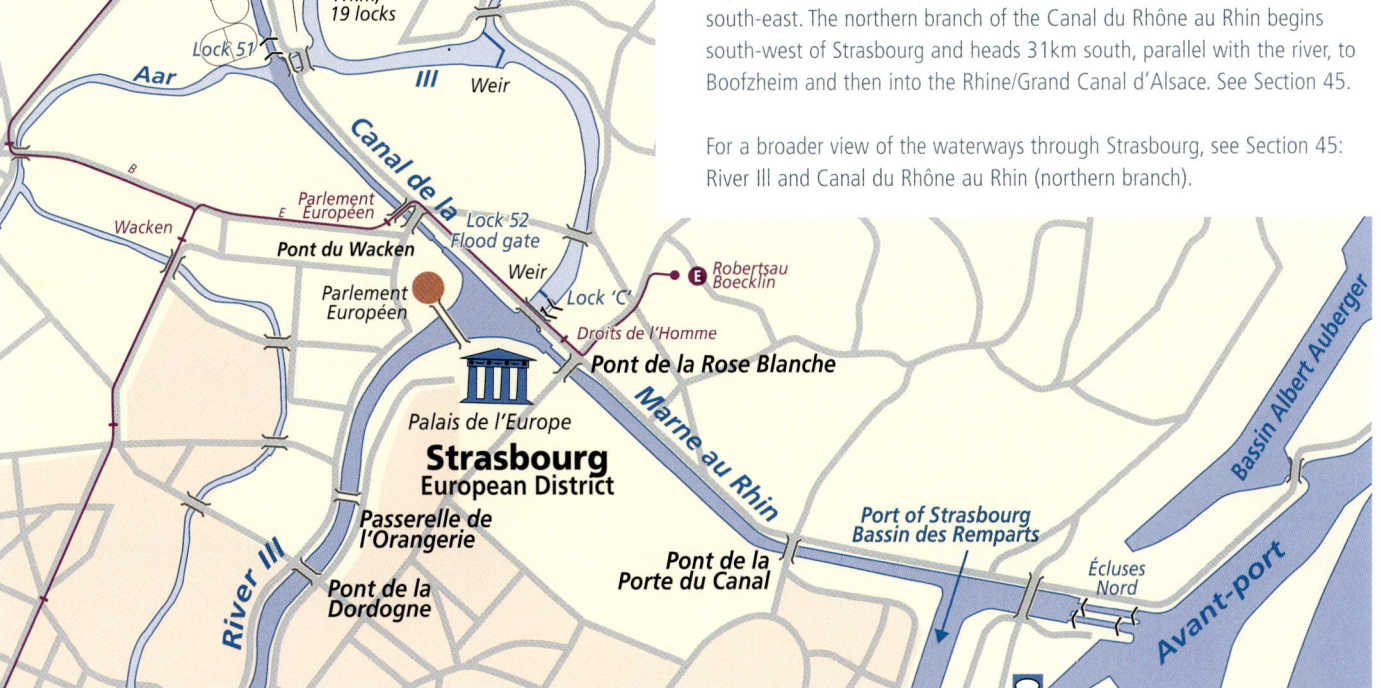

41. Canal de la Sarre and River Sarre

THE CANAL DE LA SARRE branches off from the Canal de la Marne au Rhin near Gondrexange (PK 227), and after cutting through a vast forest strewn with lakes, runs down the Sarre valley to enter the river at Sarreguemines. Navigation continues on the canalised river to the German border a short distance upstream of Saarbrücken. The canal is 63km long, and the French portion of the canalised river Sarre is 12km long, making a total of 75km. The canal was built to carry coal from the mines around Saarbrücken, hence its original name 'Canal des Houillères de la Sarre'. The canal is rural in character and charming throughout. Through navigation down to the Moselle near Trier, 90km beyond Saarbrücken, is possible, thanks to canalisation of the Saar in Germany, making the industrial centre accessible to Rhine barges. This through route offers attractive possibilities for cruising, especially the ring via the Sarre and the Moselle in Germany and back via the Canal de la Marne au Rhin. The ring was blocked for several years following closure of the first lock in Germany, at Güdingen, but is now again fully operational.

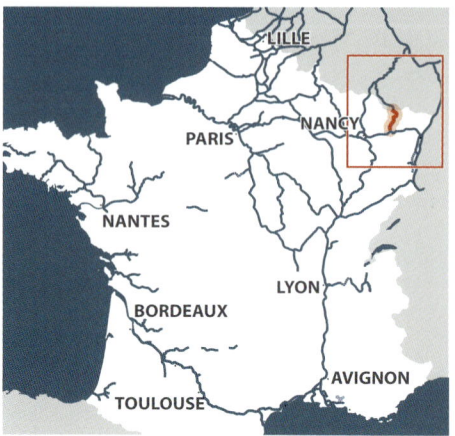

A private company was set up to build the canal in 1844, but was wound up before works could begin. The State took over the project and the works were started in 1861, to be completed in 1867. Although predating the 'Freycinet' programme by nearly 20 years, it was built directly to these generous dimensions, justified by the huge volume of coal to be exported from the Saar collieries in Germany, since the river Saar itself was unnavigable. The Saar canalisation in Germany was completed in 1986.

Navigation
No particular difficulties are to be anticipated on this tranquil rural waterway, which is popular with tourists in hire boats. Speed is limited to 8 km/h.

Locks
There are 27 locks on the canal, falling towards the Sarre, and 3 locks on the French portion of the canalised river Sarre. The least dimensions are 39m by 5.15m.

Draught
The maximum authorised draught is 1.80m.

Headroom
The fixed bridges on the canal leave a minimum headroom of 3.65m above normal water level. The least headroom on the canalised river is 4.17m, reduced to 3.42m above the highest navigable water level.

Towpath
There is a good towpath throughout, surfaced for use as a cycle path.

Authority
VNF Strasbourg
- 35 rue de Dieuze, 57930 Mittersheim 03 87 07 67 12 (PK 0-25)
- 1 rue de Steinbach, BP 122, 57216 Sarreguemines cedex 03 87 27 66 50 (PK 25-76)

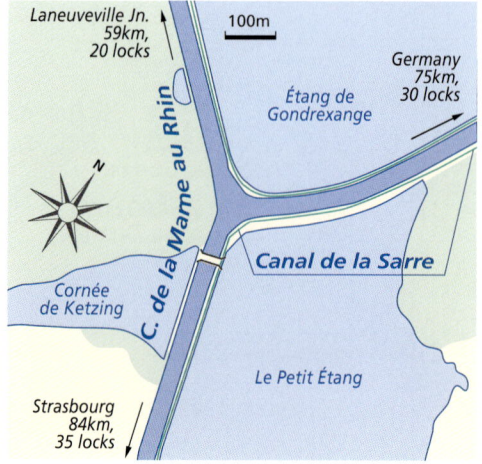

Canal de la Sarre

Key dimensions (m)	
Length	39.00
Beam	5.15
Draught	1.80
Air draught	3.65

Étang de Gondrexange viewed from the Port du Houillon, PK 2.2
© GORDON KNIGHT

Route description

Canal de la Sarre

PK 0.0	**Junction with Canal de la Marne au Rhin** (PK 228), near Gondrexange
PK 0.1	Restricted passage
PK 2.2	**Port du Houillon** *port de plaisance* l/b, moorings for 25 boats, night €15, diesel, water, electricity, shower
PK 2.3	Bridge
PK 3.1	Flood gate, bridge
PK 3.9	**Diane-Capelle** bridge, village 200m r/b
PK 5.5	Lock 1, bridge, water

Possible mooring to hard quay downstream on the left bank.

PK 6.7	Stock aqueduct, Étang du Stock extends beyond both banks
PK 8.7	Restricted passage
PK 10.4	Bridge (Albeschaux), quay u/s l/b

Delightful rural mooring, no services.

PK 11.0	Lock 2
PK 11.5	Lock 3
PK 11.9	Lock 4
PK 12.4	Lock 5
PK 12.8	Lock 6
PK 13.2	Lock 7
PK 13.6	Lock 8, bridge, quay (Vorbusch) d/s r/b, café
PK 14.3	Lock 9
PK 15.2	Lock 10
PK 16.1	Lock 11
PK 17.4	Lock 12
PK 18.1	Railway bridge
PK 19.5	Lock 13, bridge
PK 20.0	Junction with Canal des Salines (abandoned), l/b
PK 20.1	**Mittersheim** basin, municipal *port de plaisance* r/b, Canal Évasion hire base, moorings for 30 boats, night €10, water and electricity included, showers, restaurant, village 400m

Pontoon moorings for visiting craft in the hire base, but there is also a hard quay for barges to moor alongside.

PK 20.3	Lock 14, bridge
PK 22.6	Lock 15, quay (Pont-Vert) u/s l/b
PK 22.7	Bridge (D39)
PK 23.9	Quay (Burlach) l/b
PK 27.1	Lock 16, bridge, private quays u/s and d/s l/b
PK 28.3	Bridge (Neuweyerhof)
PK 29.5	Bridge (Muller), restricted width
PK 32.1	Bridge (Freywald), restricted width, **Harskirchen** 500m r/b
PK 32.8	Lock 17, bridge
PK 33.0	**Bissert-Harskirchen** basin, municipal *port de plaisance* l/b, 20 boats, 03 88 01 25 88, night €9, water, electricity, shower, slipway, pump-out, wifi, village 300m l/b
PK 33.5	Lock 18, bridge, water
PK 37.4	Bridge (Haras)
PK 37.9	Skew railway bridge

IV – Northeastern France

PK **38.8** Lock 19
PK **39.2** Bridge (Rech)
PK **39.8** Albe aqueduct
PK **40.8** Lock 20, bridge, water
PK **41.1** **Sarralbe** municipal *halte* l/b, quayside mooring for 10 boats, free (maximum 48 hours), water, electricity (free), small town 300m r/b over bridge

Halte with a 160m long concrete quay backed by an attractively landscaped public park.

PK **41.3** Towpath bridge (towpath changes from r/b to l/b)
PK **41.5** Pipeline crossing and bridge
PK **41.6** Private footbridge
PK **41.7** Solvay works, private quay r/b
PK **42.0** Private bridge and pipeline crossing
PK **42.3** Railway bridge
PK **42.9** Pipeline crossing
PK **43.0** Bridge (Niederau), restricted width
PK **44.8** Motorway bridge (A4)
PK **45.2** **Herbitzheim** bridge, quay u/s r/b, village 800m r/b
PK **45.6** Lock 21, bridge
PK **46.6** Pipeline crossing
PK **48.6** Pipeline crossing
PK **51.4** Skew railway bridge
PK **51.9** Lock 22, bridge, boatyard u/s l/b
PK **52.0** **Wittring** private *halte* for 6 visiting boats, 06 10 02 32 71, night €10, water, electricity, restaurant, village l/b

Delightful village with moorings stern-to-quay along the quay downstream of the bridge, restaurant Victoria on the quayside.

PK **53.6** Railway bridge (Dieding)
PK **57.2** Skew railway bridge (Zetting)
PK **57.6** Lock 23, bridge, **Zetting** l/b
PK **60.2** Lock 24, bridge, **Sarreinsming** 400m r/b
PK **60.4** Bridge
PK **61.1** **Remelfing** quay l/b, turning basin, village 500m d/s l/b
PK **61.5** Lock 25, bridge
PK **63.0** Lock 26, bridge and railway viaduct, moorings d/s r/b
PK **63.4** Lock 27, VHF 20, water
PK **63.4** Navigation enters canalised river Sarre

Sarre weir and mill in the village of Sarreinsming. © GORDON KNIGHT

Popular mooring in front of the casino in a former china works in Sarreguemines. © GORDON KNIGHT

Canalised river Sarre

PK **63.5** Bridge (D662, Sarreguemines southern bypass)
PK **63.7** Quays l/b (Grand Port de Sarreguemines)
PK **64.4** **Sarreguemines** footbridge, *port de plaisance* along quay in front of casino r/b, up to 30 boats, 06 89 94 68 93, night €10, fuel, water and electricity on pontoon, shower, wifi, slipway, pump-out, restaurant, town centre r/b

Excellent pontoon mooring in front of a former china works converted into a casino. So popular (particularly with German boaters) that an additional pontoon was provided below the following bridge. Both pontoons have water and electricity.

PK **64.6** Bridge (Pont des Alliés), quay d/s l/b, town centre l/b
PK **64.8** Bridge (Pont de l'Europe)
PK **64.9** Lock 28 and weir
PK **65.0** Confluence of Blies r/b (r/b in Germany from this point), moorings 03 87 98 93 00, night €10, diesel, water, electricity, slipway, pump-out
PK **65.7** Skew railway bridge
PK **66.2** Entrance to Welferding lock-cut, l/b
PK **66.4** **Welferding** bridge, village l/b
PK **66.8** Lock 29
PK **66.9** Navigation re-enters Sarre
PK **70.1** Bridge (N61bis, expressway spur)
PK **70.6** Quay for former Grosbliederstroff power station l/b
PK **71.1** Entrance to Grosbliederstroff lock-cut, l/b
PK **71.6** Grosbliederstroff footbridge, village l/b
PK **72.3** Turning basin
PK **72.7** Lock 30, bridge
PK **72.7** Navigation re-enters Sarre
PK **75.6** French-German border l/b (Saarbrücken 6km d/s)

Güdingen lock, the first encountered in Germany, has been restored after being out of operation for several years.

42. Canal des Vosges

Previously called the southern branch of the Canal de l'Est, the Canal des Vosges is a delightful waterway which extends 122km from the river Moselle at Neuves-Maisons to the Saône at Corre. It follows the Moselle valley to Épinal, then rises sharply to a summit level at an altitude of 360m, the second highest in France after that of the Canal de Bourgogne. The summit level and the descent towards the Saône, following the steep-sided Coney valley, are very picturesque. The canal has two branches: the **Nancy branch** provides a useful link, from Messein (PK 28) to the eastern section of the Canal de la Marne au Rhin, while the **Épinal branch** extends 3km to the town of Épinal from the through route at the foot of the Golbey flight of locks (PK 83). The original 'southern branch' of the Canal de l'Est started at a junction with the Canal de la Marne au Rhin at Toul, 20km east of the junction with the 'northern branch' (now the Canal de la Meuse) at Troussey. Since 1979 it has been superseded by the river Moselle over a distance of 26km to the steelworks at Neuves-Maisons, accessible to Rhine barges and push-tows.

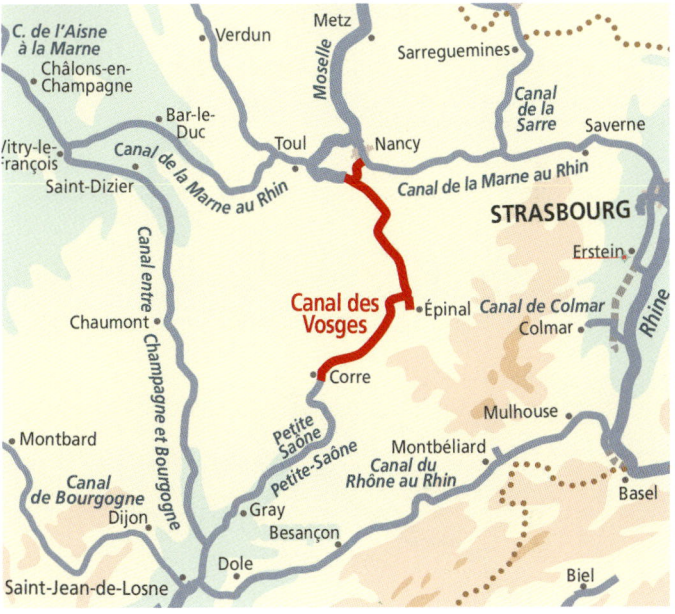

Public works were at a standstill after the Franco-Prussian War, but one canal project was immediately promoted as essential, to interconnect west of the Vosges the canals that were now intercepted by the border. The 'Canal de l'Est' was authorised by laws voted by the Assemblée Nationale in 1872 and 1874, and works began immediately. The canal was completed in 1880. Its southern branch, renamed Canal des Vosges, is now essentially devoted to tourism, with very little commercial traffic.

Navigation
The canal is an easy and delightful cruising waterway, with no particular difficulty. It sees very little commercial traffic and runs through predominantly rural areas. The town of Épinal, at the end of its 3km branch, is the exception.

Locks
There are 93 locks, of which 47 fall towards the Moselle and 46 towards the Saône. The locks are of standard 'Freycinet' dimensions, 38.50m by 5.20m, except for locks 47 to 34 on the Moselle side, which are slightly longer (41.30m). Because traffic is so light, boaters have to book passage at one of the two control offices: Messein, 03 29 66 85 05 when arriving from the Moselle or the Nancy Branch, or Bains-les-Bains, 03 29 34 26 87 when arriving from the Saône.

Draught
The maximum authorised draught is 1.80m throughout.

Headroom
All the fixed bridges leave a clear headroom of 3.50m above normal water level.

Towpath
There is a towpath throughout, but it may be overgrown if not impassable through the summit level.

Authority
VNF Nord-Est
UTI Canal des Vosges
– 1 avenue de la Fontenelle, 88000 Épinal 03 29 34 19 63
   uti.vosges@vnf.fr (PK 31-147)
UTI Moselle
– 52 rue Charles de Foucauld, 54000 Nancy 03 83 17 41 20
   uti.cmre-nancy@vnf.fr (PK 26-31)

Route description

PK 25.7 **Junction with canalised river Moselle** at upstream end of industrial port of **Neuves-Maisons**, turning basin, large industrial quays (limit of navigation by Rhine barges)

PK 25.9 Lock 47, bridge

PK 26.2 Turning basin

IV – Northeastern France

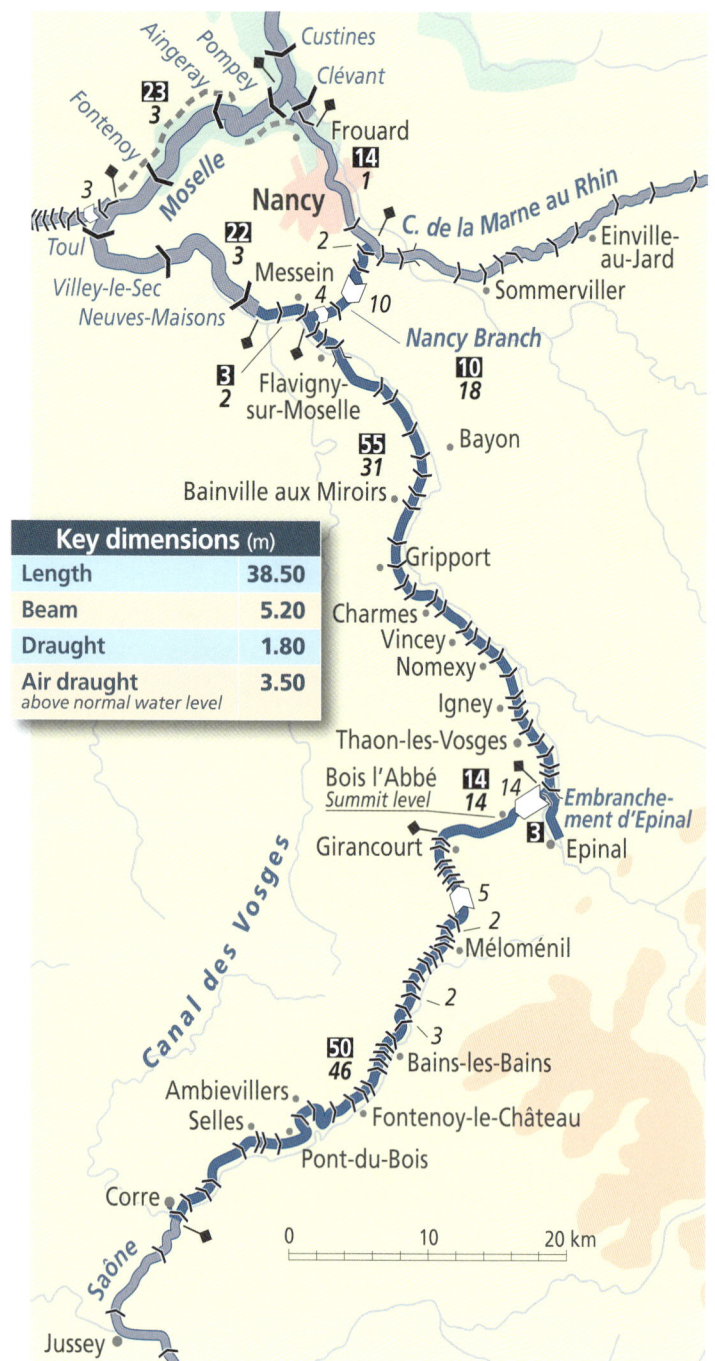

Key dimensions (m)
Length	38.50
Beam	5.20
Draught	1.80
Air draught *above normal water level*	3.50

PK 26.9 **Messein** bridge, quay u/s r/b, village 200m r/b
PK 27.9 Bridge (D331)
PK 28.2 Lock 46, VHF 20, bridge, water
PK 28.3 Junction with the Nancy branch, turning basin for commercial barges
PK 29.6 Footbridge, mooring for 9 boats u/s r/b, night €4, water, electricity
PK 30.2 **Richardménil** bridge, *halte* managed by association u/s r/b, 06 89 33 37 28, up to 12 boats, night €7, water €5 per 1000 litres, electricity €2/day (6A), village 500m r/b
PK 31.0 Motorway bridge (A330)
PK 31.5 Lock 45, bridge
PK 31.6 **Flavigny** quay and turning basin r/b, village 1200m l/b
PK 33.0 Lock 44, bridge
PK 33.8 Lock 43, Moselle aqueduct upstream (length 125m)
PK 34.6 Bridge (D570)
PK 36.2 Bridge, turning basin u/s l/b
PK 38.7 Bridge (D570), disused quay d/s, l/b
PK 39.1 Lock 42
PK 40.9 Lock 41, bridge, **Crévechamps** 200m l/b
PK 43.9 Lock 40, bridge
PK 44.6 Floating footbridge
PK 45.2 Neuviller quay and turning basin l/b, village 500m
PK 46.8 Lock 39, bridge, commercial quay u/s r/b, **Bayon** 1300m r/b, moorings d/s r/b
PK 47.9 Lock 38, bridge, Roville-devant-Bayon l/b
PK 49.2 **Mangonville** bridge, small village l/b,
PK 50.0 Lock 37, bridge
PK 51.1 Lock 36, bridge, quay d/s l/b, Bainville-aux-Miroirs l/b
PK 52.3 Turning basin l/b
PK 53.6 Lock 35, bridge
PK 54.5 **Gripport** bridge, mooring for 3 boats, village 300m l/b
PK 55.0 Lock 34, footbridge
PK 56.8 Lock 33 (Socourt), bridge, quay d/s l/b, village 1km l/b
PK 58.2 Lock 32 (Plaine de Charmes), bridge
PK 59.3 Basin l/b
PK 59.9 Lock 31 (Charmes), bridge, water
PK 60.6 **Charmes** bridge (Grand Pont), municipal *halte*, capacity 20 boats, 03 29 66 01 86, night €9, water, electricity, shower €1.50, wifi €3/72 hours, slipway, restaurant, town l/b

Charmes is a favourite overnight stopping place on the canal, with all services in the small town.

Attractive quayside halte *in Charmes, PK 61.* © MARKBECH

PK 61.4 Lock 30 (Moulin de Charmes), bridge, turning basin u/s
PK 63.9 Lock 29 (Vincey), bridge, power station and private quays r/b
PK 65.2 **Vincey** bridge, quay d/s l/b, village 200m l/b
PK 65.4 Factory and quay l/b
PK 65.6 Skew railway bridge
PK 65.8 Lock 28 (Portieux), bridge
PK 67.4 Lock 27 (Fouys)
PK 68.1 Basin l/b
PK 69.4 Lock 26 (Avière), aqueduct upstream (restricted width 6m)
PK 70.8 Lock 25 (Nomexy), bridge, water, quay u/s l/b, village 500m l/b
PK 72.1 Lock 24 (Héronnière), bridge, turning basin d/s l/b
PK 73.9 Lock 23 (Vaxoncourt), bridge
PK 74.8 Lock 22 (Igney), bridge, quay u/s l/b, village 500m l/b

Canal des Vosges

PK 75.7	Basin (loading *péniches*), r/b
PK 76.1	Lock 21 (Plaine de Thaon), bridge, private quay u/s r/b
PK 77.5	Lock 20 (Thaon), bridge, water
PK 78.0	**Thaon-les-Vosges** bridge, quay u/s r/b, town 300m l/b
PK 78.5	Bridge
PK 78.6	Lock 19 (Usine de Thaon), private quays u/s, quay d/s r/b, no services, town l/b 750m
PK 80.2	Lock 18 (**Chavelot**), bridge, water, village l/b
PK 81.2	Bridge (N57 Épinal bypass)
PK 81.4	Commercial basin r/b (construction materials)
PK 81.6	Lock 17 (Prairie Gérard), bridge
PK 82.4	Lock 16, bridge, quay for restaurant u/s r/b
PK 83.2	Lock 15 (Côte-Olie), VHF 20, water, bridge (D157)
PK 83.3	**Junction with embranchement d'Épinal**, r/b

Since there are no locks on the Épinal Branch, there is every reason to make the detour up to the dynamic town of Épinal, famous for its printed images. This printing tradition led to *image d'Épinal* becoming a common French expression, meaning a preconceived or commonly accepted image that is disconnected from reality. Épinal is the last town to take on provisions before Bains-les-Bains. See branch description p.59.

PK 83.4	Lock 14 (Golbey), footbridge
PK 83.5	Lock 13 (Golbey), basin u/s
PK 83.7	Lock 12 (Golbey), basin u/s
PK 84.0	Lock 11 (Golbey), skew railway bridge, basin u/s
PK 84.5	Lock 10 (Golbey), bridge, water, basin u/s, town 1 km r/b
PK 84.8	Lock 9 (Golbey), former loading quay u/s r/b
PK 85.1	Lock 8 (Golbey), bridge, basin u/s
PK 85.3	Lock 7 (Golbey), basin u/s

Between locks 6 and 7 on the Golbey flight, PK 85. © WIKIMEDIA COMMONS

PK 85.4	Lock 6 (Golbey), basin u/s
PK 85.6	Lock 5 (Golbey), bridge, water, basin u/s
PK 85.8	Lock 4 (Golbey), basin u/s
PK 86.0	Lock 3 (Golbey), basin u/s
PK 86.1	Lock 2 (Golbey), basin u/s
PK 86.4	Lock 1 (Bois-l'Abbé), bridge, beginning of summit level
PK 87.0	Skew bridge (Bois l'Abbé)
PK 88.7	Turning basin and quay
PK 89.2	**Les Forges** bridge, moorings south bank, village 150m r/b
PK 90.6	Bridge
PK 91.1	**Sanchey** bridge, small village
PK 92.4	Aqueduct
PK 92.9	Basin
PK 94.2	**Chaumousey** aqueduct, basin d/s l/b, village l/b
PK 96.8	Bridge (Gare de Girancourt)
PK 97.2	Lock 1 (Trusey), VHF 20, bridge, end of summit level
PK 97.8	Lock 2 (**Girancourt**), bridge, basin r/b, village l/b
PK 98.3	Turning basin r/b
PK 99.0	Lock 3 (Barbonfoing), bridge
PK 99.7	Lock 4 (Launois), water
PK 100.9	Lock 5 (Void de Girancourt), bridge
PK 101.5	Lock 6 (Void de Girancourt), basin u/s r/b
PK 102.3	Lock 7 (Void de Girancourt), basin u/s r/b
PK 102.8	Lock 8 (Void de Girancourt), basin u/s r/b
PK 103.1	Lock 9 (Void de Girancourt), basin u/s r/b
PK 103.4	Lock 10 (Void de Girancourt), basin u/s r/b
PK 103.7	Lock 11 (Void de Girancourt), basin u/s r/b
PK 104.0	Lock 12 (Brennecôte), basin u/s r/b
PK 104.5	Lock 13 (Thiélouze), basin u/s r/b
PK 104.9	**Thiélouze** bridge, small village r/b
PK 105.5	Lock 14 (Port de Thiélouze), basin u/s r/b
PK 106.1	Lock 15 (Thillots)
PK 106.7	Lock 16 (**Méloménil**), bridge, small village l/b
PK 107.7	Lock 17 (Reblangotte)
PK 108.3	Lock 18 (**Uzemain**), bridge, basin d/s r/b, village 3 km l/b
PK 109.1	Lock 19 (Charmoise-l'Orgueilleux)
PK 110.4	Lock 20 (Coney), basins u/s r/b
PK 110.8	Basin r/b
PK 111.4	Lock 21 (Pont Tremblant), bridge, water, basin u/s r/b
PK 112.1	Lock 22 (Thunimont), bridge, water
PK 112.9	Lock 23 (Usine de Thunimont), private quay d/s r/b
PK 113.2	Swing bridge
PK 114.2	Lock 24 (Harsault), bridge, basin u/s r/b
PK 115.0	Basins r/b
PK 115.4	Lock 25 (Colosse), water
PK 116.3	Lock 26 (Forge Quénot), basin u/s r/b
PK 116.7	Basins r/b
PK 117.3	Lock 27 (Basse-du-Pommier), basin d/s r/b
PK 118.4	Lock 28 (Basse Jean-Melin), basin u/s r/b
PK 118.8	Basin r/b
PK 119.4	**Bains-les-Bains** bridge (Pont du Coney), municipal *halte* d/s r/b, 1.50 m draught, water, town 2.5 km l/b

Attractive spa town worth the detour on foot or by bike from the canal.

PK 119.6	Lock 29 (Pont du Coney)
PK 120.7	Lock 30 (Montroche)
PK 121.3	Lock 31 (Manufacture des Bains), bridge, quay d/s l/b
PK 122.3	Lock 32 (Grurupt), VHF 20, bridge, quay d/s l/b
PK 123.8	Footbridge (Pipée), quay u/s l/b
PK 124.0	Lock 33 (Pipée), basin d/s r/b
PK 124.6	Lock 34 (Fontenoy Amont)
PK 125.6	**Fontenoy-le-Château** bridge, *port de plaisance* and Le Boat hire base u/s l/b, visitor moorings not guaranteed, 03 29 30 43 98, night €10, fuel to order, water €2, electricity €2, showers, wifi, crane to order, restaurant, village 300m l/b, *fontenoy@leboat.com*

IV – Northeastern France

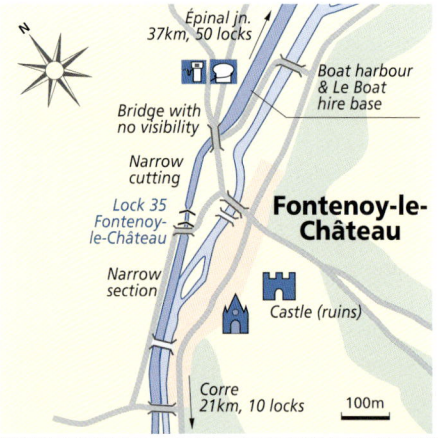

Selles swing bridge, PK 137. © DAVE DOBEL

PK **144.1** Private quay r/b
PK **145.9** Lock 45 (Vougécourt), bridge, quay d/s r/b
PK **146.6** Bridge
PK **146.9** Corre bridge, municipal *halte* d/s r/b, 07 86 60 13 21, up to 15 boats, night €12, water and electricity included, showers (€1 for 10 minutes), restaurant
PK **147.3** Lock 46 (Corre), VHF 20, water, junction with canalised river Saône, Corre *port de plaisance* 400m u/s (see Section 43, Petite Saône)

The port de plaisance *at Fontenoy-le-Château, PK 126* © LORRAINE VOIE VERTE

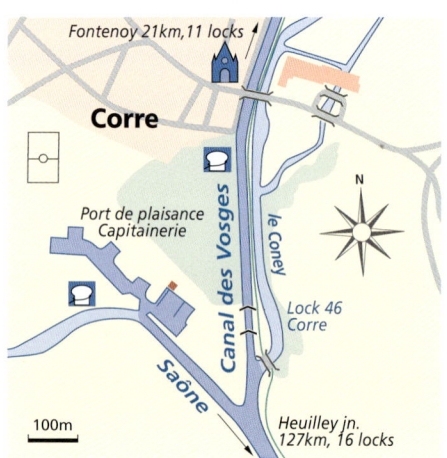

Delightful village in a remarkable setting, with its ruined château dating from the early 11th century on the narrow spur between the Coney and Châtelain valleys. The lock is in a narrow cutting which debouches (coming from the south) into the wide canal basin, with restaurants and all services in the small market town. The 15th/16th century flamboyant gothic church of Saint-Mansuy is also worth visiting.

PK **125.8** Lock 35 (Fontenoy-le-Château), bridge
PK **126.1** Footbridge
PK **126.2** Bridge (D434)
PK **127.7** Lock 36 (Montmotier), bridge
PK **129.9** Lock 37 (Gros-Moulin), bridge, basin u/s r/b
PK **130.2** Basin r/b
PK **130.8** Lock 38 (Ambiévillers)
PK **132.5** Freland château, former swing bridge, quay d/s r/b
PK **134.0** Footbridge
PK **134.2** Pont-du-Bois bridge, quay d/s r/b, small village 1200m r/b
PK **134.4** Lock 39 (Pont-du-Bois), water
PK **136.2** Lock 40 (Bois de Selles)
PK **136.7** Lock 41 (Carrières de Selles), bridge, quay u/s r/b
PK **137.4** Selles swing bridge, village r/b
PK **138.6** Lock 42 (Village de Selles), bridge, dry dock and basin u/s r/b
PK **140.1** Footbridge
PK **140.9** Bridge
PK **141.5** Passavant-la-Rochère basin r/b, village and historic glassworks 3 km r/b
PK **142.6** Lock 43 (Basse-Vaivre)
PK **143.6** Lock 44 (Demangevelle), bridge, village 700m l/b

Canal des Vosges

Nancy Branch

Looking from the bottom lock (13) of the Nancy branch at Laneuveville towards the Canal de la Marne au Rhin © AVINCENT V

PK 0.0	Junction with Canal de la Marne au Rhin (PK 169)
PK 0.2	Lock 13 (versant Meurthe), bridge, **Laneuveville-devant-Nancy** 200m r/b

The remote control issued here, or at lock 46 downstream of the junction, will be used for all the locks on the branch.

PK 0.4	Lock 12, railway bridge u/s, private quay u/s r/b
PK 2.5	Lock 11, bridge
PK 3.9	Lock 10, basin u/s r/b
PK 4.2	Lock 9, bridge

Looking down from lock 8 to 9 on the branch, PK 4 © LETIR

PK 4.5	Lock 8, bridge (D71)
PK 4.7	Lock 7, basin u/s r/b
PK 4.9	Lock 6, basin u/s r/b
PK 5.1	Lock 5, basin u/s r/b
PK 5.3	Lock 4, basin u/s r/b
PK 5.4	Lock 3, basin u/s r/b
PK 5.6	Lock 2, basin u/s r/b
PK 5.7	**Fléville-devant-Nancy** bridge, mooring possible downstream, small town and château 900m

Mooring is also possible in the other basins between locks 8 and 2.

PK 5.8	Lock 1 (versant Meurthe), bridge, beginning of Mauvais Lieu summit level
PK 6.0	Motorway bridge (A33)
PK 7.1	Bridge and railway bridge (siding)
PK 8.2	Motorway bridge (A330)
PK 8.5	Lock 1 (versant Moselle), bridge (D570), end of summit level
PK 9.2	Lock 2
PK 9.3	Railway bridge
PK 9.6	Lock 3
PK 9.9	Lock 4
PK 10.1	Lock 5, bridge (D115)
PK 10.2	Junction with Canal des Vosges, turning basin

Épinal Branch

PK 0.0	Junction with through route at bottom of Golbey flight
PK 0.2	Bridge (D157)
PK 0.3	Moselle aqueduct, narrow passage, heavily wooded, proceed with caution
PK 2.2	Bridge (D46)
PK 2.7	Footbridge
PK 3.3	**Épinal** basin, municipal *port de plaisance* l/b, 30 berths, *capitainerie* 03 29 81 33 45, night €6, fuel on request, water and electricity included, showers, restaurant, town centre 800m, *lacapitainerie@gmail.com*

Épinal, surrounded by wooded hills, is a pleasant town with all services and resources within walking distance of the canal basin: admire the majestic Place des Vosges, the 11th century basilica church, the fine architecture in the historic centre and many attractions.

The port de plaisance in Épinal, showing the water intake from the Moselle to supply the canal. The capitainerie is the large building towards the end of the esplanade © POSTOO.COM

IV – Northeastern France

43. Petite Saône

The Petite Saône is navigable over a distance of 165km from Corre, where it is continues from the Canal des Vosges (formerly called the Canal de l'Est, southern branch), to the important junction of Saint-Jean-de-Losne, where the Canal de Bourgogne enters on the right bank. The 205km onwards from Saint-Jean-de-Losne down to the confluence with the Rhône at Lyon-La Mulatière are described under Section 47, Grande Saône. The Petite Saône is another of the author's favourite five waterways in France, for the delightful landscapes, with gently rolling hills and the constant interest of the waterway itself, alternating between broad river sections and boldly engineered lock-cuts, including two tunnels. In this sparsely-populated area of France, there is only one small town, Gray, but there are many welcoming villages with good moorings and services. Overall, the Saône forms the backbone of the French waterway network, being joined by four major canals linking with the other main river basins, of which three join the Petite Saône: the Canal entre Champagne et Bourgogne (PK 255), the Canal du Rhône au Rhin (PK 219) and the Canal de Bourgogne (PK 215). The kilometre distances are those of the original river, counting from KP 0 at the former Mulatière lock just downstream of the confluence with the Rhône in Lyon, up to KP 407 in Corre. The route description gives the distances as observed on the kilometre posts, while the actual distances are indicated at the end of each lock-cut.

The Saône has always been the most navigable of French rivers, with a very gentle gradient and regular flow, albeit subject to floods which can make the broad valley look like an inland sea. The Roman general Vetus envisaged a canal from the Saône to the Moselle. Natural navigability made merchants an easy prey for local lords and tax collectors, and chains were laid across the river in many locations, to collect tolls. Colbert declared them illegal in 1664, but it seemed to Delalande – writing in 1778 – that 'the easier the navigation, the more its natural advantages have been abused by exactions of all sorts'. Navigability in the industrial era was introduced, as on the other major rivers, after the movable weir was invented by Poirée. By 1847 there were five weirs and locks on the Saône. The canalisation as completed above Auxonne has not changed, while development of the high-capacity waterway downstream meant the replacement of 12 early weirs and locks by only five in the 215km. The last, at Seurre, was completed in 1980. The entire waterway remains in the national priority network, and may one day be adapted to form the high-capacity Saône-Moselle waterway (Vetus' dream!)

Navigation
The Petite Saône is completely unspoilt and ideal for cruising: navigating the river should not present any difficulties to normal pleasure craft, with the exception of the occasional fallen tree and branches, both on the banks and floating on the current. There may also be waterlogged trunks just below the surface, so keep a good look-out.

The river's longer meanders are bypassed by lengths of canal incorporating standard 38.50m locks. As mentioned above, these canals cut almost 30km from the natural length of the river (407km from Corre to Lyon). There are two tunnels: Saint-Albin (PK 48) has a length of 681m, a width at water level of 6.55m and a maximum height of 4.10m, while Seveux-Savoyeux (PK 76) has a length of 643m, width 6.50m and headroom 3.60m. In both cases, the canal cutting is no wider than the tunnel for some distance beyond each entrance and one-way traffic is enforced, controlled by lights. At certain other locations, identified in the route description, passing and overtaking are forbidden. The right-angle junction with the Canal entre Champagne et Bourgogne is controlled by lights from Heuilley lock.

Locks
There are 19 locks plus flood locks at Cubry-les-Soing and Ferrières-les-Ray, which are normally open. There are also flood gates protecting most of the lock-cuts. The first 15 locks (Corre to Gray) have a length of 38.50m with a width of 5.20m. The remaining four are 40m by 8m. Many of the

Petite-Saône

Port de plaisance *at Corre* © GORDON KNIGHT

Key dimensions (m)	
Length	38.50
Beam	5.20
Draught	1.80
Air draught	3.50

Regulations
The maximum authorised speed is 15km/h in river sections (although there are some local restrictions), and 6km/h in the lock-cuts.

Navigation
Entering lock-cuts from upstream can be difficult during flood conditions.

Authority
VNF Rhône-Saône
- 2, quai du canal, BP 2, 70170 Port-sur-Saône, 03 84 91 51 99 (PK 0-62)
- 5, quai Vergy 8, 70101 Gray 03 84 65 11 02 (PK 62-127)
- Avenue Pierre Nugues, 71100 Châlon-sur-Saône, 03 85 97 19 40 (PK 127-150)

locks are electrified and equipped for automatic operation. In general, in season, opening hours are from 06:00 to 21:00. The last two, Poncey and Auxonne, open later at 09:00, close between 12:30 and 13:30, and close at 19:00. These two operate via a *perche* (twist the pole hanging above the river); the others are manned.

Draught
The maximum authorised draught is 1.80m.

Headroom
The minimum headroom is 3.50m.

Towpath
There is no continuous towpath. The lock-cuts have a towpath, but not the river sections.

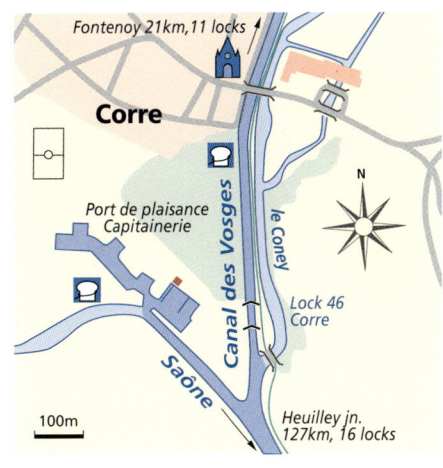

IV – Northeastern France

Route description

PK **407.0** Junction with Canal des Vosges d/s of Corre lock, *port de plaisance*, basin off river u/s l/b, 85 berths, 15 visitor moorings, 06 08 34 96 62, *fluvialoisirs.com*, night €13, water and electricity included, showers, slipway, crane 25t, repairs, wifi, restaurant 400m in village

PK **404.4** Entrance to Ormoy lock-cut, l/b
PK **403.0** Flood gate, bridge
PK **402.7** **Ormoy** bridge, village l/b
PK **401.9** Bridge (Devez)
PK **401.5** Ormoy lock (automatic), bridge
PK **401.4** End of lock-cut, river PK 400.7 (difference = 0.7km)
PK **400.2** Entrance to Denon meander cutoff l/b
PK **400.1** Denon bridge
PK **400.0** End of cutoff l/b, river PK 398,7 (difference = 1.3km, 2km total from Corre)
PK **398.4** Rond Pré meander cutoff (l/b)
PK **396.9** Vaivre meander cutoff (l/b)
PK **395.8** Entrance to Cendrecourt lock-cut, l/b, flood gate, bridge
PK **393.8** **Cendrecourt** lock (automatic), bridge, village 500m l/b
PK **393.5** End of lock-cut, 25m long timber quay and slipway 200m up the Saône at campsite, no services, mooring for **Jussey** 1km, small town 2km, river PK 392 (difference = 1.5km, 3.5km total from Corre)

The long walk from the rural mooring is rewarded by all basic shops and restaurants in this small market town, also with a station on the main line from Paris to Vesoul, which may be useful in this very remote area.

PK **391.8** Cendrecourt bridge
PK **390.6** Jussey railway viaduct
PK **390.2** Confluence of Amance, r/b
PK **386.1** La Hang meander cutoff, passing forbidden
PK **385.8** La Hang Bridge and end of cutoff l/b, river PK 385.6 (difference = 0.2km, 3.7km total from Corre)
PK **384.5** **Montureux-lès-Baulay** *halte* l/b, pontoon 24m, water (on request)

Approaching Montureux-lès-Baulay from downstream © GORDON KNIGHT

PK **383.7** Montureux bridge, entrance to Montureux lock-cut l/b
PK **383.3** Montureux lock (automatic), bridge, quays u/s and d/s l/b
PK **383.2** End of lock-cut, river PK 382.6 (difference = 0.8km, 4.5km total from Corre)
PK **381.8** **Fouchécourt** *port de plaisance* r/b (Le Petit Port) in small basin r/b, 03 84 68 77 74, *lepetitport.fr*, 17 berths, night €15, water, electricity, shower, restaurant
PK **380.1** **Baulay** bridge, timber quay, pontoon moorings u/s l/b, water, village 300m l/b
PK **376.6** **Port d'Atelier** bridge, limited moorings l/b, village r/b
PK **372.6** Conflandey bridge and lock
PK **372.5** Confluence of Lanterne l/b, tip of island, downstream-bound boats follow r/b arm, quay r/b, water, electricity
PK **372.1** **Conflandey** footbridge, village r/b
PK **371.8** Tip of island, u/s-bound boats follow l/b arm
PK **370.5** Island (Île du Cul du Chaudron), keep to l/b side
PK **368.5** Beleau island
PK **367.1** New viaduct (N19 Port-sur-Saône bypass)
PK **367.0** Entrance to Port-sur-Saône lock-cut, l/b
PK **366.9** Bridge (old main road) and flood gate, narrow cut, no mooring (proceed to basin), town l/b
PK **366.4** **Port-sur-Saône** basin and Franche-Comté Nautic hire base, 06 07 33 19 25, *fcnautic.com*, 120 berths, 10 visitors' moorings, night €13, water and electricity included, diesel, showers, crane 25t, slipway, pump-out, repairs, wifi, VNF office, restaurant l/b

A substantial port in a busy little town, which has a station on the main line from Paris to Basle: a rare resource in this otherwise poorly served area.

Port-sur-Saône quay, conveniently closer to the town than the large basin on the near side © GORDON KNIGHT

PK **366.1** Bridge (Maladière)
PK **365.5** Port-sur-Saône lock (automatic)
PK **365.4** End of lock-cut, river PK 364 (difference = 1.4km, 5.9km total from Corre)
PK **364.7** Gilley island (keep to r/b side)
PK **361.0** Entrance to Chemilly lock-cut, r/b, bridge
PK **360.4** Chemilly lock (automatic)
PK **360.3** End of lock-cut, river PK 360.0 (difference = 0.3km, 6.2km total from Corre)
PK **357.4** Entrance to Scey lock-cut, l/b, flood gate, proceed down Saône for access to **Scey-sur-Saône** pontoon moorings for 6 boats along campsite r/b, open mid-June to early September, night €5, water, electricity, town r/b
PK **356.8** Quay formerly used by sand-barges, r/b

Petite-Saône

PK **356.7 Scey-sur-Saône** bridge, basin d/s r/b, Locaboat hire base, 03 84 68 88 80, 10 visitors' moorings, night €10, water €3, electricity €2, shower, crane 8t on request, restaurant opposite basin, town 1km

One of the author's favourite mooring places on the Petite Saône, another small town with some interesting Spanish-looking buildings and most services, as well as a good supermarket and restaurants.

PK **356.4** Scey lock (automatic)
PK **356.1** End of lock-cut, river PK 353.1 (difference = 3km, 9.2km total from Corre)
PK **352.9** Entrance to Rupt lock-cut, r/b
PK **352.6** Bridge and flood gate, lights controlling tunnel entrance (canal narrows to one barge's width)

Entering the tunnel at Saint-Albin © PIERRE GLEIZES

PK **352.5** Saint-Albin tunnel (northern entrance)
PK **351.9** Saint-Albin tunnel (southern entrance)
PK **351.8** Bridge with lights controlling tunnel entrance, end of narrow section
PK **351.2** Rupt lock, water
PK **350.6** End of lock-cut, river PK 343.5 (difference = 7.1km, 16.3km total from Corre), access to **Traves** 5km, Saône Valley *port de plaisance*, in basin on l/b 800m upstream from bridge, 06 81 85 65 85, 10 boats, night €8, water €4, electricity €4, showers €3, slipway, wifi, *saonevalley.com*

The detour up to the village of Traves is synonymous with a deep immersion in nature, the tall trees being home to many herons. The village has a restaurant and *boulangerie*.

PK **342.8 Chantes** bridge, mooring possible d/s r/b, no services, village 1km l/b, **Rupt-sur-Saône** r/b, 500m
PK **342.1** Island, channel follows r/b arm
PK **341.1** Entrance to Chantes lock-cut, r/b, flood gate, bridge
PK **341.0** Chantes lock
PK **340.3** End of lock-cut, river PK 340.0 (difference = 0.2km, 16.5km total from Corre)
PK **338.2** Entrance to Cubry lock-cut
PK **338.1 Cubry-les-Soing** flood lock, usually open, bridge village 1.5km l/b
PK **337.4** End of lock-cut, river PK 336.6 (difference = 0.8km, 17.3km total from Corre)
PK **334.1** Narrow passage, no passing and overtaking
PK **334.0** End of narrow passage
PK **333.8** Entrance to Soing lock-cut, r/b, flood gate
PK **333.5** Bridge (Soing)
PK **332.5** Soing lock, bridge
PK **332.3** End of lock-cut, river PK 329.0 (difference = 3.3km, 20.6km total from Corre), possible to proceed u/s staying close to l/b to basin at **Soing**, 2.5km, moorings for 5 boats, campsite 03 84 78 45 17, night €3 (maximum 4 days), water, electricity, showers €2.20 at camp site, town l/b 100 m
PK **328.2** Entrance to Charentenay lock-cut, l/b (moorings adjacent to camp-site on l/b of Saône just d/s)
PK **327.7 Charentenay** bridge, flood gate, village and restaurant l/b
PK **326.0** Charentenay lock (automatic), bridge, VHF 20
PK **325.8** End of lock-cut, **Ray-sur-Saône** 1km up the river keep to l/b of island, municipal *halte*, pontoon for 5 boats, free, water, river PK 324.2 (difference = 1.6km, 22.2km total from Corre)
PK **323.9** Ray bridge
PK **323.7** Entrance to Ferrières lock-cut, r/b (Saône also navigable)
PK **323.4** Ferrières-lès-Ray, bridge
PK **322.4** Recologne bridge
PK **320.6** End of lock-cut, r/b (upstream-bound boats may also keep to Saône), river PK 318.5 (difference = 0.9km, 23.1km total from Corre)
PK **317.8 Recologne**, r/b, quay for sand-barges
PK **315.0** Entrance to Savoyeux lock-cut, r/b, flood gate, bridge
PK **313.8 Savoyeux** basin, moorings, Saône-Plaisance hire base, 03 84 67 00 88, 60 berths, 15 visitor berths, night €12, diesel, water €2, electricity €2, showers €2, crane 30t, slipway, repairs, wifi, *saone-plaisance.com*
PK **313.6 Seveux** bridge, village 1km l/b, canal narrows, sound horn for tunnel (controlled by lights)
PK **314.7** Savoyeux tunnel (northern entrance)
PK **314.0** Savoyeux tunnel (southern entrance)
PK **313.8** Railway bridge
PK **313.7** Bridge (with lights controlling tunnel entrance), end of narrow section
PK **313.3** Savoyeux lock, VHF 22
PK **313.3** End of lock-cut, river PK 306.8 (difference = 6.5km, 29.6km total from Corre)
PK **302.0 Quitteur** bridge, quay d/s l/b, restaurant r/b, **Autet** 1km r/b (shops)
PK **301.0** Confluence of Salon, r/b
PK **298.4** Entrance to Vereux lock-cut, l/b
PK **297.6** Flood gate, bridge
PK **296.3** Vereux lock, VHF 20

63

IV – Northeastern France

PK **296.2** End of lock-cut, river PK 296.0 (difference = 0.2km, 29.8km total from Corre)
PK **294.0** Prantigny bridge
PK **291.8** Carosse island (keep to l/b arm)
PK **289.3** Entrance to Rigny lock-cut, l/b, flood gate, bridge
PK **288.4** **Rigny** lock, VHF 22, moorings d/s r/b, village with shops 300m r/b
PK **288.3** End of lock-cut, river PK 287.5 (difference = 0.8km, 30.6km total from Corre)
PK **287.0** Commercial quay r/b
PK **283.8** Camp-site and *halte* l/b, moorings for 10 boats, May-October, night €5, water, electricity, showers
PK **283.3** **Gray** *halte nautique* l/b, 03 84 65 18 15, 25-30 boats, free, water €4 for 2 hours, electricity €5/day, wifi

Gray is a bustling market town proud of its Burgundian-style glazed tile town hall roof, and offers all services. The biggest town on the Petite Saône, it has a popular campsite and riverside park. The quayside moorings above the lock offer a good view of the town rising steeply on the opposite bank.

The Pont de Pierre at Gray   © GORDON KNIGHT

PK **283.2** Gray lock, VHF 20, and bridge (Pont de Pierre)
PK **283.0** **Arc-lès-Gray** *halte* on pontoon for 5 boats r/b, 03 84 65 18 15, water, electricity
PK **282.3** Bridge (Pont Neuf)

PK **282.1** Grain loading basin, r/b
PK **281.0** Restaurant, pontoon moorings r/b
PK **276.0** **Mantoche** *halte* on quay backed by grass, 8 boats, night €1.50, water only in season, village r/b
PK **275.0** Entrance to Apremont lock-cut, r/b
PK **275.1** Flood gate, bridge
PK **274.1** Apremont bridge (basin silted up)
PK **271.9** Apremont lock, bridge, VHF 22
PK **271.9** End of lock-cut, river PK 270 (difference = 1.9km, 32.5km total from Corre)
PK **268.5** Island (keep to r/b arm), Cecey quay, r/b
PK **263.5** Confluence of Vingeanne, r/b
PK **262.6** Montseugny island (keep to r/b arm)
PK **260.2** Quays for sand-barges, l/b
PK **259.0** River divides, take r/b arm (Île de Fley)
PK **258.0** Entrance to Heuilley lock-cut r/b, flood gate, bridge, mooring to bollards u/s r/b, **Heuilley-sur-Saône** 800m
PK **257.6** Heuilley basin, silted up, village r/b
PK **257.2** Bridge
PK **255.5** Junction with Canal entre Champagne et Bourgogne (controlled by lights), see Chapter III, Section 26
PK **255.4** Heuilley lock, bridge, VHF 20, restaurant

This is the first lock heading south after the Canal entre Champagne et Bourgogne. The lock sequence activated by turning the suspended pole.

Pontailler-sur-Saône, with its port de plaisance and hire base in the sheltered basin. The horse-chestnut trees gave the name of the Restaurant des Marronniers beside the basin. The Vieille-Saône continues from here through the town and on downstream, returning to the Saône at Vonges, but is open only to light craft **bouger-nature-en-bourgogne.com**

Petite-Saône

PK **255.3** End of lock-cut, river PK 254.3 (difference = 1km, 33.5km total from Corre)

PK **251.5** Entrance to Vieille Saône r/b, access to Pontailler *port de plaisance*, Canalous-Plaisance hire base, 03 80 47 43 50, 54 berths, 14 visitor berths in season, night €7, water €3.50, electricity €2, showers €2, crane 15t, slipway

The *port de plaisance* is through a bridge (adequate headroom, but check) and into a side channel where there is a waiting pontoon, then a marina basin. *Capitainerie* with showers..

PK **251.3** **Pontailler-sur-Saône** bridge, mooring d/s r/b, suitable for small vessels only, water, town r/b

Alternative mooring is the long stretch of quayside on the river itself. Charming village, with Atac supermarket through the village centre, then turn right (1.3 km).

PK **249.7** Vieille Saône enters r/b, caution, silted up
PK **249.5** Vonges explosives factory, r/b
PK **247.6** Basin, r/b, completely silted up
PK **246.0** Pontoon moorings r/b

Logis-Hôtel le Saint-Antoine set back from the river and restaurant Le Nymphéa beside the mooring. Hotel 03 80 47 11 33, riverside restaurant 03 80 32 02 50.

PK **245.5** **Lamarche-sur-Saône** bridge, municipal *halte* l/b, 4 boats, free, water and electricity by tokens, pump-out, village r/b
PK **242.0** Entrance to Poncey lock-cut, l/b, flood gate, bridge
PK **241.1** Poncey lock, bridge, VHF 22
PK **241.0** End of lock-cut, river PK 239.5 (difference = 1.5km, 35km total from Corre)
PK **238.9** Railway viaduct (Saône, TGV Rhin-Rhône)
PK **235.0** Island (Île de la Bouillie)
PK **233.6** **Auxonne** *port de plaisance* 'Port Royal' in basin l/b, 06 02 34 40 75, 150 berths, night €10, water and electricity (metered), slipway, repairs
PK **233.1** Bridge (Auxonne), public *halte* u/s l/b on pontoon for 30 boats (stern to pontoon), free, water, electricity, town centre, tourist office and all services l/b, water-skiing and bathing areas u/s

The *port de plaisance at Auxonne viewed from the ramparts of the former garrison town*

PK **233.0** Entrance to Auxonne lock-cut, l/b, and railway bridge
PK **232.8** Bridge and flood gate, office of sub-divisional engineer
PK **230.4** Auxonne lock, bridge, VHF 20
PK **230.5** End of lock-cut, river PK 229.5 (difference = 1km, 26km total from Corre)
PK **229.1** Motorway bridge (A39)
PK **223.7** Bridge (Maillys)
PK **222.0** Confluence of Tille, r/b, shoals
PK **221.6** Quay for sand-barges, r/b
PK **220.9** Island, channel in l/b arm
PK **219.0** Junction with Canal du Rhône au Rhin, l/b, mooring to stone quay d/s l/b,

A stylish lock-keeper's house makes the otherwise discreet entrance lock to the Canal du Rhône au Rhin a landmark on the Saône.

Designed as a work of art, the lock control cabin at Saint-Symphorien entrance lock; the Saône flows past in the background © PHILEAS FOTOS/VNF

PK **218.2** Saint-Symphorien village 400m l/b (no shops)
PK **216.7** Effective u/s limit of high-capacity waterway
PK **214.8** **Saint-Jean-de-Losne** bridge, moorings on both banks, small town r/b, **Losne** l/b
PK **214.6** Junction with Canal de Bourgogne, see Grande Saône

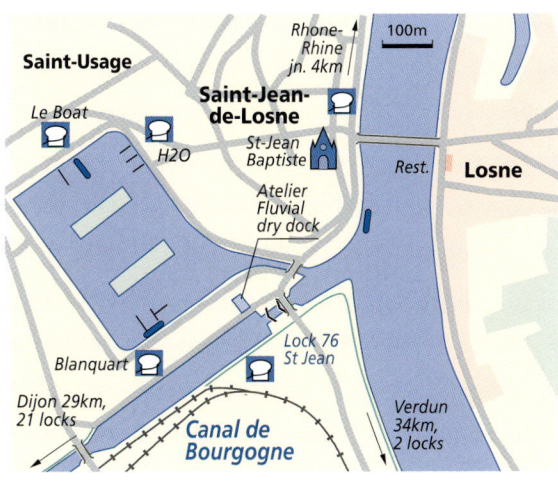

IV – Northeastern France

44. Rhin (Rhine)

THE RHINE HAS ITS SOURCES in the Swiss Alps southwest of Chur. Passing through Lake Constance, it retains its alpine character along the Swiss-German border down to the Basle region, where navigation begins at Rheinfelden. Just below the busy inland port of Basle the river leaves Switzerland and forms the French-German border over a distance of 184km, down to Lauterbourg. The Rhine then runs north and northwest through Germany and the Netherlands to discharge into the North Sea, 1320km from its source. The Upper Rhine (from Basle down to Bingen in Germany) has always been a difficult and often a dangerous river to navigate. Large-scale channel improvements were carried out between 1840 and 1860, but they had the effect of increasing the current speed and bed erosion. A meandering channel formed within the corrected 250m-wide bed and rocky bars were gradually exposed, the most notorious being at Istein near Kembs. Further works were required, to fix the channel by means of transverse groynes, but Basle was still only accessible to 600-tonne barges under favourable conditions. A more effective solution for navigation was already being envisaged before the 1914-1918 war. This was the construction of a canal stretching down the left bank from Basle to Strasbourg, the Grand Canal d'Alsace, designed as a series of hydroelectric power schemes, with benefits for agriculture as well as navigation. France was authorised to undertake the project under the the Treaty of Versailles and the works were conceded to Electricité de France. The first section of the canal, avoiding the Istein bar, was opened in 1932. By 1956 three further schemes had been completed. The project was then modified under a new agreement between the French and German governments, to limit the serious environmental impact on the Rhine itself. Subsequent schemes took the form of diversion canals of varying length, with a dam on the Rhine and power station and locks towards the downstream end of the canal. In the 1970s two further schemes were completed downstream of Strasbourg. As a result, the Rhine is canalised almost throughout its course on the French border.

Distances on the river are counted from the Rheinbrücke at Constance (under international agreement). The route description here covers the section of the river shared by France between PK 352.1 and PK 168.5. The Grand Canal d'Alsace extends over a distance of 53km, from PK 226.6. to PK 173.6.

There are connections with the Canal du Rhône au Rhin, Niffer branch, at Niffer (PK 185), with the Canal de Colmar (formerly a branch of the Canal du Rhône au Rhin) at PK 226, with the Canal du Rhône au Rhin, northern branch at PK 257.9 and with the Canal de la Marne au Rhin at Strasbourg (PK 291 or 295, see plan p. 242).

Navigation

The Rhine is a challenging fast-flowing river from the German border up to Iffezheim lock. The winding channel, the ferries, the current and the incessant traffic all require

Gambsheim Locks, on the Rhine, the busiest in France.
© JEAN MARX/MRW-ZEPPELINE ALSACE/DOC VNF

Rhine

Key dimensions (m)	
Length	185.00
Beam	11.50
Draught	2.70
Air draught	7.00

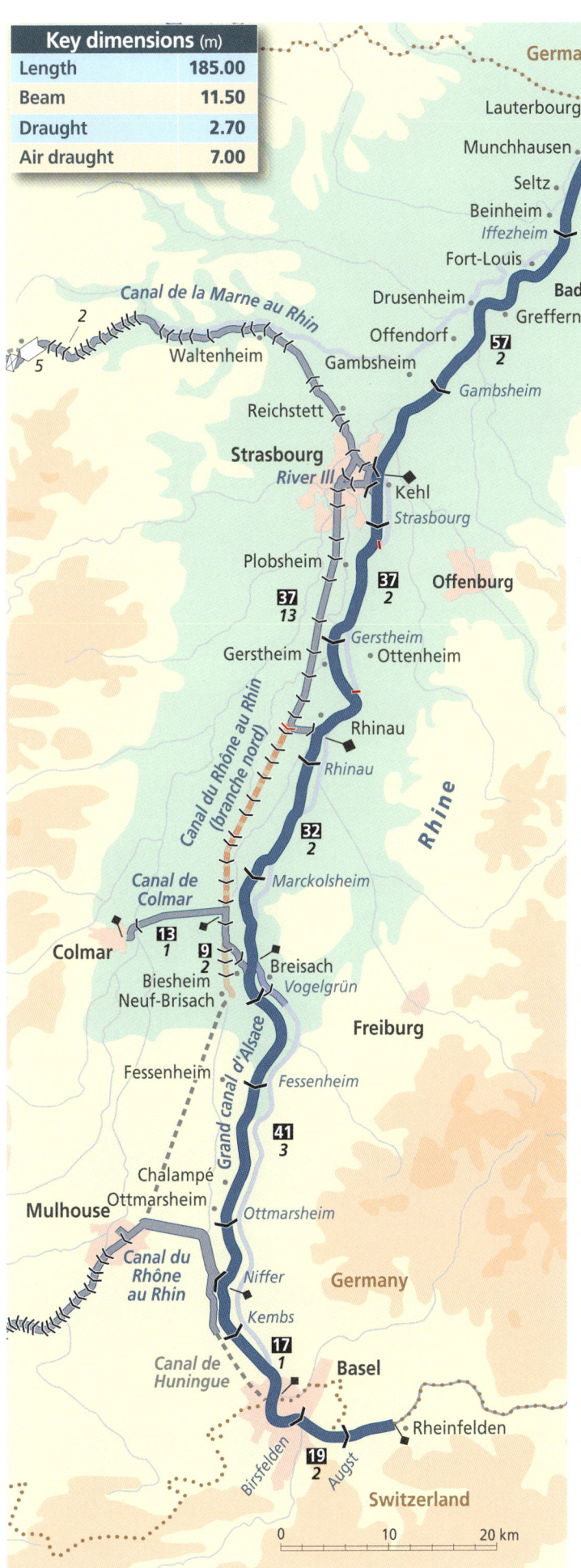

Canalisation of the Rhine for hydropower and navigation was authorised under the Treaty of Versailles in 1919 for the exclusive benefit of France. The twin Kembs locks, built in the 1930s, were 182.50m by 25m and 100m by 25m. After World War II, construction of the Grand Canal d'Alsace continued, until pressure from Germany, supported by environmental studies, called for a change in design. Subsequent schemes, with locks 185m by 12m and 185m by 23m (later widened to 24m), were built on diversion canals. Below Strasbourg, the locks built in the 1970s at Gambsheim (on the French side) and Iffezheim (on the German side) each have two identical chambers 270m by 24m.

constant attention. From Iffezheim upstream to Basle the dams and locks make the river easy to navigate, but it is forbidden to hire boats. Fast currents will also be encountered on the approach to the Swiss border and the port of Basle. The blue flag protocol applies on the Rhine, allowing craft to pass starboard to starboard instead of port to port, so that upstream craft can choose the inside of bends where the current is not so strong. Smaller craft do not have to display a blue flag, but should of course be out of the main channel and attentive to what may be incorrectly interpreted as erratic zigzagging by commercial traffic. Editions du Breil's guide No. 22 covers the Rhine in France and Switzerland, with detailed navigational advice and recommendations.

Locks

There are 10 locks, all built as part of important hydroelectric power schemes. The first four are on the Grand Canal d'Alsace, the remaining six on diversion canals. Each lock comprises two chambers side by side, one 185m by 24m, the other 185m by 12m. In view of the heavier traffic downstream of the busy port of Strasbourg (12 million tonnes per year), the two most recently-built locks, at Gambsheim and Iffezheim, each have two 270m by 24m chambers. The other variations are not significant.

Draught

There is a guaranteed draught of 3.00m between Huningue and the downstream end of the Grand Canal d'Alsace. On the canalised river the available draught at the normal stage of the river is 2.70m down to Strasbourg and 2.90m between Strasbourg and Lauterbourg.

Headroom

All the fixed bridges offer a clear headroom of 7.00m above the highest navigable water level between Basle and Strasbourg, 9.10m between Strasbourg and Lauterbourg.

IV – Northeastern France

Authority

VNF Strasbourg, UT Rhin
- 60 rue du Grillenbreit, BP 40545, 68021 Colmar
  03 89 41 21 53 *subdi-colmar.sn-strasbourg@developpement-durable.gouv.fr* (PK 168-258)
- 2, route de l'Ill, BP 19, 67761 Gambsheim cedex
  03 88 59 76 00 *emr.ut-rhin.s2r2e.dt-strasbourg@vnf.fr* (PK 258-352)

Route description

PK 352.1 Mouth of Vieille-Lauter l/b, French-German border
PK 349.2 **Lauterbourg** industrial harbour l/b, 03 88 94 80 08, restaurant, village 2 km
PK 344.0 **Munchhausen** 700m l/b, access by river Sauer
PK 341.6 Entrance to gravel basins l/b
PK 340.4 **Seltz** pendulum ferry, village 2.5 km l/b

Care is required approaching the ferry when in operation.

PK 339.0 Entrance to gravel basin, l/b
PK 335.7 Road bridge (formerly railway), Beinheim-Wintersdorf
PK 335.5 **Beinheim** *port de plaisance* l/b (Cercle Nautique de l'Alsace du Nord), 03 88 53 01 37, 15 visitors' berths, night €14, water, electricity, showers, slipway, restaurant on barge, village 3.5 km

One of the popular ports on the Rhine used by *plaisanciers* from France, Germany and Switzerland.

PK 334.5 Confluence of Moder, l/b
PK 334.0 Iffezheim locks (lift 10.30m), VHF 18, and power station, r/b, dam l/b, bridge
PK 326.9 **Fort-Louis** 1 km l/b (gravel basins u/s and d/s)
PK 321.3 **Greffern** gravel loading basin and boat club moorings, r/b
PK 319.8 Entrance to gravel loading basin, l/b
PK 318.3 **Drusenheim** ferry, village 1.5 km l/b
PK 317.6 Entrance to basin, l/b
PK 317.3 Entrance to gravel loading basin, r/b
PK 313.7 **Offendorf** gravel loading basin l/b, three private *ports de plaisance*: Port O'Rhin, 06 07 62 76 73, one visitor mooring, night €10, water and electricity included, shower €1.50, *mt-stenger@t-online.de*; Nautic Port, 03 88 96 74 58, 200 berths, 10 visitor berths, night €20, *contact@nautic-port.fr*; B.N.O., 07 82 54 67 69, 6 visitor berths, night €10, water, electricity, showers €1, pump-out, slipway, clubhouse in season, *base.nautique67@orange.fr*

Ports located along the perimeter of a still active gravel lake, offering calm moorings in a delightful forest setting.

PK 311.7 Entrance to diversion canal, l/b
PK 308.8 Gambsheim locks (lift 10.35m), VHF 20, and hydropower plant, bridge (cross-border road)
PK 307.2 End of diversion canal, navigation re-enters Rhine
PK 303.3 Entrance to gravel loading basin r/b
PK 297.7 Entrance to port of Kehl, r/b
PK 295.6 Junction with northern entrance to port of **Strasbourg** and Canal de la Marne au Rhin, l/b

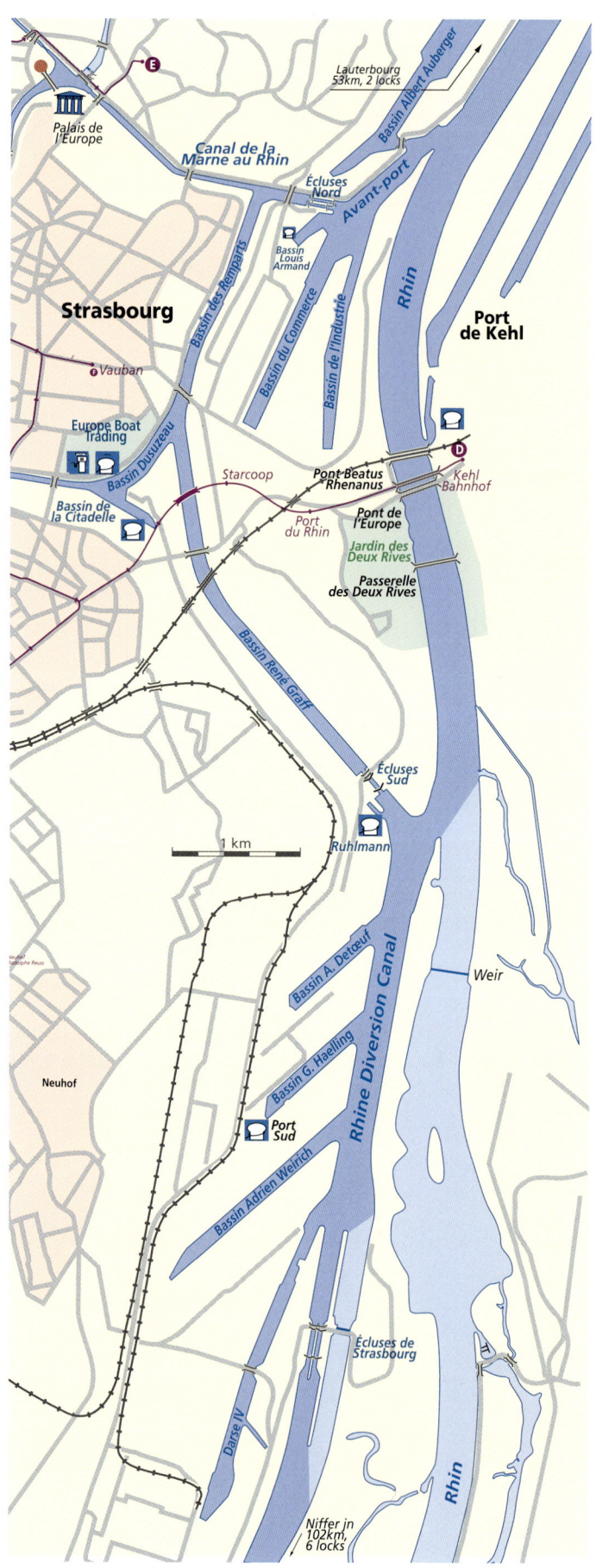

The Port of Strasbourg and the alternative route for Rhine barges and other large vessels through the basins, from PK 296 to PK 291. The Avant-Port gives access to the Bassin Louis-Armand and boat club moorings (Plaisance Club de Strasbourg), with 6 visitor moorings.

Rhine

PK **293.7** Railway bridge, **Kehl** boat club harbour d/s r/b
PK **293.5** Bridge (Pont de l'Europe, Strasbourg-Kehl)
PK **293.0** Footbridge (Deux Rives)
PK **291.4** Entrance to diversion canal, junction with southern entrance to port of Strasbourg and Canal du Rhône au Rhin l/b, *port de plaisance* (Ruhlmann), 06 64 85 38 87, 50 berths, by reservation only, water, electricity, crane 25t, slipway, repairs
PK **290.6** Basin 1 (Auguste Detœuf)
PK **289.8** Basin 2 (Gaston Haelling), *port de plaisance* at end of basin, 06 08 17 69 43, 65 berths, 4 visitor berths, €14, water and electricity included, restaurant Le Container, *club.du.port.de.plaisance@gmail.com*
PK **289.1** Basin 3 (Adrien Weirich)
PK **288.3** **Port of Strasbourg**, basin 4, l/b
PK **287.4** Strasbourg locks (lift 10.80m), VHF 22, and hydropower plant, bridge
PK **283.1** End of diversion canal, navigation re-enters Rhine
PK **283.0** Main road bridge (Pierre Pflimlin), N353
PK **282.5** **Plobsheim** compensating basin (used for water sports) l/b
PK **276.6** Entrance to gravel loading basin r/b
PK **274.1** Entrance to diversion canal, l/b
PK **272.2** Gerstheim locks (lift 10.98m) VHF 20, and power station, bridge
PK **267.5** End of diversion canal, navigation re-enters Rhine
PK **261.0** **Rhinau** ferry, village 800m l/b
PK **260.1** Entrance to diversion canal, l/b
PK **257.9** Junction with link canal to Canal du Rhône au Rhin , l/b

Heading downstream, boats will enjoy relief from the Rhine and its incessant traffic by entering this small canal and continuing on it down to Strasbourg.

PK **256.2** Rhinau-Sundhouse locks (lift 12.30m) VHF 22, and power station, bridge
PK **248.2** End of diversion canal, navigation re-enters Rhine
PK **242.5** Entrance to diversion canal, l/b
PK **239.9** Marckolsheim locks (lift 13.80m), VHF 20, and power station, bridge
PK **234.3** End of diversion canal, navigation re-enters Rhine
PK **230.8** Industrial quay (Kaysersberg) l/b
PK **228.6** Industrial quay (Rhenalu) l/b
PK **226.6** Entrance to Grand Canal d'Alsace, l/b
PK **225.9** **Biesheim** *port de plaisance* on Rhine l/b (access from end of diversion, next line), 06 81 48 95 63, 220 berths, night €14, water and electricity included, fuel, showers, crane 28t, slipway, repairs, *rhin-plaisance.com*
PK **226.3** Junction with Canal de Neuf-Brisach , l/b, connecting with the Canal du Rhône au Rhin, branche Nord, and its Colmar Branch, see Section 45, River Ill and Canal du Rhône au Rhin.
PK **225.8** Port of Colmar-Neuf-Brisach l/b
PK **224.5** Vogelgrün locks (lift 11.80m) VHF 22, and power station, bridge
PK **210.5** Fessenheim locks (lift 15.10m) VHF 20, and power station, bridge
PK **209.6** Fessenheim nuclear power plant (decommissioned 2020)
PK **199.6** **Chalampé** l/b
PK **199.3** Railway and road bridge (Neuenburg-Chalampé)

PK **199.0** Industrial quay (Rhône-Poulenc) l/b
PK **197.0** Industrial quays l/b
PK **196.0** Port of Mulhouse-Ottmarsheim l/b
PK **194.3** Motorway bridge (A36)
PK **193.7** Ottmarsheim locks (lift 14.70m) VHF 22, and power station, bridge
PK **191.9** Turning basin (Hombourg), 600 x 200m
PK **185.4** Junction with Canal du Rhône au Rhin, Niffer branch , l/b, **Niffer** 600m (*port de plaisance* see under section 46)

The control tower on the older lock at Niffer was designed by Le Corbusier.

PK **181.0** Gravel loading quay r/b
PK **180.5** Gravel loading quay l/b
PK **179.8** Overhead power transmission lines
PK **179.1** Kembs locks (lift 13.20m) VHF 20, power station, bridge
PK **173.7** End of Grand Canal d'Alsace, Kembs dam r/b, navigation re-enters Rhine
PK **171.3** Bridge (Palmrain), industrial quay d/s l/b
PK **170.2** Footbridge (Trois Pays)
PK **170.0** French-German border r/b
PK **169.9** Port of Basel, Kleinhüningen basin, r/b
PK **169.7** Entrance to former Huningue branch of Canal du Rhône au Rhin, l/b (navigable 2km to *port de plaisance* at Kembs), **Huningue** quay and small town l/b
PK **169.2** Mouth of Wiese river, r/b
PK **168.5** French-Swiss border l/b (Basel centre 2 km u/s)

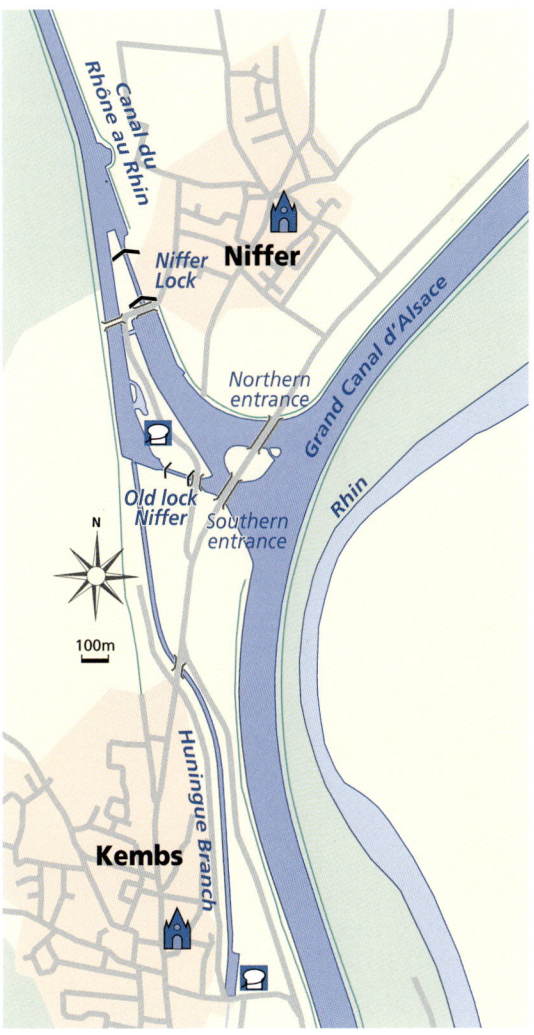

IV – Northeastern France

45. River Ill and Canal du Rhône au Rhin (northern branch)

Navigation in Strasbourg is a tale of two waterways, plus the basins of the port of Strasbourg. For convenience, they need to be considered as a single regional network. The network is formed by the river Ill, a tributary of the Rhine, navigable over a length of nearly 13km from the junction with the Canal de la Marne au Rhin (PK 312) at the European Parliament building in Strasbourg, through the city and the Alsace plain to Ostwald. After the cross-Strasbourg link (4.5km long) with its two arms flowing round the historic centre, the river connects with the northern branch of the Canal du Rhône au Rhin, which retains this name despite being severed from the main canal (see the following Section 46). The canal, managed by VNF, extends from the western end of the Dusuzeau basin of the port of Strasbourg through to Rhinau lock, where it connects with the Rhine. This Freycinet canal effectively continues the through routes, whether via the River Ill or the basins of the port of Strasbourg, making a continuous waterway that is 39.3 km long via the Ill, just 600m longer if starting from the Bassin des Remparts in the port of Strasbourg. See the detailed map on p. 72.

Key dimensions (m)	
Length	34.85
Beam	5.10
Draught	1.80
Air draught	3.50
[upper river Ill	2.60]

The River Ill has been navigated since time immemorial. Strasbourg was established on its islands, and from here upstream the river was equipped with *pertuis* (flash locks) for nearly 100km. The present navigation was incorporated into the city's fortifications as early as the 11th century. In the 14th century the *ponts couverts* were built to protect the city. Vauban built his famous barrage in the late 17th century to further protect the city. The existing locks were built at the turn of the 19th century and enlarged under the Becquey programme (1820-1830).

The northern branch of the Canal du Rhône au Rhin originally ran from the through route at Mulhouse to Strasbourg, a distance of 96km. A motorway junction north of Mulhouse severed the old canal in the late 1950s, but it is planned to restore two abandoned lengths extending over a length of 66km south to the picturesque fortified town of Neuf-Brisach. The works were begun in 2005, but interrupted in late 2007 when it was discovered that full restoration was going to cost almost double the originally budgeted amount of €7 million. The region was also unwilling to budget for operating and maintenance costs. This is one of the many difficulties caused by the government's policy of transferring secondary inland waterways to regional or local authorities.

River Ill and Canal du Rhône au Rhin

An additional system inherited from the old canal, and a worthwhile excursion for private boats, is the link from the Rhine to Colmar, using a 1960s connecting canal (the Canal de Neuf-Brisach), a length of the old northern branch of the Canal du Rhône au Rhin, and the Colmar branch of that branch, a route that is 23km long.

These two waterways are at present connected only by the Rhine, but the author has contributed to the project to restore the canal in the disused section, 23km long with 12 locks (one new), so that Colmar could be reached by hire boats. This is the dotted orange line on the maps. Pending completion of this project, the Colmar access route is described separately, with its own PK starting from the Rhine, and breaking down into three sections: first the 6km Neuf-Brisach link canal, built as part of the upper Rhine development works, then a 3km length of the former canal maintained for navigation, finally the original branch of the Canal du Rhône au Rhin, 13km long.

In short, there are two 'regional' systems based on the same original canal, but severed until further notice, to the deepest regret of Colmar and its Chamber of Commerce, who rightly see great potential for developing waterway tourism with the rest of Alsace and Lorraine.

The 'dead end' section of the river Ill upstream of the cross-Strasbourg link is 8.3km long, leading to factories and a large gravel pit that formerly made use of barge transport. This section also gave access to the now disused Canal de la Bruch.

Navigation
Navigation on the cross-Strasbourg link is not encouraged by the Strasbourg Port Authority. This is a pity, because it is possibly the most attractive urban waterway in France. In practice, private boats are allowed to cruise through the Petite-France, but downstream only, thus using Lock A in the opposite direction to the incessant traffic of trip-boats, which systematically do the ring clockwise. The navigable length of the river is shown on the detailed plan of Strasbourg on the next page. Navigation on the Canal du Rhône au Rhin is straightforward, except when crossing the River Ill in flood at PK 115.

Locks
There are two locks on the River Ill, A and B, one on each of the alternative routes through Strasbourg. The first is on the Ill in the heart of the Petite France district, while the second is on the Canal des Faux Remparts The latter is used by the Strasbourg trip-boats to make the round cruise through the city. A third lock (C) gives access to the 400m long 'dead end' section of the river north of the level junction with the Canal de la Marne au Rhin. It is used only by waterway maintenance vessels. Lock dimensions are 34.85m by 5.32m. Trip-boats have priority at the locks.

On the Canal du Rhône au Rhin from the port of Strasbourg to Rhinau there are 12 locks, plus a flood lock (normally open) at the crossing of the Ill flood diversion canal (PK 17). The lock connecting with the Rhine at Rhinau is 40m by 6.00m. The others are 38.80m long and 5.10m wide.

The Colmar branch has 3 locks. The new lock on the Neuf-Breisach link canal measures 40m by 6.00m. The second lock (38.80m by 5.10m) is on the former through route of the canal, while the third (38.85 by 5.30m) is at the crossing of the River Ill near Colmar.

Draught
The maximum authorised draught is 1.80m, but silting has occurred on the upper reaches of the Ill towards Ostwald, and caution is required when heading upstream on the river from the junction with the Canal du Rhône au Rhin.

Headroom
The least headroom on the cross-Strasbourg link is 3.90m, reduced to 3.50m above highest navigable water level. On the upper reaches, headroom is reduced to 3.15m (2.60m above highest navigable water level). On the Canal du Rhône au Rhin the fixed bridges offer a minimum headroom of 3.70m.

Towpath
There is no towpath along the river Ill, but attractive riverside walks have been developed throughout the navigable ring in Strasbourg. There is a good towpath along the canal, paved to serve as a cycle route.

Authority
VNF Strasbourg
- 46, quai Jacoutot, 67000 Strasbourg, 03 88 45 50 20 (Ill PK 8.2-12.8, canal PK 134-98)
- 60 rue du Grillenbreit, 68021 Colmar cedex, 03 89 41 21 53 (canals from Rhine to Colmar)
  subdi-colmar.sn-strasbourg@developpement-durable.gouv.fr

Région Alsace, Service de l'Ill
- Parc du Murgiessen, 67150 Erstein, 03 88 59 89 99 (Ill PK 0-8.2)

Route description

River Ill
PK 12.8 **Junction with Canal de la Marne au Rhin**, in front of European Parliament building

Boats from Nancy and the Vosges turn right here into the Ill, boats from the Rhine and the Port of Strasbourg turn left, while on the other (north) side of the canal are La Robertsau weir and lock C of the river Ill, for works craft only.

PK 12.6	Private footbridge (European Parliament)
PK 12.1	Footbridge (Passerelle de l'Orangerie)
PK 11.8	Bridge (Pont de la Dordogne)
PK 11.3	Bridge (Pont de la Forêt Noire)
PK 11.1	Bridge (Pont d'Auvergne), river Aar (not navigable) l/b
PK 11.0	Bridge (Pont Royal), tramway lines C, E
PK 10.8	**Junction with Canal des Faux Remparts**, l/b
PK 10.7	Bridge (Pont Saint-Guillaume)
PK 10.5	Footbridge (Passerelle de l'Abreuvoir)
PK 10.4	Bridge (Pont Sainte-Madeleine)
PK 10.0	Bridge (Pont Saint-Nicolas), tramway lines A, D

The swing bridge (Pont du Faisan) is opened for a trip boat coming

IV – Northeastern France

This view of the European Parliament is taken from the bridge over the at present inaccessible section of the Ill; the Ill to Strasbourg is on the left, the Canal de la Marne au Rhin to the right.
© FRÉDÉRIC-GENEVIÈVE

River Ill and Canal du Rhône au Rhin

The 'Ponts couverts' at the entrance to Strasbourg's 'Petite France' quarter, viewed from Vauban's fortified bridge. Lock B is to the left, while the route through Strasbourg takes the arm to the left of the first tower. © WAKE FOREST UNIVERSITY VIA WIKIPEDIA

Canal du Rhône au Rhin, branche nord

The first 3.5 km to the entrance to the Bassin d'Austerlitz are part of the Port of Strasbourg. This gives the effective through route from the Canal de la Marne au Rhin.

PK **137.5**	Junction with Canal de la Marne au Rhin, northern end of Bassin des Remparts
PK **136.1**	Bridge over Bassin des Remparts (Pont d'Anvers)
PK **135.9**	Junction with Bassin Vauban r/b, connection to Rhine via Écluses Sud
PK **135.4**	Bassin Dusuzeau, junction with Bassin de la Citadelle r/b, *port de plaisance* l/b, 06 07 21 82 45, 20 visitor berths, night €17, diesel, water, electricity, pump-out, crane 30t, repairs **europe-boat-trading.fr**
PK **135.0**	Bridge (pont du Danube)
PK **134.7**	Bridge (pont Winston Churchill)
PK **134.4**	Footbridge
PK **134.0**	Junction with Bassin d'Austerlitz of port of Strasbourg
PK **133.9**	Bridge (d'Austerlitz)
PK **133.8**	Bridge (de la Bourse), tramway lines A & D
PK **133.5**	Lock 86, automatic, bridge (Porte de l'Hôpital), Strasbourg centre 800m north

out of Lock A in the Petite-France. Space is limited, dissuading boats from using the river Ill heading downstream, while navigation in the same direction as the trip boats is forbidden.

PK **10.2**	Bridge (Pont du Corbeau)
PK **9.7**	Bridge (Pont Saint-Nicolas)
PK **9.5**	Bridge (Pont Saint-Thomas), *halte* Finkwiller u/s r/b for 2 boats, limited to 48 hours, water and electricity payable by credit card, pump-out
PK **9.4**	Lock A (drop 1.90m)
PK **9.3**	Swing bridge (Faisan)
PK **9.1**	Junction with Canal des Faux Remparts, l/b, Quartier des Moulins, take l/b channel, bridge (Ponts Couverts)
PK **9.0**	Barrage Vauban (part of former fortifications), 13 arches, navigation through l/b arch
PK **8.8**	Bridge (Pont des Frères-Matthis)
PK **8.5**	Bridge (Pont Louis Pasteur)
PK **8.4**	Canal du Rhône au Rhin leaves Ill, r/b
PK **8.3**	Canal du Rhône au Rhin enters Ill, r/b

The following route description starts with the alternative (and 'normal') route south from the Canal de la Marne au Rhin via the basins of the port of Strasbourg and the first 1.5 km of the Canal du Rhône au Rhin, branche nord. The official distances of the canal (from the original junction in Mulhouse) are continued for convenience.

View from the Pont Winston Churchill towards the Presqu'île André Malraux, a major urban development around the Bassin de l'Hôpital. The canal starts just after the entrance to this basin. © CRISTINA SÁENZ DE MIERA

73

IV – Northeastern France

PK **133.0** Basin r/b (Bassin de l'Hôpital), boat harbour (Plaisance Club Strasbourg), visitor moorings 6 boats, 03 88 84 50 54, water, electricity, showers
PK **132.6** Flood gate (Heyritz), bridge and footbridge
PK **132.5** Junction with the river Ill , l/b (route through the centre of Strasbourg)
PK **132.4** Railway bridge
PK **132.3** Expressway bridge (D1004)
PK **132.2** *Port de plaisance* 'Marinest', 50 berths, 06 64 85 38 87, water, electricity (metered), slipway, crane 40t, repairs
PK **132.1** Rail and road bridges
PK **132.0** Lock 85, automatic, lift bridge, quay u/s r/b
PK **130.9** Pipeline crossing and overhead power lines
PK **129.5** Lock 84, bridge
PK **129.2** Bridge (D468)
PK **128.9** Footbridge
PK **128.5** Main road bridge (D1083), limited moorings on stone quay l/b, **Illkirch-Graffenstaden** l/b
PK **127.5** Bridge (Lixenbuhl), tramway line A
PK **126.6** Bridge
PK **125.4** Lock 83, bridge
PK **124.2** Basin (Illkirch-Graffenstaden)
PK **123.7** Expressway bridge (N353)
PK **123.1** Conveyor bridge
PK **122.3** **Eschau** bridge, quay d/s r/b, village l/b
PK **121.6** Lock 82, bridge
PK **120.3** **Plobsheim** bridge, quay d/s r/b, no services, village 400m r/b

PK **110.2** Bridge
PK **109.0** Lock 77
PK **108.3** **Obenheim** bridge, village 1 km r/b
PK **105.8** **Boofzheim** quay and Le Boat hire base r/b, 2 visitor moorings, night €20, water and electricity included, 06 72 13 37 09 , shower, quay u/s r/b, village 1200m r/b
PK **105.7** Lock 76, bridge (D5)
PK **103.4** Lock 75, VHF 18, bridge
PK **102.5** Junction with currently disused section of the canal towards Colmar l/b

Pending restoration of the connecting length to Colmar, the route here continues, to connect with the Rhine at Rhinau. The PK are continued accordingly.

Friesenheim-Rhinau link canal
PK **100.2** Bridge (D468), **Friesenheim** 1 km north
PK **99.3** Crossing of river Ischert on the level, quays d/s
PK **98.2** Lock (Rhin), bridge, VHF 18
PK **97.7** Entrance to river Rhine d/s of Rhinau locks (Rhine PK 258)

See under the Rhine for the connection to the Colmar route, 32 km and two locks further south.

A lone Dutch barge at winter moorings beside the Notre Dame-du-Chêne chapel, PK 119

The entrance lock from the Rhine at Rhinau, PK 98.

PK **119.0** Quay r/b, Notre Dame-du-Chêne chapel
PK **118.1** Lock 81, bridge, aqueduct u/s
PK **117.7** Bridge (D788)
PK **115.8** **Erstein-Krafft** bridge, *halte* d/s r/b, moorings for 5-6 boats, 1 *péniche*, free (maximum 48 hours), water
PK **115.5** Flood lock 80
PK **115.4** Crossing of Ill flood diversion canal on the level, junction with Erstein branch (disused, restoration proposed in a study carried out in 2006 but not approved)
PK **114.8** Lock 79, bridge
PK **113.8** **Erstein** bridge, sugar refinery quay d/s l/b and conveyor bridges, town 3 km l/b
PK **111.8** Lock 78, bridge
PK **111.3** **Gerstheim** quay r/b, no services, village 1200m r/b

Branch off the Canal du Rhône au Rhin

From the Rhine to Colmar
Neuf-Brisach junction canal and Colmar Branch (Canal de Colmar)

Distances are given cumulatively from the Rhine to Colmar for convenience, since neither of the intermediate junctions offers a choice of route at present.

PK 0.0	**Entrance to link canal from the Rhine** d/s of Vogelgrün locks (Rhine PK 226)
PK 0.3	Lock (Écluse du Rhin), VHF 8, bridge
PK 1.6	**Biesheim** *halte* l/b, Rhône au Rhin Plaisance, 10 berths up to 15m, 06 32 41 50 00, night €10, water and electricity included, slipway
PK 1.9	Footbridge
PK 2.1	Bridge
PK 2.2	Rail and road bridges, Biesheim 1.5 km l/b
PK 2.7	Weir r/b (river Giessen leaves canal)
PK 2.8	Bridge (Bœbbels)
PK 5.0	Bridge (D468)
PK 6.0	**Kunheim** bridge, village r/b
PK 6.1	**Junction with former main route of Canal du Rhône au Rhin, southbound** (PK 59.3), moorings for 16 boats, 03 89 47 40 40, night €6, water, electricity, shower, pump-out, navigation continues north on the original canal

In addition to the Artzenheim-Friesenheim section, the author's study in 1999 recommended restoration of the canal southbound to Neuf-Brisach, a distance of 6 km with four locks, where there is a large basin ideal for development as a *port de plaisance*. Regrettably there is currently no momentum for this project.

PK 7.9	Lock 63, bridge (D9)
PK 9.3	**Junction with former main route of Canal du Rhône au Rhin, northbound**, (PK 56.1), bridge, navigation north towards Strasbourg projected (restoration partially completed), sharp left turn on branch west towards Colmar
PK 9.7	Bridge
PK 11.1	Footbridge
PK 11.3	Pipeline crossing
PK 12.2	Bridge
PK 13.1	Bridge
PK 14.0	Bridge (D9), **Muntzenheim** 600m south
PK 15.0	Bridge
PK 15.6	Aqueduct
PK 16.3	Bridge, **Wickerschwihr** 500m north
PK 17.1	Bridge
PK 18.1	Bridge
PK 18.8	Bridge
PK 19.5	Bridge
PK 20.4	Lock (Ill) with flood gate, bridge d/s
PK 20.6	Crossing of river Ill, weir on north side, navigation enters the river Lauch

Beware of the cross-current.

PK 20.7	Motorway bridge (A35)
PK 20.8	Footbridge
PK 21.5	Footbridge
PK 22.4	Turning basin, industrial quays d/s l/b
PK 22.7	**Colmar** basin (head of navigation) *port de plaisance*, 06 80 25 44 63, 58 berths, 15 visitor berths, night €17, fuel, water, electricity, showers, crane 18t, pump-out, repairs, town centre 1 km

Colmar is a very picturesque town, with its half-timbered houses and the winding streams of the river Ill. These make a delightful boat excursion, less than 1 km from the *port de plaisance*.

The port de plaisance *in Colmar, with its imposing* capitainerie *and the 300m-long basin heading up towards the town centre. The town and its port look forward to a new lease of life when the canal section between Artzenheim and Friesenheim can be finally restored, after years of hesitation by the region.* © GSV

The boat trip through Colmar's answer to Strasbourg's 'Petite-France' is thoroughly recommended. © HORST KÜHN

IV – Northeastern France

46. Canal du Rhône au Rhin

THE CANAL DU RHÔNE AU RHIN, built between 1784 and 1833, is a magnificently scenic route through the Jura, with wooded cliffs and blueish ranges of hills in the background. The two historic towns, Dole and Besançon, both have spectacular settings. It is used by boats heading south from Germany and Switzerland to the Mediterranean, but it is also a cruising waterway in its own right, especially in the picturesque valley of the Doubs, which makes up for nearly two thirds of the route. Commercial traffic in 38.50m barges has practically disappeared. The long-standing project to open up a new large-scale waterway on the line of the canal, providing a continuous route for Rhine barges from the North Sea to the Mediterranean, was abandoned in 1997.

The canal links the upper Rhine (in fact the Ottmarsheim reach of the Grand Canal d'Alsace) at Niffer (PK 185) to the Saône at Saint-Symphorien, 4km upstream of the junction with the Canal de Bourgogne at Saint-Jean-de-Losne. The length of the canal is 237km.

Officially the canal starts at the Saône and ends at the Rhine, but the route description is here presented in the reverse direction, to make it more comprehensible for navigators heading towards the Saône. From Mulhouse to Niffer, navigation follows the former Kembs-Niffer branch of the canal, which was upgraded to the 1350-tonne barge standard as part of the Upper Rhine development works. A higher-capacity (Class Vb) lock was added in the 1990s. From Mulhouse (PK 18) to l'Isle-sur-le-Doubs (PK 96) navigation is almost exclusively in man-made cut, crossing the Saône-Rhine watershed by a summit level at an altitude of 340m. From l'Isle-sur-le-Doubs (PK 141) to Dole (PK 220), the navigation then uses the course of the river Doubs for long section. This requires care in the river sections, where the fixed masonry weirs are difficult to see for boats heading downstream. However, navigation aids have been improved considerably in recent years. Finally, from Dole to Saint-Symphorien, a 17km canal section leads to the River Saône (Petite Saône).

The **Belfort branch**, 10km long, connects to Botans, a small town in the suburbs of Belfort, but is practically disused.

[A 'northern branch' of this canal, 66km long, extending from Neuf-Brisach to the port of Strasbourg, and its Colmar branch, 23km long, are isolated from the main route from the Rhine to the Saône. Details are given in Section 45 common to this canal and the river Ill.]

There are two tunnels, at Thoraise (PK 59) and under the citadel at Besançon (PK 74), although boaters will often prefer to cruise through the town. Thoraise tunnel is 185m long, while that at Besançon is 394m long. Both are for one-way traffic only (6m wide). There are also numerous narrow bridge-holes (as little as 5.18m wide), aqueducts and cuttings allowing one-way passage only.

Navigation

All locks and channels were renovated in the period 2000-2005, but sections of the River Doubs form much of the route, and particular care must be taken to keep to the marked channels, and to avoid rocks and shallows, and of course the man-made weirs. All dangers are clearly marked and should not otherwise cause problems, unless the river is running fast. From the Rhine at Niffer through to the Île Napoleon docks in Mulhouse, the canal sees some very large Rhine barges and push-tows.

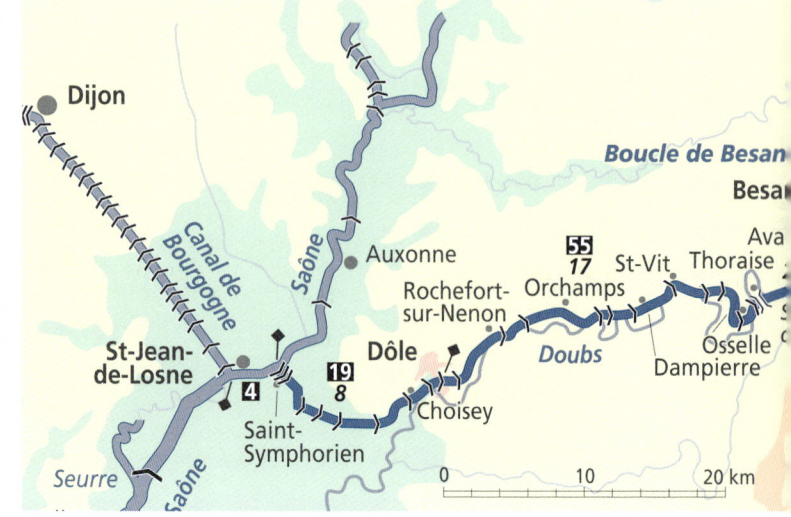

Canal du Rhône au Rhin

The first section of the Canal de Franche-Comté (as it was then called) was authorised by Burgundy Council in 1783 and completed in 1802 from the Saône to Dôle. Napoleon was seeking to develop inland waterway connections throughout the country, and the Rhône-Rhine link was of such strategic importance that he gave his name to the project. He wrote to Crétet, director of Ponts et Chaussées in 1805: 'It is not palaces or buildings the Empire needs: it is canals and navigable rivers'. Hence the Canal Napoléon. The problem was funding. The Emperor's administration conceived the predecessor of today's public-private partnership model, selling existing canals to private companies, to provide funds for new links. The proceeds were diverted for the war effort, and it was not until the Becquey programme was finalised in 1821 that this vital project, now renamed 'Canal Monsieur', could be reactivated by the canal company created for this purpose, and completed in 1833 by the engineer Claude-François Perret. Upgrading to Freycinet standards started in 1882, and the summit level was lowered, reducing the number of locks. Works were completed in 1904. The new high-capacity Rhine-Rhône waterway would have made the canal obsolete, but the environment minister Dominique Voynet cancelled that project in 1997. The Government then funded – as compensation – the backlog of maintenance works and other improvements. The canal is to be transferred to the regions, but no timetable has been set for this operation.

Throughout the rest of the canal the occasional commercial *péniche* must of course be given priority at the locks. The maximum permitted speed is 10km/h in the river sections and 6km/h in canal sections.

Locks

There are 112 locks, of which 40 climb from the Rhine to the summit, and the remaining 72 fall towards the Saône (including two double staircase locks). There are also four flood locks that are normally open to navigation, generally situated at the entrances to certain lock-cuts in the Doubs valley. The lock numbers do not conform to these totals, because of various changes made since the canal was first built. At the end of the last century the summit level was lowered and the first locks on either side eliminated.

In the 1980s, locks 12 and 13 at Sochaux were replaced by a single lock at the end of a section upgraded to high-capacity standards as part of the (now abandoned) Rhone-Rhine waterway past the Peugeot car factory. The first locks at Niffer are of Rhine barge dimensions (new chamber 190m by 12m and an older chamber 85m by 12m). The 39 up to the summit level to Mulhouse are 38.80m by 5.10m.

Key dimensions (m)	
Length	38.50
Beam	5.20
Draught	1.80
Air draught *above normal water level*	3.50

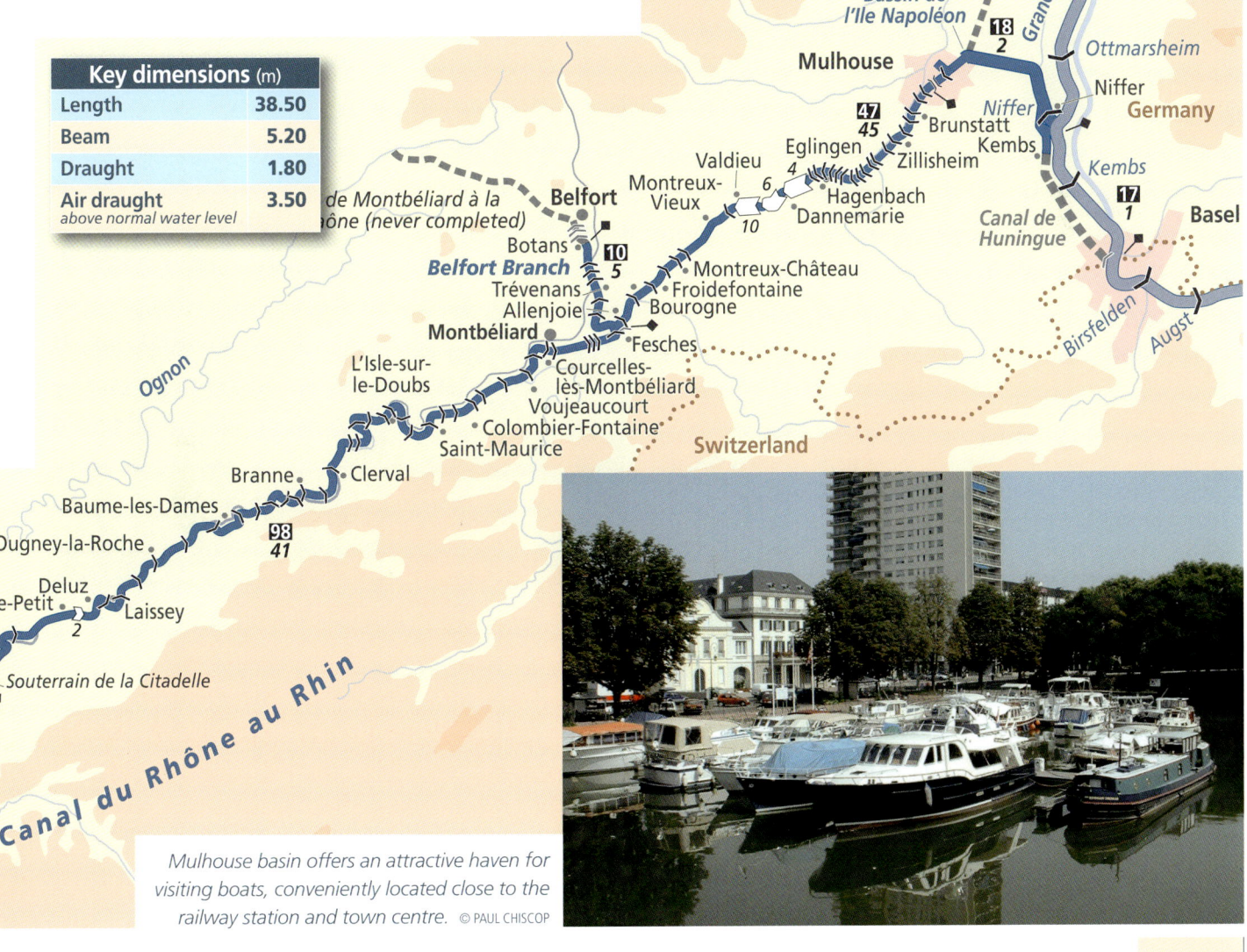

Mulhouse basin offers an attractive haven for visiting boats, conveniently located close to the railway station and town centre. © PAUL CHISCOP

IV – Northeastern France

The first five down from the summit level to PK 175 (Allenjoie) are of larger dimensions (40.70m by 6.28m).

The last 68 locks from Allenjoie to Saint-Symphorien are 38.70m by 5.25m.

Draught
The maximum authorised draught is 1.80m.

Headroom
The maximum authorised air draught is 3.50m, reduced to 3.40m above the highest navigable water level when the Doubs is in flood.

Towpath
There are service paths along all the canal sections, but not along the sections in the river Doubs.

Authority
VNF Strasbourg
– Subdivision de Belfort: 6, rue Alfred Engel, BP 06, 90800 Bavilliers 03 84 21 00 88 **subdi-mulhouse-belfort. sn-strasbourg@developpement-durable.gouv.fr** (PK 0-65)

VNF Rhône-Saône
– Subdivision de la Vallée du Doubs: Moulin Saint-Paul, 18, avenue Goulard, BP 429, 25019 Besançon cedex 03 81 25 00 30 **vallee-du-doubs.subdivisions.sn-rhone-saone@ developpement-durable.gouv.fr** (PK 65-177)
– Subdivision de Dole: 2, rue Général Béthouard, BP 83, 39108 Dole 03 84 70 80 05 **dole.subdivisions.sn-rhone-saone@ developpement-durable.gouv.fr** (PK 177-237)

Besançon Loop
This loop provides an alternative route for boats through the attractive town, bypassing the 500m length of the through route of the canal through the Citadelle tunnel. The loop is 4km long, from the upstream tunnel entrance (flood gate 50a) to the downstream entrance (lock 50, Tarragnoz), and includes lock 51a (Saint-Paul). Navigational characteristics are the same as for the rest of the canal.

Belfort Branch
The Belfort branch leaves the through route at PK 172, near Allenjoie, and may be navigated up to PK 9.7 at Botans. Just beyond this village on the outskirts of Belfort, a motorway crosses the canal. The canal was originally projected to extend through a series of watersheds and connect with the Saône at Port-sur-Saône. Works were completed up to the main summit level, with 13 locks, 20.6km beyond Botans. The first lock on the Saône side was also built, as well as two tunnels on the summit level, before the project was abandoned.

Navigation
The canal sees little traffic, and VNF must be contacted by 16:00 the day before the intended passage, to mobilise an itinerant lock-keeper

Locks
There are 5 locks, with minimum dimensions 38.70m by 5.20m.

Draught
The maximum authorised draught is 1.20m.

Headroom
The bridges offer a minimum headroom of 3.50m.

Towpath
There is a towpath throughout the length remaining open to navigation.

Authority
VNF Strasbourg
– Subdivision de Belfort: 6, rue Alfred Engel, BP 06, 90800 Bavilliers 03 84 21 00 88 **subdi-mulhouse-belfort. sn-strasbourg@developpement-durable.gouv.fr**

Route description

PK 0.0 **Two junctions with the Grand Canal d'Alsace**, Ottmarsheim reach, southern entrance to smaller lock, northern entrance to high-capacity lock

PK 0.2 Bridge (D468) over both branches

PK 0.3 Niffer old lock on southern branch, bridge, private port Alsace Plaisance, 06 80 75 56 15, 2 visitor berths (by reservation only), night €12, water and electricity included, shower, slipway

The smaller southern Niffer lock is often – but not always – used by pleasure craft. Coming from the Rhine stop just before the old lock and call the lock-keeper via VHF 22 or 03 89 74 57 44 for instructions. Coming from Mulhouse it is also courteous to call the lock-keeper to advise of your intention to head down the Huningue Branch or to use the attractive moorings just short of the old lock rather than pass the lock. To use these moorings, call Alsace Plaisance in advance.

Contrasts in lock control cabins at Niffer: on the left, the building designed by Le Corbusier in 1960 for the first large lock; right, the less modest statement by Italian architect Bernardo Fort-Brescia, for the new lock opened in 1996. © PISTACHIO 67/ERIC PITISI

PK 0.5 **Junction with Huningue branch**, navigable 2km to Kembs boat harbour (see plan opposite), 06 83 89 18 50, 48 berths, 6 visitor berths, night €15, water, electricity, shower, restaurant

PK 1.1 Footbridge

PK 1.2 Niffer large lock, VHF 22, village 1km r/b, bridge

PK 1.4 **Junction of the two lock-cuts**

Canal du Rhône au Rhin

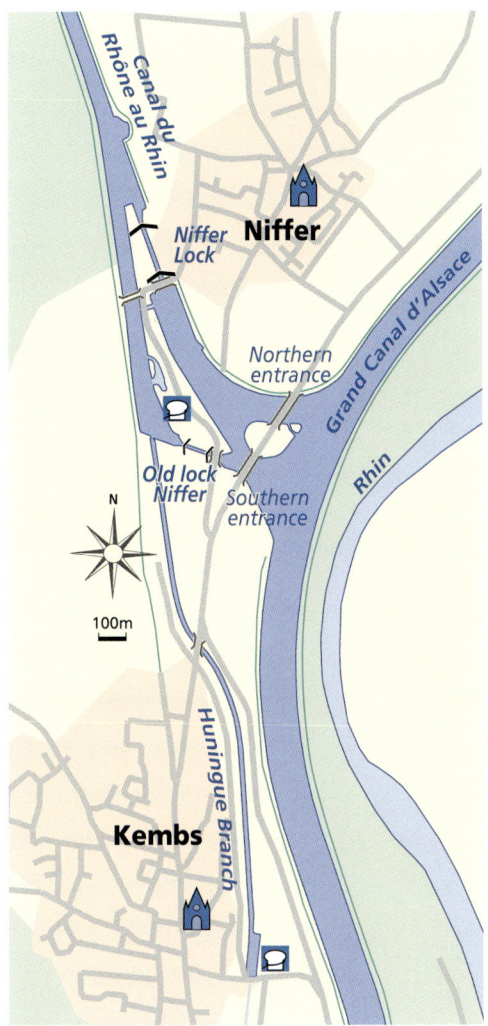

PK 1.6	Overhead power line
PK 3.4	Bridge (Route de Petit Landau)
PK 9.5	Bridge (Bouc), D108
PK 11.7	Motorway bridge (A35), Peugeot factory d/s l/b
PK 13.3	Railway bridge
PK 13.5	**Île Napoléon** basin, junction with former through route, chandlery, bridge

The canal originally proceeded north from the Île Napoléon basin to Colmar and then Strasbourg. It was replaced by the Grand Canal d'Alsace (River Rhine lateral canal).

PK 14.3	Oil terminal basin, short-term mooring
PK 14.9	Water point and customs post, l/b
PK 15.4	Railway bridge
PK 15.8	Bridge
PK 16.3	Basin l/b (length 1900m, silted up, no access)
PK 16.4	Former lock, bridge (Bâle)
PK 16.8	New lock 41, bridge

This lock-keeper close to the centre of Mulhouse controls the chain westwards from locks 39 to 28 at PK 31.7. It is important to give notice of intended passage the day before (before 16:00).

PK 17.9	Bridge (Bonnes Gens)
PK 18.1	Tunnel (canal covered for 140m in front of SNCF railway station, and tramway line 1)
PK 18.2	**Mulhouse** basin and *port de plaisance* Pro'Bateaux l/b, 06 17 03 31 50, 35 berths plus one barge mooring, night €15, water, electricity (€0.24/kWh), shower €1, wifi, pump-out, town centre 500m l/b
PK 18.3	Bridge (Jules Ehrmann)
PK 18.5	Bridge (Altkirch)
PK 18.9	Bridge (Noyers)

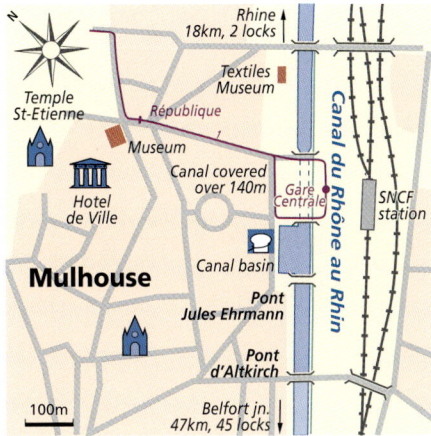

Port de Plaisance in the Vieux Bassin, all facilities. Railway museum, Electrical engineering museum, ceramics museum and textile museum. And home of the Schlumph brothers' phenomenal Bugatti Museum.

PK 19.1	Bridge (Fonderie)
PK 19.2	Railway bridge, footbridge
PK 19.4	Lock 39

This lock marks the start of mobile lock-keeper service.

PK 20.4	Lock 38, bridge
PK 21.7	Lock 37, bridge
PK 21.8	Bridge (D433)
PK 22.7	Lock 36, bridge
PK 23.2	Turning basin
PK 24.3	Lift bridge
PK 24.5	Lock 35
PK 24.9	**Zillisheim** lift bridge, village r/b
PK 25.8	Lock 34, bridge
PK 27.0	Lock 33
PK 28.3	Lock 32 (flood lock), bridge and footbridge, moorings d/s r/b, no services, bollards u/s, **Illfurth** 400m r/b
PK 29.0	Lock 31
PK 30.2	Lock 30, bridge, **Heidwiller** r/b
PK 31.0	Lock 29, bridge
PK 31.7	Lock 28, change of mobile lock-keepers
PK 31.9	Bridge (D466)
PK 33.3	Lock 27, bridge
PK 34.1	Lock 26, bridge
PK 35.3	Lock 25, bridge, mooring d/s, **Eglingen** 100m r/b
PK 35.9	Lock 24
PK 37.4	Bridge
PK 37.5	Lock 23
PK 37.7	**Hagenbach** *halte* Alsace Plaisance r/b, 16 berths, 2 visitor berths, night €12, water and electricty included
PK 38.4	Lock 22
PK 38.9	Lock 21, footbridge

IV – Northeastern France

PK **39.4**	Lock 20
PK **40.1**	Lock 19, bridge
PK **40.8**	Lock 18, bridge
PK **41.3**	Lock 17, end of mobile lock-keeper's service
PK **41.6**	**Dannemarie** bridge, *relais nautique* d/s managed by Sud-Alsace Largue District, 50 berths, 10 visitor berths, 06 80 73 67 10, night €12, water, electricity (metered), showers, wifi, slipway, larger vessels moor to grass bank close to bridge opposite restaurant, village 700m r/b

Port of Dannemarie © GORDON KNIGHT

PK **41.7**	Lock 16
PK **41.8**	Aqueduct
PK **42.2**	Lock 15, bridge, beginning of mobile lock-keepers' service
PK **42.6**	Lock 14, D419 parallel to r/b
PK **43.6**	Lock 13, bridge, Retzwiller r/b
PK **44.0**	Lock 12, beginning of regulated flight
PK **44.4**	Lock 11
PK **44.8**	Lock 10
PK **45.0**	Lock 9
PK **45.2**	Lock 8
PK **45.4**	Lock 7
PK **45.6**	Lock 6
PK **45.7**	Lock 5
PK **45.9**	Lock 4
PK **46.1**	Lock 3
PK **46.2**	**Valdieu** bridge (D419) and railway bridge, basin l/b
PK **46.3**	Lock 2, beginning of summit level, end of flight and mobile lock keepers' service
PK **49.0**	**Montreux-Vieux** bridge, village 200m north
PK **49.9**	Turning basin, bollards, no services
PK **51.6**	Lock 3, bridge, end of summit level, **Montreux-Château** 400m, *halte* u/s for 8 boats, 06 60 05 83 46, night €7, water and electricity included

Good moorings with services. Quayside also at Montreux-Vieux. Locks 3 to 15 (Dannemarie) are a chain and an lock-keeper will accompany boats passing through them. Boats may be invited to lock through in groups.

PK **53.4**	Lock 4, bridge
PK **55.2**	**Brebotte** bridge, turning basin d/s, village 600m
PK **55.6**	Lock 5
PK **57.7**	**Froidefontaine** swing bridge, village l/b
PK **58.0**	Lock 6, bridge
PK **58.5**	Bridge (N1019)
PK **58.7**	Quays l/b, bollards, no services
PK **59.1**	Railway bridge
PK **59.3**	**Bourogne** bridge, former coal unloading quays d/s l/b, village 800m r/b
PK **61.0**	Lock 7
PK **61.2**	Navigation enters river Allan (at confluence with Bourbeuse, crossed by towpath on r/b)
PK **62.1**	Navigation re-enters canal, Allan weir l/b
PK **63.0**	Lock 8 (Fontenelles), bridge, Allenjoie 500m r/b
PK **63.7**	Disused lock 9 down to Allan, l/b
PK **63.9**	Bridge (Allenjoie)
PK **64.5**	Towpath bridge (Moulin-de-Boise)
PK **65.3**	**Junction with Belfort branch**, for through route turn sharp left (see plan)

Lock 9 Allenjoie and aqueduct over rhe Allan

Canal du Rhône au Rhin

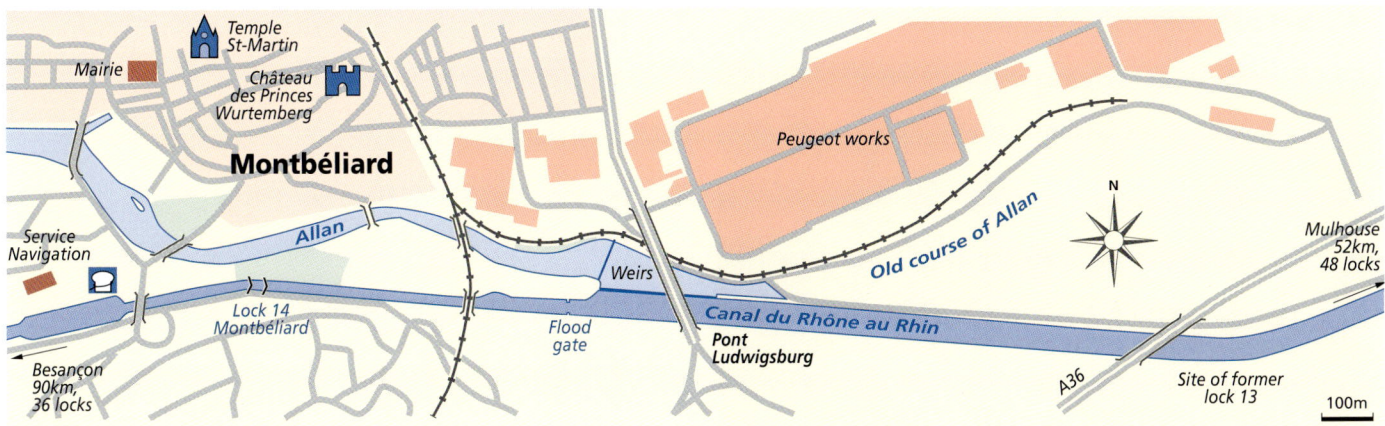

PK 65.3	Fesches aqueduct over the river Allan
PK 65.4	New lock 9 (Allenjoie)
PK 65.6	Former canal to Fesches, l/b
PK 65.8	Lock 10 (Marivées), bridge
PK 66.9	Bridge (D61)
PK 67.6	Lock 11 (Étupes), bridge, village 700m l/b
PK 68.3	Lock 12 (Étupes new lock) leading into 3km section of high-capacity waterway (Allan diversion canal)
PK 69.1	Bridge (Exincourt), D437, motorway junction r/b
PK 69.7	Suspension bridge (Peugeot works)
PK 70.3	Motorway bridge (A36), skew
PK 71.3	Bridge (Ludwigsburg), Sochaux motorway spur, weir r/b
PK 71.7	Flood gate
PK 71.8	Railway bridge, industrial quay u/s l/b, end of large-scale waterway section
PK 72.3	Lock 14 (Montbéliard)
PK 72.6	New road bridge (replacing former lift bridge)
PK 72.8	**Montbéliard** basin, *port de plaisance*, quay 55m with 3 perpendicular pontoons, 03 81 94 45 60, 30 berths, night €10, water €3, electricity €3, shower, slipway, VNF office, all services in town centre 800m r/b

Once a Roman stronghold, now the home of Peugeot vehicles. *Port de Plaisance*, all services, but possibly noisy.

PK 73.4	Lock 15 (Côteau Jouvent)
PK 74.5	Courcelles-lès-Montbéliard lift bridge
PK 75.0	Lock 16 (Courcelles-lès-Montbéliard)
PK 75.8	Canal narrows, one-way traffic
PK 75.9	Footbridge (Bart)
PK 76.8	Canal narrows, one-way traffic
PK 77.2	Lock 17 (Voujeaucourt), bridge, quay u/s l/b
PK 77.8	Canal crosses Doubs on the level, keep to towpath side during floods

Doubs crossing, beware of cross-current.

PK 78.0	Flood lock 18a (Voujeaucourt), bridge (Moulin)
PK 79.0	Bridge (Berche)
PK 79.7	Lock 18 (Dampierre), waiting bollards d/s r/b
PK 80.0	Bridge (Dampierre-sur-le-Doubs)
PK 81.5	Lock 19 (Plaine de Dampierre)
PK 83.1	Lock 20 (Raydans), bridge (D126)
PK 84.1	**Colombier-Fontaine** lift bridge, village l/b, commercial quay d/s l/b
PK 85.3	Lock 21 (Colombier-Fontaine)

PK 87.2	Lock 22 (Saint-Maurice), bridge
PK 88.7	Railway bridge
PK 89.6	Lock 23 (Colombier-Châtelot), bridge, basin u/s silted up
PK 91.2	Lock 24 (Blussans), bridge
PK 94.4	Canal narrows, one-way traffic
PK 94.6	Lock 25 (Côteau-Lunans)
PK 95.3	Railway bridge
PK 96.3	**L'Isle-sur-le-Doubs** lock 26 (lock-keeper also operates lock 27), bridge, *halte* in basin u/s r/b, 03 81 99 37 80, 8 berths, night €15, water and electricity (by credit card), shower at camp site, pump-out, town centre l/b

Quayside moorings above the lock, close to a fuel service station.

PK 97.0	Bridge (D683)
PK 97.4	Lock 27 (Papeteries), water, navigation enters river Doubs
PK 98.6	Lock 28 and weir (Appenans)
PK 101.1	Lock 29 and weir (Goulisse)
PK 102.9	Entrance to Pompierre lock-cut, r/b, flood gate 30a (Rang), bridge
PK 103.4	Railway bridge
PK 105.0	Lock 30 (Plaine de Pompierre), bridge
PK 106.6	Lock 31 (Pompierre), bridge, navigation re-enters Doubs
PK 107.4	Motorway bridge (A36)
PK 108.0	Santoche island (keep to r/b)
PK 109.3	Entrance to Clerval lock-cut, r/b
PK 109.9	Lock 32 (Clerval)
PK 110.2	Navigation re-enters Doubs
PK 110.5	**Clerval** bridge, mooring u/s r/b, pontoons l/b 06 75 39 50 68, 10 berths, water, electricity, showers, crane, suitable for small craft only, village l/b
PK 111.7	Entrance to Branne lock-cut, r/b, flood lock 33a, bridge
PK 113.9	Lock 33 (Chaux-lès-Clerval)
PK 115.3	**Branne** towpath bridge, small village r/b

Locks in this section of the river are located immediately next to weirs and can be tricky when heading downstream. For this reason, they are generally made ready for downstream boats. Lock 35 (Hermite) at PK 117.5 has gaps in the walls where the old gates were; take care when rising in the lock.

PK 116.0	Lock 34 (Branne), navigation re-enters Doubs
PK 117.5	Lock 35 and weir (Hermite)
PK 118.5	Lock 36 and weir (Hyèvre-Magny)
PK 118.8	Hyèvre-Magny bridge
PK 121.0	Lock 37 and weir (Grand-Crucifix)
PK 123.1	Lock 38 and weir (Raie-aux-Chèvres)

81

IV – Northeastern France

Excellent mooring at the municipal halte in Baume-des-Dames, associated with the campsite © GORDON KNIGHT

PK **125.1** Entrance to Grange-Ravey lock-cut, l/b, campsite r/b, small pontoons, services
PK **125.4** Lock 39 (Lonot), navigation re-enters Doubs
PK **126.4** Confluence of Cusancin l/b, towpath bridge
PK **126.7** Entrance to Baume-les-Dames lock-cut, l/b, narrow section, one-way traffic
PK **127.4** Bridge (D50)
PK **127.5** Flood lock 40a (Baume-les-Dames), bridge
PK **127.7** **Baume-les-Dames** municipal *halte* l/b (managed by campsite), capacity 15 boats, 06 26 14 40 84, night €20 including water/electricity, shower €2.50, slipway, pump-out, Service Navigation, town centre 1200m r/b
PK **129.1** Bridge (Grange Villotey), canal narrows for 140m
PK **130.0** Lock 40 (Baumerousse), bridge, bollards r/b, navigation re-enters Doubs
PK **133.5** Lock 41 and weir (Fourbanne), water
PK **135.7** Lock 42 and weir (Ougney), water, bridge
PK **136.1** Ougney bridge
PK **137.4** **Ougney-la-Roche** restaurant l/b, pontoon for shallow-draught vessels, water and electricity

Restaurant pontoon in a lovely stretch of the river

PK **138.1** Lock 43 and weir (Douvot), bridge, bollards u/s
PK **140.4** Lock 44 and weir (Laissey)
PK **140.6** Laissey bridge
PK **142.4** Lock 45 and weir (Aigremont)
PK **143.8** Entrance to Deluz lock-cut r/b, flood lock 46a
PK **144.5** Bridge (Papeteries), paper mill, weir on river
PK **144.7** **Deluz** *halte* l/b, Doubs Plaisance, 06 71 17 91 29, 30 berths, 10 visitor berths, night €12.10, water and electricity included (shut off November to March), wifi, slipway, boatyard, crane 17t, repairs

Moorings beside a charming village. This is a dramatic section of the river past high cliffs.

PK **146.7** Double staircase lock 46/47 (Deluz), electric, bridge, navigation re-enters Doubs
PK **148.8** Bridge (Vaire)
PK **149.3** Former quay for La Rochette-Cenpa paper mill (Novillars) r/b
PK **151.9** Entrance to Roche lock-cut, r/b, flood gate 48a, bridge
PK **154.4** Lock 48 (Chalèze), bridge, navigation re-enters Doubs
PK **157.4** Overhead power lines
PK **160.8** Lock 49 and weir (Malâte)
PK **162.3** Private industrial quays r/b
PK **162.6** Footbridge (Prés-de-Vaux)
PK **163.0** Entrance to tunnel (Souterrain de la Citadelle) l/b flood gate 50a (Rivotte), bridge, straight on for **Besançon** centre and *halte fluviale* then passing through lock 51bis (Saint-Paul), recreational traffic only (see plan opposite and route description for 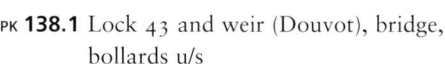)

The birthplace of Victor Hugo was traditionally a centre of clock-making. There is a spectacular view from the hilltop *Citadelle* over the Doubs valley. Take the very attractive 3km river loop through the historic town, or the 400m long Tarragnoz tunnel that by-passes it (available depth 2.10m, height 4.30m). For the route round the loop (next page), note that the available depth is limited to 1.30m.

PK **163.4** Lock 50 (Tarragnoz) in downstream tunnel entrance, junction with Besançon loop
PK **163.5** **Besançon** bridge (Tarragnoz), moorings in Doubs u/s and d/s, night €15, water and electricity, access to town centre see plan
PK **163.6** Lock 51 (Tarragnoz), navigation re-enters Doubs

A hire boat manœuvring to enter the Citadelle tunnel in Besançon, through Lock 50 © GORDON KNIGHT

Canal du Rhône au Rhin

Lock 50 and the entrance to the tunnel under the Citadelle © F-W

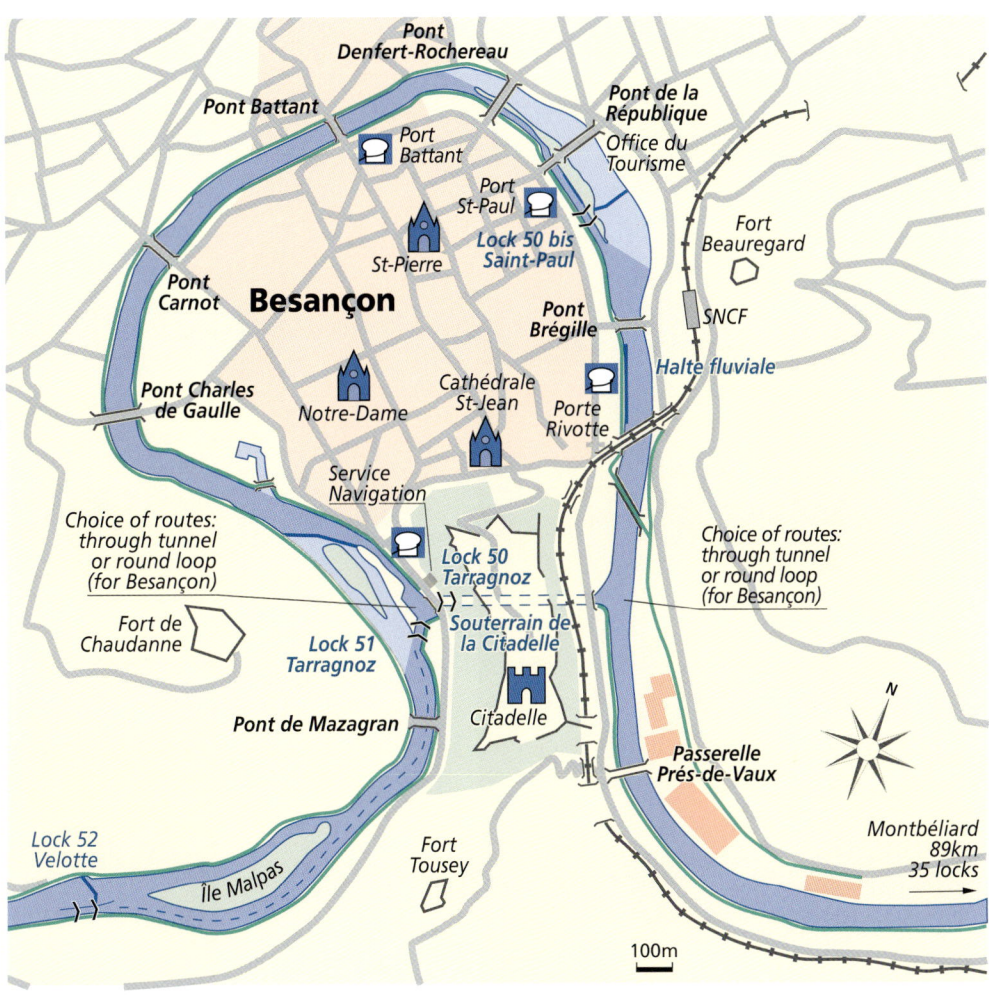

Besançon Loop

PK 0.0	**Upstream junction with through route** at PK 163.0 (entrance to Citadelle tunnel l/b)
PK 0.3	Skew bridge
PK 0.5	Railway bridge
PK 0.8	Bridge (Brégille), restaurant with quay d/s r/b
PK 0.9	**Besançon** halte 'La Cité des Arts' l/b, Doubs Plaisance, 06 71 17 91 29, 20 berths on 250m pontoon, night €12.10, water and electricity included, showers, diesel, pump-out
PK 1.0	Entrance to lock-cut, l/b
PK 1.1	Lock 50bis (Saint-Paul) adjacent to hydropower plant, bridges, halte Doubs Plaisance d/s r/b for 24 boats, 8 visitor berths, 06 71 17 91 29, night €12.10, water and electricity included, shower, wifi, pump-out
PK 1.2	Bridge (République), quay d/s r/b, water
PK 1.5	Bridge (Denfert-Rochereau)
PK 1.6	Navigation re-enters Doubs
PK 2.0	Bridge (Battant)
PK 2.6	Bridge (Canot)
PK 3.0	Bridge (Charles De Gaulle)
PK 3.6	Weir on r/b, keep towards l/b
PK 4.0	**Downstream junction with through route** (above lock 51)

The halte downstream of the lock at Moulin Saint-Paul in Besançon
© GORDON KNIGHT

Navigation continues on main route

PK 163.8	Bridge (Mazagran)
PK 165.1	Lock 52 and weir (Velotte)
PK 165.5	Bridge (Velotte)
PK 166.3	Floating chandlery l/b opposite island
PK 167.3	Bridge (Beure), N273 Besançon ring road
PK 168.7	Lock 53 and weir (Gouille)
PK 170.7	Entrance to Aveney lock-cut, l/b, flood lock 54a
PK 171.0	**Avanne-Aveney** bridge, village with restaurant
PK 173.0	Canal narrows for 400m, one-way traffic

IV – Northeastern France

PK **174.0** Double staircase lock 54/55 (Rancenay), electrically operated, bridge, navigation re-enters Doubs
PK **176.8** Entrance to Thoraise lock-cut, l/b, flood-lock 56a, bridge
PK **177.4** Thoraise tunnel, length 185m, winding basin at u/s entrance

Short tunnel with waterfall curtains at each end (operated by your remote control) and lighting display inside. Depth 2.8m, height 4.1m+. Good mooring between the tunnel entrance and the following écluse.

Artistic illuminations in Thoraise tunnel, PK 177. © VNF

PK **177.8** Lock 56 (**Thoraise**), bridge, mooring u/s r/b, water, electricity, shower, navigation re-enters Doubs
PK **179.4** Bridge (Torpes-Boussières)
PK **180.1** Entrance to Osselle lock-cut, r/b
PK **180.5** Flood lock 57a (Torpes)
PK **182.2** Railway bridge
PK **182.3** Bridge (Portail de Roche)
PK **183.2** Lock 57 (Osselle), bridge, village 400m
PK **183.7** Bridge (Osselle)
PK **185.6** Bridge (Moulin d'Arenthon), canal narrows for 40m
PK **187.3** New lock 58 (Routelle)
PK **188.4** Bridge (Roset-Fluans)
PK **188.6** Old lock 58 (Roset-Fluans), bridge, navigation re-enters Doubs
PK **191.3** Lock 59 (Saint-Vit) and weir, bridge, water
PK **191.5** **Saint-Vit** halte on pontoon in mill stream l/b for 4 boats, water, electricity, shower, village 1.5 km
PK **191.8** Bridge (Salans-sur-le-Doubs)
PK **192.0** Island, keep to r/b
PK **194.0** Small towpath bridge, r/b
PK **194.2** Entrance to Dampierre lock-cut, r/b
PK **194.8** Flood gate 60a (Fraisans), bridge, village 1 km l/b
PK **195.9** Bridge (Dampierre)
PK **196.4** Lock 60 (Dampierre), navigation re-enters Doubs
PK **197.5** Entrance to Ranchot lock-cut, r/b, narrow section to lock
PK **197.7** Flood gate 61a, bridge

PK **197.8** **Ranchot** bridge, timber quay (25m) r/b for 5 boats, 06 75 32 87 39, night €8, water, electricity, showers at campsite, village 100m r/b, **Rans** 500m l/b
PK **198.5** Lock 61 (Ranchot)
PK **199.3** Lift bridge (Moulin des Malades)
PK **199.5** Lock 62 (Moulin des Malades), navigation re-enters Doubs
PK **201.9** Entrance to Orchamps lock-cut, r/b, bridge
PK **203.3** **Orchamps** bridge, moor well u/s for village r/b
PK **203.5** New flood lock 63 (Orchamps), bridge
PK **205.7** Bridge (Lavans)
PK **207.4** Lock 63 (Moulin-Rouge), navigation re-enters Doubs
PK **208.5** Entrance to Audelange lock-cut, r/b, flood gate 64a, bridge
PK **209.5** Lock 64 (Audelange), navigation re-enters Doubs
PK **211.1** **Rochefort-sur-Nenon**, mooring under cliff r/b, pontoon moorings along bank, water, also at restaurant u/s r/b

Take care to keep to the channel on the river section east of the village.

Approaching the flood lock at Rochefort-sur-Nenon, PK 211.

PK **211.3** Entrance to Rochefort-Dole lock-cut, new flood lock 65, bridge
PK **215.0** Lock 65 (Baverans), bridge, village 600m r/b
PK **215.3** Railway bridge
PK **215.9** Bridge (Brevans)
PK **217.3** Railway bridge
PK **217.7** Lock 66 (Charles-Quint), bridge, quiet arm of the Doubs with steep banks d/s l/b, possible mooring
PK **217.9** Navigation enters small arm of Doubs
PK **218.1** Bridge (Pasquier), towpath crosses to l/b
PK **218.5** **Dole** footbridge, basin, Port Le Prélot and Nicols hire base r/b, 06 08 89 10 48, 60m pontoon, 35 berths, night €8.50, water €3.50, electricity €3.50, showers €3.50 (tokens purchased from *capitainerie*), slipway, larger vessels moor to quay l/b, VNF depot l/b, town centre r/b

Birthplace of Louis Pasteur. Well-equipped moorings. The section following the port is shaded by plane trees, like the Canal du Midi.

PK **218.7** Bridge (Pont de la Charité)
PK **218.8** Lock 67 (Jardin-Philippe) in short lock-cut r/b, bridge, navigation re-enters Doubs
PK **220.1** Entrance to Doubs-Saône canal r/b, flood lock 68, bridge
PK **220.3** Main road viaduct (Corniche), D405
PK **221.3** Bridge (Saint-Ylie)

Canal du Rhône au Rhin

PK 222.8 Choisey bridge, village r/b
PK 224.4 Lock 69 (Bon Repos), bridge (D905), quay d/s r/b, no services
PK 224.9 Motorway bridge (A39)
PK 225.5 Railway bridge
PK 225.7 Bridge (Beauregard)
PK 226.6 **Tavaux-Cité** quay r/b (factory)
PK 226.7 Lock 70 (Belvoye), bridge former freight office
PK 227.2 Solvay works, basin l/b
PK 227.7 Conveyor bridge
PK 228.1 Private bridge
PK 228.4 Pipeline crossing
PK 228.8 Lock 71 (Ronce), bridge and pipeline crossing
PK 230.3 Lock 72 (Abergement-la-Ronce), bridge
PK 230.7 **Abergement-la-Ronce** municipal *halte* l/b, 3 berths, free, water, electricity, shops l/b
PK 232.2 Bridge (Samerey)
PK 233.3 Motorway bridge (A36)
PK 235.4 Basin (silted up)
PK 236.1 Lock 73 (Tuilerie)
PK 236.2 Bridge (Laperrière)
PK 236.7 Lock 74 (Laperrière), **Saint-Symphorien** basin u/s l/b, *port de plaisance* formerly managed by Bourgogne Marine, 45 berths, water, electricity, repairs, village 800m

This long-established *port de plaisance* and boatyard, offering repairs and maintenance, is waiting for a new operator to be selected by the Rives de Saône tourist office in 2021.

PK 237.1 Lock 75 (Saône), VHF 18, bridge, basin u/s with permanent moorings, abandoned dry dock, *junction with Saône* (PK 160)

A modest entry/exit point for the canal route that connects the Rhine with the Saône and the Rhône. The recent white, angular control tower is very noticeable.

Belfort branch

PK 0.0 *Junction with main canal* (PK 65.3)
PK 0.9 Bridge (Jonchets)
PK 1.8 Brognard bridge, small village 300m l/b, motorway r/b
PK 2.9 Lock 1 (Brognard)
PK 3.6 Dambenois bridge, small village 200m l/b
PK 4.1 Lock 2 (Dambenois), bridge
PK 5.2 Bridge (D25)
PK 6.1 Lock 3, bridge, basin d/s r/b, moorings for 3 boats, 0607 31 13 41, night €5, water, electricity, shower, crane on request, slipway, **Trévenans** 400m l/b
PK 6.9 Lock 4, bridge
PK 7.1 Railway viaduct (Savoureuse, TGV Rhin-Rhône)
PK 7.7 Lock 5, bridge, aqueduct u/s
PK 7.9 Bridge (Bermont)
PK 8.3 Bridge (N1019)
PK 8.5 Bridge (Dorans)
PK 9.7 **Botans** lift bridge, basin d/s l/b, quay (200m), water, electricity, small village r/b, **Belfort** 4 km l/b
PK 9.9 Motorway bridge (A36), head of navigation (3.6km length beyond bridge, comprising three locks, abandoned)

The superb location of the port de plaisance *at Dole* © GORDON KNIGHT

CHAPTER V – SOUTHEAST FRANCE

From Burgundy to the Mediterranean – the Grande Saône and Rhône

We now enter the 'common trunk' of the waterway network, the all-important itinerary that starts in the traditional barge town of Saint-Jean-de-Losne and links north and south, Burgundy to Provence, the North Sea to the Mediterranean. This 'water highway' for *plaisanciers* is also a high-capacity waterway plied by a sizeable fleet of motor barges, push-tows and more than 20 river cruise ships, and is home to the famous *mistral* wind that blows south and has slowed many a boat's progress.*

This commercial function of the Saône-Rhône axis is not obvious where the route starts, but first appears a few kilometres downstream at the port of Pagny. Even here, traffic remains for the time being relatively light. The cruise ships also rarely come this far upstream.

There are branches to explore from Seurre (the bypassed river Saône) and Verdun-sur-le-Doubs (the Doubs), before the junction with the Canal du Centre at Chalon. From here there is the strong sense that one is no longer in deepest rural France, but in a prosperous and dynamic transport corridor. That means towns, *ports de plaisance*, services, even night life if desired, at frequent intervals, as well as countless waterside restaurants. Another significant difference with cruising 'over the top' on any of the central or north-eastern canals is that there are very few locks, hence more time to spend enjoying the places you stop at.

Allow at least two weeks to make the transit down to the Mediterranean, and more to allow for getting side-tracked to Louhans, at the end of the navigable river Seille, in delightful pastoral landscapes, or Pont-de-Vaux with its splendid port, while Lyon itself is a destination which now at last welcomes visiting boats, in the *Bassin Nautique*, the centrepiece of the new and trendy Lyon-Confluence quarter. Continuing downstream from Lyon, there are excellent moorings at regular intervals, and some well-equipped *ports de plaisance*. Favourites are Les Roches de Condrieu (especially for the location), Valence l'Épervière, Viviers and Vallabrègues.

Once the delta is reached at Arles, there are fewer choices than suggested by the map, for the Canal d'Arles à Fos is used only to enter the basin in Arles, while the high-capacity Canal de Barcarin striking east to the port of Fos is for commercials only.

The Mediterranean is reached through the short canal at Port-Saint-Louis-du-Rhône, with the possibility of continuing east beyond Martigues (but not all the way to Marseille through the Rove Tunnel, closed since 1963). The Petit-Rhône is the route to the Southern waterways, especially the Canal du Midi (*Midi* meaning south).

* Seriously adverse navigable conditions are in fact quite rarely encountered: essentially a combination of flood flows on the Rhône and the southward-blowing *mistral*.

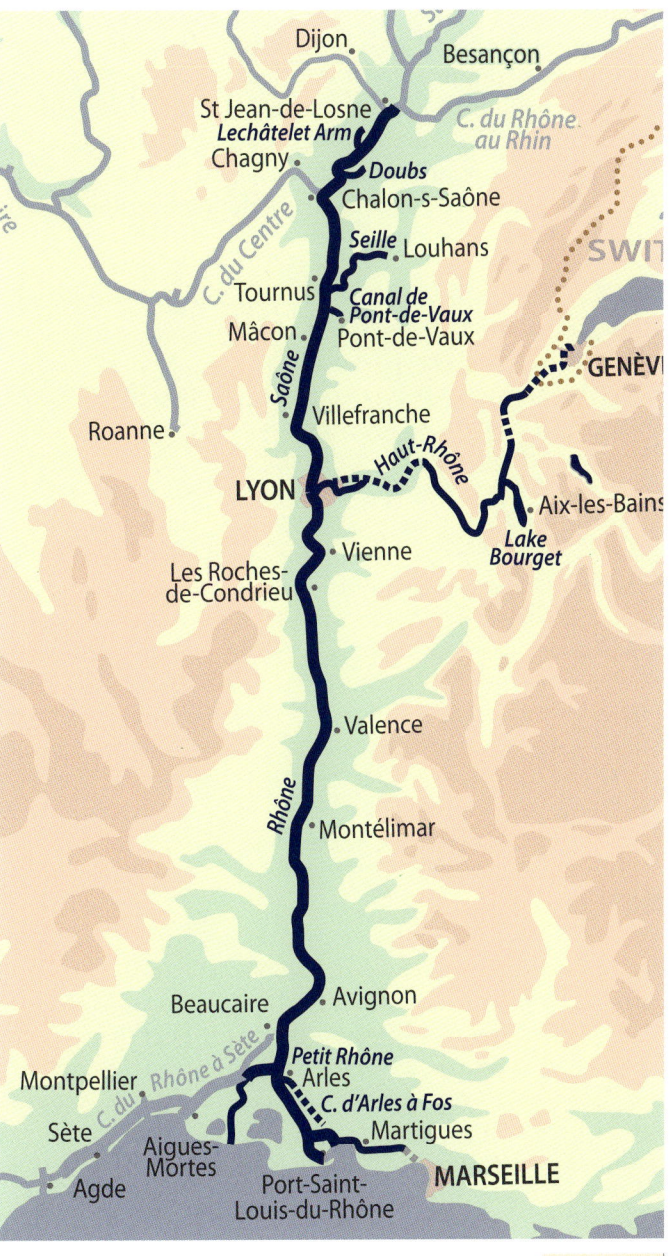

Early morning, out of season calm at Tournus on the Grande Saône

V – Southeast France

47. Grande Saône

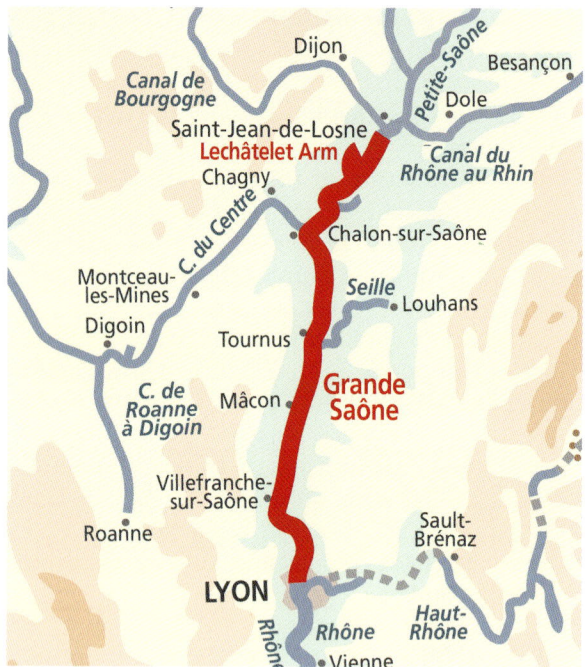

The high-capacity (*grand gabarit*) waterway from Saint-Jean-de-Losne to Lyon amply justifies this separate section, not just for the character of the river and dimensions of its locks and channels, but also as an itinerary. All the canals of northern, central and north-eastern France, including the 'Petite Saône', lead into this single route funnelling boats towards the Mediterranean.

The formal division between the two sections of the Saône used to be just below Saint-Symphorien (PK 209), but that was when the new Rhône-Rhine canal was planned to be dug from this point. The important junction of Saint-Jean-de-Losne, where the Canal de Bourgogne joins the Saône, is the more logical 'hub' (PK 205), as well as being the effective upstream limit of *grand gabarit* navigation: barges carrying up to 3000 tonnes, as well as the increasingly popular 'floating hotels' – the 110m long river cruise ships. The Saône becomes wider and no longer has the intimate charm of the upper reaches. Another important route from the Seine basin, the Canal du Centre, enters the river at Chalon-sur-Saône. The 3.5km-long Mâcon bypass was built to allow commercial traffic to avoid the low arched Saint-Laurent bridge – a historic monument – at Mâcon, but boats continue to use the Saône to reach the town centre, and the route description here follows the natural course of the river.

> The Saône has always been the most navigable of French rivers, with a very gentle gradient and regular flow, albeit subject to floods which can make the broad valley look like an inland sea. The Roman general Vetus envisaged a canal from the Saône to the Moselle. Natural navigability made merchants an easy prey for local lords and tax collectors, and chains were laid across the river in many locations, to collect tolls. Colbert declared them illegal in 1664, but it seemed to Delalande – writing in 1778 – that 'the easier the navigation, the more its natural advantages have been abused by exactions of all sorts'. Navigability in the industrial era was introduced, as on the other major rivers, after the movable weir was invented by Poirée. By 1847 there were five weirs and locks on the Saône. The canalisation as completed above Auxonne has not changed, while development of the high-capacity waterway downstream meant the replacement of 12 early weirs and locks by only five in the 215 km. The last, at Seurre, was completed in 1980, and gives big barges and river-sea ships access to the modern port 'Aproport' at Pagny.

Navigation

The Grande Saône carries regular commercial traffic: big barges, impressive container vessels and occasional push-tows plying the Rhône and Saône up to Mâcon or Chalon, less frequently up to the 'Aproport' harbour at Pagny above Seurre, as well as 38.50m *péniches* making the south-north transits through central France, moving grain, limestone aggregate and cement. There is now a dedicated VHF frequency (18) for Lyon and environs, where the many bridges are the trickiest 'pinch points'. Normally, commercial traffic uses VHF 10 and a listening watch on that channel can provide useful warnings. There are a number of places to refuel alongside the river itself, as well as various service stations nearby. And, in addition to the various places detailed below, there are many other places to moor, although the river is shallow in many places. The channel is marked, as necessary, on the right-bank side by red-and-white stakes or red cylindrical buoys, and on the left-bank side by green-and-white stakes or green conical buoys. Care should be taken to avoid the submerged groynes or dykes that are encountered especially downstream of Chalon-sur-Saône, and use of a detailed navigation guide is recommended. These structures were part of the 19th century improvements. The river narrows in Lyon, and during floods alternating one-way navigation is enforced.

Locks

There are five locks over the 216km of high-capacity waterway (originally nine before the modernisation works started). Seurre is the first of the new locks and is situated at the end of a 10km long diversion canal which cuts almost 11km from the natural length of the Saône. The other modern locks are at Écuelles, Ormes, Dracé and

Grande Saône

Key dimensions (m)	
Length	185.00
Beam	12.00
Draught	3.00
Air draught	6.00

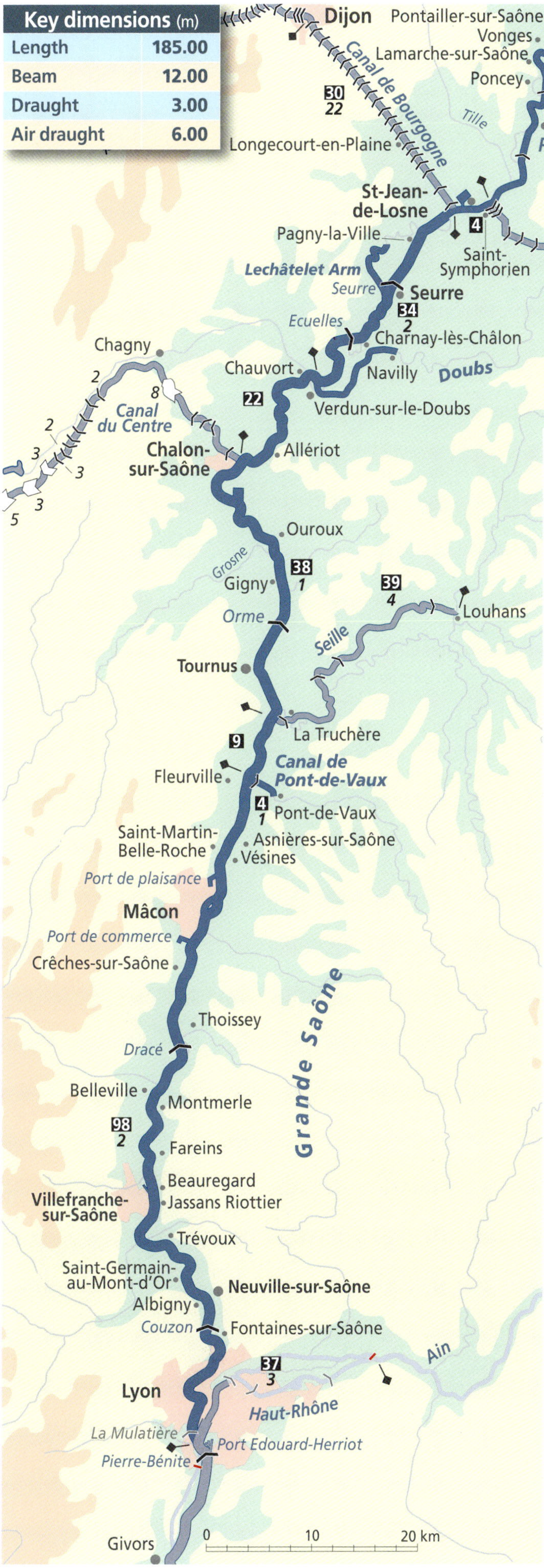

Mooring on the stepped quay at Saint-Jean-de-Losne

Couzon (adjacent to the former lock). All the new locks measure 185m by 12m and are controlled by lights. Boats are locked through after a maximum wait of 20 minutes if no commercial barge has appeared in the meantime. There are several mooring dolphins on the approach to each lock, some of which have gangways for access to the bank. However, these were designed for vessels exceeding 38m, making mooring awkward for smaller craft. Otherwise there is no difficulty in negotiating these big locks, which have step bollards set into the chamber walls.

Draught
Following completion of the dredging works between Chalon and Saint-Jean-de-Losne, the authorised draught is 3.00m throughout this section.

Headroom
The lowest bridge in this section is the Pont Saint-Laurent, at Mâcon, a listed public monument, with a headroom of 7.20m (over a width of 10m) above the normal level and 3.70m above the highest navigable water level. As noted above, the 3km long bypass at Mâcon allows commercial traffic to avoid this bridge. All other bridges offer a minimum headroom of 6.00m.

Towpath
There is no continuous length, but between Auxonne and Corre the lock-cuts all have service roads, and rough tracks are available along many intermediate reaches of the river.

Authority
VNF Rhône-Saône
- Port fluvial, 71100 Châlon-sur-Saône 03 85 97 19 40
  (PK 150-235)
- Subdivision de Mâcon: 6, rue de la Poste, 01750 Saint-Laurent-sur-Saône 03 85 39 91 91   (PK 235-334)
- 4, rue Jonas Salk, 69007 Lyon 04 78 69 69 10
  (PK 334-365)

V – Southeast France

Route description

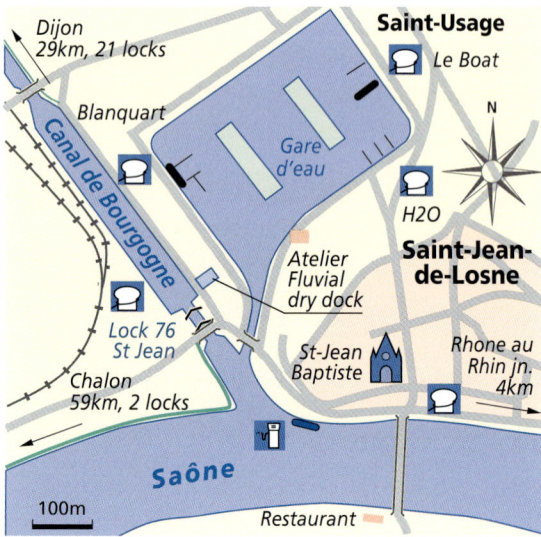

PK **204.9** **Saint-Jean-de-Losne** bridge, moorings on both banks, Quai National stepped quay on r/b, for 7 boats, free (maximum 48 hours), water €3.20 per 500 litres, electricity €3.20 per 4 hours (by tokens), small town r/b, **Losne** l/b

PK **204.7** Junction with Canal de Bourgogne , r/b, large basin (Gare d'Eau) entered at junction, Le Boat hire base 03 80 27 03 50, H2O 03 80 39 08 08 and Blanquart 03 80 29 11 06 boatyards, night from €10, new fuelling dock at entrance (replaces former barge), water, electricity, shower, crane, slipway, pump-out, repairs at Atelier Fluvial, 03 80 27 03 00, chandleries, restaurants, wifi

This enormous harbour of the Gare d'Eau lies off the river, adjacent to the first lock on the Canal de Bourgogne. Within the basin there are three potential moorings, divided by small islands: firstly Blanquart's pontoons immediately on the left, then H2O's pontoons along the southeast bank, then Le Boat's hire boat basin on the far bank. There is a signed route to follow around the harbour basin. Blanquart is reputed to give good service and has excellent security, but is also often full; H2O is the most popular and largest port. Le Boat's pontoon is the least hemmed-in but is not available at weekends or change-over days when it is full of returning hire boats. In addition to the quay and the Gare d'Eau, tree-lined bankside mooring is possible a short way along the Canal du Bourgogne at Saint-Usage. Private barges can berth in the former lock-cut PK211 by arrangement with H2O. Both Blanquart and H2O have excellent chandleries. There are three boatyards for repairs and maintenance, located around the Bourgogne basin above the lock. H2O's is on the west side. Blanquart's to the north and Atelier Fluvial immediately by the lock-keeper's house. H2O and Blanquart can lift out for work to be done 'on the hard'. Atelier Fluvial is a professional (commercial and private) *péniche* yard, with a large dry dock, and another repair yard on the river upstream from the quays, with a sideways ramped haul-out. Shops in the village include a Casino supermarket, Intermarché, Bricomarché and a building materials yard (all excellent). Bars and restaurants including the authentically tatty and very friendly PMU bar opposite the cannon-strewn monument to Saint-Jean's brave defenders of 1636. Railway station about 1km westwards along the river, regular trains to Dijon (thence TGV trains to Paris). Saint-Jean is a popular over-wintering place with a lively international community.

PK **203.6** Railway viaduct (Saint-Usage)

PK **203.3** Commercial quays, r/b

PK **203.3** Former entrance to Saint-Jean-de-Losne lock-cut, replaced by a new meander cutoff

PK **202.7** End of meander cutoff (river dammed), H2O residential barge moorings in lock-cut r/b

PK **196.6** Entrance to Seurre diversion canal, l/b (difference = 1.3km, river PK 199.2) (Pagny dam)

PK **194.2** Bridge (Pagny)

PK **192.5** Entrance to Port de Pagny, multimodal port and industrial platform, l/b

Large new commercial harbour, upstream limit of navigation for the biggest barges.

PK **192.1** Bridge (Labruyère)

PK **190.9** Motorway bridge (A36)

PK **189.4** Bridge (Chamblanc)

PK **187.3** Seurre lock, lift 3.75m, VHF 22, bridge, water on mooring pile d/s

PK **186.8** End of diversion canal, junction with Lechâtelet arm r/b (see below, at end of Grande Saône), **Seurre** *port de plaisance* in basin d/s l/b, 60 berths, 03 80 20 31 05, night €15.50, water and electricity included, showers €2, wifi at *capitainerie*, slipway, pump-out, larger vessels moor 100m d/s to bollards and rings in stone wall l/b

Seurre is a lovely riverside small town with a number of possible mooring places. The *port de plaisance* offers excellent services, but the pontoons beside the stepped quay just downstream, opposite the small island, are also ideal for a short stay. It is possible to cruise 10km along the by-passed river from Seurre and moor at Lechâtelet – there are some shoals to be avoided on the way.

All part of the fun: going shopping from the pontoon moorings at Seurre

PK **186.4** Bridge (Seurre)

PK **186.3** Island (Île aux Princes), new channel on r/b side,

PK **184.6** Former entrance to Seurre lock-cut l/b

Grande Saône

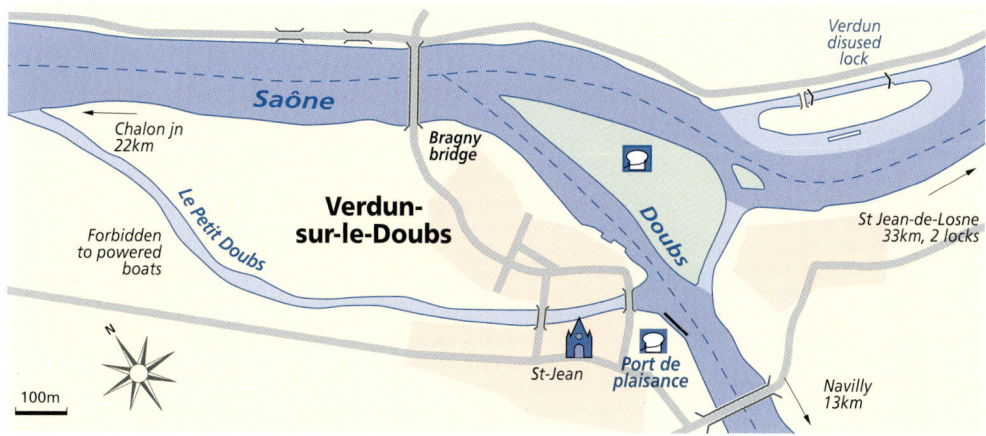

- PK **183.6** Seurre lock (disused), l/b, and end of lock-cut
- PK **182.2** Chivres viaduct (railway converted to road), D35d
- PK **181.0** **Chazelles**, l/b, quay, restaurant
- PK **176.7** Entrance to new lock-cut, r/b (difference = 1.3km, river PK 178) (Charnay-les-Chalon 700m l/b)
- PK **175.5** Écuelles lock, lift 3.20m, VHF 20, bridge, water on dolphins u/s and d/s, vessels and push-tows longer than 90m report here to arrange passage through tight bends u/s
- PK **175.2** End of lock-cut
- PK **174.5** **Écuelles** quay and village r/b
- PK **167.8** Former Verdun lock, r/b

This old Saône lock above the village has 'no entry' and 'no mooring' signs prominently displayed from all angles. This is unfortunate, because other old locks on the Saône have been made into ideal moorings.

- PK **167.0** Confluence of Doubs , l/b, access to **Verdun-sur-le-Doubs** private *port de plaisance*, 03 85 91 80 81, moorings for 25 boats, 15 visitor moorings, night €15 (€18 if more than 4m beam), water, electricity, showers €2.50 *lacapitainerieduconfluent@orange.fr*

Another lovely riverside village, just off the Saône on the River Doubs (which is fearsome in winter spate, otherwise benign). Limited pontoon space with water and electricity. It is possible to cruise up the Doubs for 14km to Navilly; good depth and width but bankside mooring difficult.

Port de plaisance at *Verdun-sur-le-Doubs*, PK 167.

- PK **166.8** Bragny bridge
- PK **165.2** Chauvort, r/b, (bridge destroyed)
- PK **164.8** Chauvort viaduct

- PK **159.5** **Gergy** bridge, municipal *halte* u/s r/b, 03 45 28 82 93, managed by Guinguette bistrot, 7 boats, free, water €5 per 500 litres, electricity €2/night (on pontoon), showers at camp site, slipway

Halte by a café/restaurant and 3-star camp-site.

- PK **157.0** Former oil depot, quay r/b
- PK **150.7** Alleriot, l/b, restaurants, anchor only (shoal)
- PK **144.9** Junction with Canal du Centre , r/b, commercial boatyard and slipway d/s r/b

A commercial *péniche* repair yard able to haul (slide) out sideways and repair the biggest barges. Opposite, the sailing club basin does not welcome visiting plaisanciers.

- PK **144.1** Yacht Club de Chalon moorings in rowing regata basin l/b, 03 85 48 83 38, night €18, water, electricity, showers, crane, slipway, repairs, visitors' berths
- PK **143.0** Chalon-sur-Saône commercial port, r/b
- PK **142.0** Bridge (Bourgogne, Chalon ring road)
- PK **141.9** Bridge (Saint-Laurent), Chalon town centre r/b

V – Southeast France

PK **141.7** **Chalon** *port de plaisance* in Génise arm l/b, 03 85 48 83 38, 150 berths, 20 visiting boats on outer pontoon, night €19, fuel, water, electricity €2.50/night, showers, crane 5t, slipway, restaurant 100m

This port is a constantly busy marina, with lots of boats and pontoons as well as a full range of services. From the river one must approach from the south side of the island, on the Bras de la Génise, and leave to the north. Excellent big supermarket and brico very near the port. It is deservedly popular and may be full, so it is advisable to phone in advance and/or get there before mid-afternoon. New pontoon moorings have also now been installed on the Quai Sainte-Marie above the Saint-Laurent bridge. Other moorings are reserved for the cruise ships that dock here each day; avoid those big dolphin moorings at all times! Chalon is a great small city, with plenty to see and do. It was the birthplace of photography, and the Brothers Niepce museum by the river is thoroughly recommended. Chalon marked the boundary between Occupied and Vichy France during WWII.

Mooring to the new halte at Quai Saint-Marie in Chalon, with Saint-Laurent island and bridge in the background. ©JACQUES BONDU

PK **141.4** Bridge (Jean Richard), moorings u/s and d/s r/b to steps and wall

PK **140.8** Chalon railway viaduct
PK **138.7** Road bridge (Pont Sud de Chalon), N80
PK **137.6** New port of Chalon, basin 1500m by 350m, l/b
PK **129.9** Port d'Ouroux, l/b
PK **129.8** Ouroux bridge, quay at campsite d/s l/b, restaurant
PK **128.6** Confluence of Grosne, r/b
PK **124.8** Thorey bridge
K **123.2** **Gigny-sur-Saône** *port de plaisance* and Saône Bateaux hire base in former lock, r/b, 03 85 44 76 84, 15 boats, night €10, diesel, water, electricity, shower, wifi, slipway, repairs, restaurant

A delightful harbour in a disused lock. Small supermarket nearby, and a *boulangerie* van turns up every morning at 8:30. The *capitaine* is friendly.

PK **119.2** Ormes lock (in lock-cut on l/b), lift 2.90m, VHF 22, bridge

Tied up in Ormes lock

PK **112.2** **Tournus** bridge, municipal *halte* on 150m pontoon d/s r/b, night €13, water and electricity included, 06 08 92 64 64, town centre r/b

Tournus is a charming historic town. The abbey of Saint-Philibert was founded in AD1000 and is well worth a visit.

PK **111.9** Hôtel de Saône pontoon l/b
PK **111.2** Tournus bridge (D975)
PK **106.7** **Confluence of river Seille**, l/b

The Seille is navigable for 39km from its junction with the Saône to Louhans (see separate section).

PK **103.2** **Uchizy** bridge
PK **97.7** **Fleurville** bridge
PK **97.7** **Junction with Canal de Pont-de-Vaux** l/b, quay d/s r/b reserved for commercial and passenger boats, restaurant, village 1.5km

See Section 49 for this short canal leading to an excellent *port de plaisance*.

PK **97.2** Confluence of Reyssouze, l/b

Grande Saône

PK 90.2 Asnières-sur-Saône, restaurant with *halte* on landing stage l/b, for 3 boats, free, water, slipway (for small craft)

A good pontoon, with water, but depth limited to 1.50m.

PK 89.1 Saint-Martin-Belle-Roche, restaurant, r/b

PK 87.7 Vésines, restaurant with landing stage (draught 1m) l/b, for 3 boats, water, slipway

Less attractive mooring than Asnières, and only 1m depth.

PK 84.7 Motorway bridge (A40), tip of island (Île Palme), channel in l/b arm

PK 83.3 Mâcon *port de plaisance*, entrance to basin, r/b, 03 85 38 35 71, 06 65 51 42 61, 425 berths, 30 visitor berths, night €16.50, fuel, water, electricity €2/night, showers, crane 5t, slipway, gastronomic restaurant 100m

Mâcon is a fine, historic town with a number of potential mooring places. This is the marina basin (Mâcon marina/*port de plaisance* website), off the river and a little distant from the town centre, but in a pleasant parkland setting and with fuel. It was significantly enlarged and modernised in 2013.

PK 82.4 U/s entrance to diversion canal, l/b (commercial traffic only, boats continue on Saône)

PK 80.9 Saint-Laurent boat moorings on 40m pontoon l/b, restaurants on quay

Just by the bridge on the island is this welcoming little pontoon, but beware of the shallows that lie immediately to the north; they are clearly marked in the chart-guides. On the opposite (town) bank, good new pontoons with water and electricity. Do not moor at the cruise ship pontoon!

Pontoon moorings at Saint-Laurent, opposite Mâcon

PK 80.6 Mâcon bridge (Saint-Laurent), mooring d/s r/b
PK 79.7 Bridge (Pont Urbain Sud)
PK 79.0 D/s entrance to diversion canal, l/b
PK 78.6 Port of Mâcon, commercial basin r/b
PK 78.4 Mâcon railway viaduct
PK 77.4 New port of Mâcon, commercial basin r/b
PK 76.7 Motorway bridge (A406)
PK 75.6 Island (Damprun), channel in l/b arm
PK 75.2 Railway viaduct (TGV Paris-Lyon)

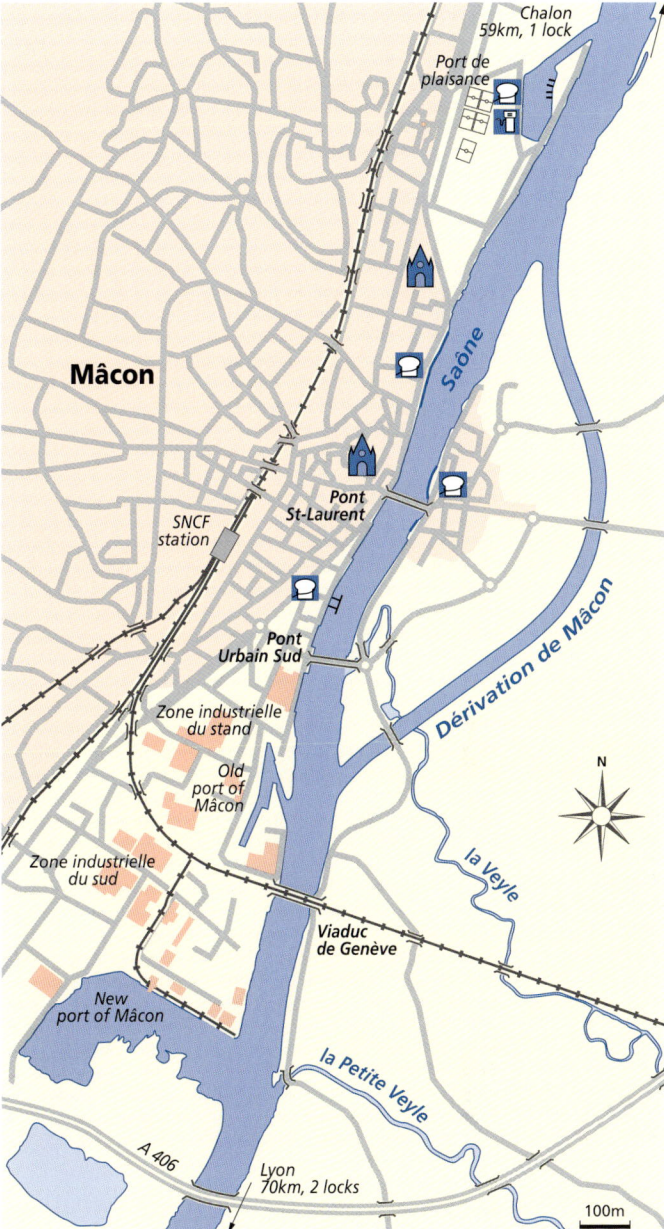

PK 72.9 Arciat bridge, quay and pontoon for 6 boats at camp-site d/s r/b, 03 85 37 11 83, night €20.60, water, electricity, shower, wifi (at campsite), restaurant, **Crèches-sur-Saône** 1.5 km r/b

Good pontoons at a camping site. All facilities, including access to a water-sports lake.

PK 66.4 Saint-Romain-des-Îles bridge, small *port de plaisance* (Port Jean Savoyet) d/s r/b, 03 85 35 51 97, water

This attractive small basin is for smaller boats only.

PK 63.3 Thoissey bridge, *halte* d/s l/b for 4 boats, 06 58 72 90 52, mid-June to end-September, night €12, water and electricity included, wifi

PK 62.4 Dracé lock, r/b, lift 2.90m, bridge, VHF 20
PK 61.4 Former Thoissey lock (disused), l/b
PK 57.4 Islands (buoyed channel)
PK 56.0 Belleville island

V – Southeast France

PK **55.3** **Belleville-sur-Saône** bridge, mooring for hotel boats d/s r/b (dolphins) and municipal *halte* on pontoon for 5-6 boats, free (maximum 72 hours), water, electricity, slipway, restaurant (town with all services 800m r/b)

In the middle of the Beaujolais terroir, a good *halte*. Bustling small town, with a hospital museum in the Hôtel-Dieu.

PK **54.7** Northern tip of Montmerle island (channel on l/b side)
PK **52.7** Southern tip of Montmerle island
PK **52.4** **Montmerle-sur-Saône** bridge, municipal *halte* on pontoon d/s l/b for up to 8 boats, 06 86 16 60 80, night €10, water, electricity, showers at camp site, slipway, small town and restaurant l/b

This is an ideal *halte* by the village square, with a small supermarket. Approaching the adjacent bridge, when heading downstream (i.e. on the west side), it is important to keep well away from the bank. There is a shallow spit that extends beyond the two red port-hand marker poles.

PK **47.7** Port Rivière, r/b
PK **43.4** **Fareins** quai l/b, restaurant
PK **42.6** Beauregard bridge
PK **41.9** New road bridge (Villefranche, D131)
PK **41.6** **Villefranche-sur-Saône** industrial port, r/b
PK **40.9** **Jassans-Riottier** *halte* l/b, pontoon for up to 8 boats, free (maximum 72 hours), water, electricity €5/day, slipway, village 400m
PK **40.6** Frans bridge, commercial quays (sand) d/s r/b
PK **35.3** **Saint-Bernard** bridge, castle l/b
PK **31.3** **Trévoux** suspension bridge, *halte* on pontoon u/s l/b for up to 8 boats, night €15, water, electricity, showers (€2) at campsite, wifi €3.50/day

Historic and very pretty, Trévoux was once capital of its own small principality of the Dombes. Good moorings by the campsite, grass, trees, walks along the river.

Passing Trévoux

PK **30.9** Bridge (Général de Gaulle D87), boatyard and moorings u/s r/b

PK **26.5** Former Bernalin lock l/b, boat harbour, 54 boats, 06 22 82 39 26, 1 visitor mooring, night €25, water and electricity included, repairs, wintering, **Parcieux** 1.5 km

The old lock chamber is so crammed full with boats that even the announced visitor mooring may not be available.

PK **25.4** Motorway bridge (A46)
PK **24.1** **Genay** port de plaisance l/b, Nautic Auto, 06 67 59 54 72, *nautic-auto.fr*, 40 berths, night €15, water, electricity, showers, crane 14t, slipway, wintering, repairs
PK **22.9** **Saint-Germain-au-Mont d'Or** boat harbour r/b, 06 99 06 50 00, 50 berths, 5 visitor berths, night €40, water, electricity, shower, crane 20t, slipway, repairs, *leyacht2020@gmail.com*

Another large *port de plaisance* and boatyard, but no fuel.

PK **20.4** **Neuville-sur-Saône** bridge, municipal *halte* on quay d/s l/b for up to 4 boats, 04 72 08 70 00, free (maximum 96 hours), water, electricity, slipway
PK **19.7** Pontoon r/b for 2 visiting boats r/b for restaurant Les Planches
PK **19.0** **Albigny** port de plaisance behind islands r/b, 60 berths, 04 72 08 83 97, 2 visitor berths on pontoon, night €12, water, electricity, showers, crane 14t, slipway, repairs, restaurant *albigny-bateaux@wanadoo.fr*
PK **17.5** Couzon lock, l/b, lift 4.00m, VHF 22

Just below the lock on the east bank, a quay close to a service station and convenience store, opposite a stretch of private moorings on the west bank.

PK **17.3** Couzon suspension bridge
PK **15.0** **Fontaines-sur-Saône** bridge
PK **14.4** Tip of island (Île Roy), d/s-bound boats take l/b channel
PK **13.4** Tip of island, upstream-bound boats take r/b channel
PK **12.4** Collonges railway viaduct
PK **12.3** **Collonges** bridge, Bocuse restaurant r/b

A good small pontoon between piles. The famous five-star Paul Bocuse restaurant is close by.

PK **10.4** Island (Île Barbe), channel in l/b arm
PK **10.0** Bridge (Île Barbe)

A canoe rally organised by Lyon Canoë passes the Île Barbe, where an abbey was founded in the 5th century. © LYON CANOË

Grande Saône

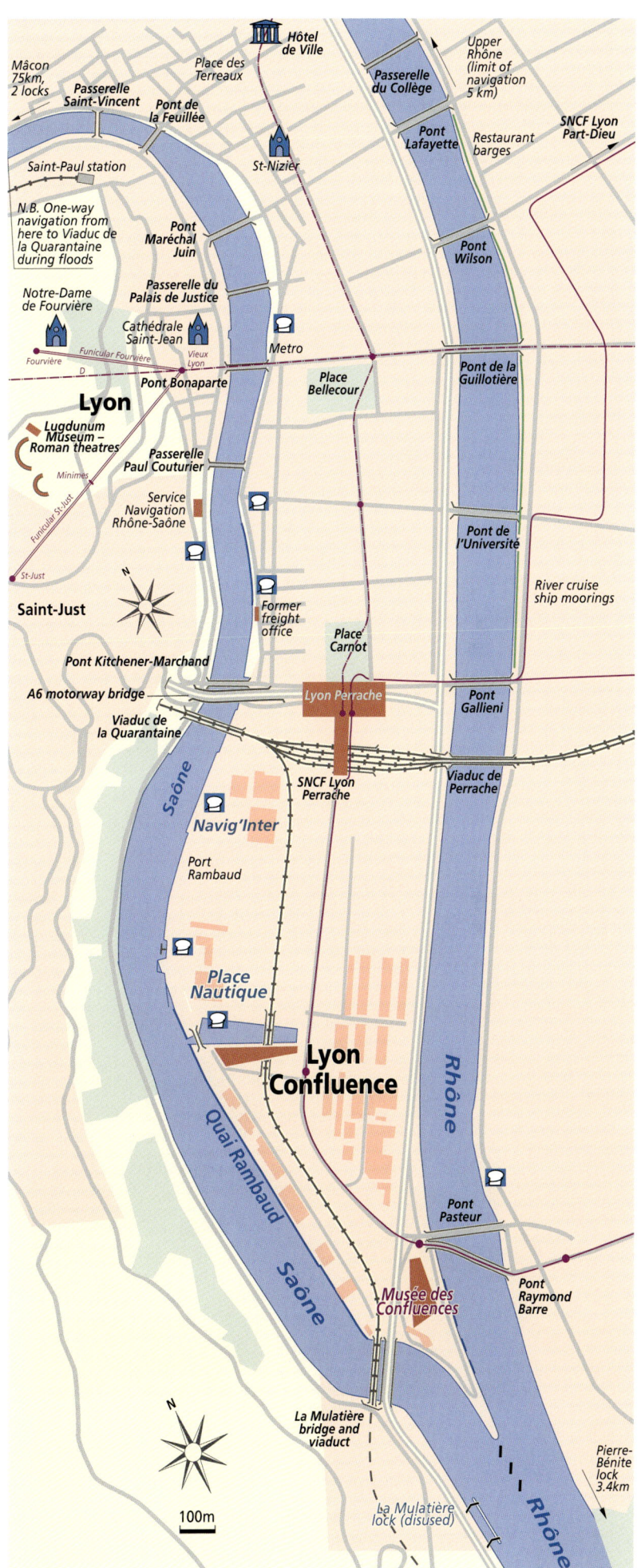

PK 9.8	Former Île Barbe lock, l/b
PK 7.5	New bridge (Pont Schuman)
PK 7.3	Bridge (Mazaryk), beginning of alternating one-way navigation through Lyon during floods
PK 6.9	Bridge (Clemenceau)
PK 6.3	Bridge (Maréchal Kœnig)
PK 5.5	Footbridge (Homme de la Roche)
PK 5.0	**Lyon** footbridge (Saint-Vincent), city centre l/b, Vieux Lyon r/b

Lyon is France's second city; fine buildings, old buildings, public squares and a long history dating back before the Roman city, which was itself very important. The walking tour of La Fourvière is recommended. As in almost every French city, town or village, the Tourist Office) that includes visiting the 'secret' houses, their courts and passages or *traboules*. Also the modern and engrossing Lugdunum archeological museum near the Fourvière basilica that dominates the skyline.

Visiting by boat is an equally memorable experience. From the river perspective, the city falls into three sections.

Firstly, the Mont d'Or northern approach, roughly starting at Belleville-sur-Saône at PK 55, including the picturesque Île Barbe, where there is the disused Bernalin lock.

Secondly, the city itself, 5km of the river with twists and turns, many bridges and almost continuous public quaysides. Keep a visual watch (and listen on VHF 18) for large commercial vessels and cruise ships, especially approaching the bridges. There are plenty of mooring possibilities, but selecting a location that is completely safe might be a problem.

Finally, there is the 2km southern tip. Formerly a huge national food market and railway depot south of Perrache railway station, it has been comprehensively redeveloped as the 'Lyon Confluence' district, with a new basin and *port de plaisance* at its centre, described on the next page.

PK 4.8	Bridge (La Feuillée)
PK 4.5	Bridge (Maréchal Juin)
PK 4.3	Footbridge (Palais de Justice)
PK 4.1	Quay l/b boat harbour, mooring possible in the heart of Lyon, l/b
PK 3.9	Bridge (Bonaparte)
PK 3.6	Footbridge (Saint-Georges, or Paul Couturier)
PK 2.9	Bridge (Kitchener-Marchand)
PK 2.8	Motorway bridge (A6)
PK 2.7	Railway bridge (Viaduc de la Quarantaine)
PK 2.4	Navig'Inter passenger boat operator l/b, 0478429681, 10 annual berths, water, electricity, subject to space available **naviginter.fr**

Another boat operator and events organiser Yachts de Lyon also has its vessels moored along the Quai Rambaud.

PK 1.9	Port Rambaud, former commercial quays l/b

The landmark vestiges of the former port are the former customs building, the sugar depot (*La Sucrière*) which now houses the biennial contemporary art exhibition, two cranes and the railway track.

V – Southeast France

PK **1.6** **Lyon-Confluence** harbour entrance l/b, *halte nautique* on the northern quay, 33 berths for boats up to 28m (barges moor on southern quay), *capitainerie* open 11:00 to 19:00, 06 89 99 45 11, night €19 (maximum 4 nights), water and electricity included, showers, pump-out, VHF 18. Open May 1-September 30.
capitainerie-lyonconfluence@gmail.com

This is the third mooring possibility in Lyon. Formerly a huge railway depot and national market, it has now been completely redeveloped as 'Lyon Confluence', and this excellent new halte fluviale is now the preferred mooring place for many boaters, with easy access throughout Lyon by the tram (Line T2) at the end of the basin. The swinging footbridge over the entrance is now maintained in the open position following structural failures.

Many péniches and boats also berth along the river here; there is an excellent fuel barge and chandlery (Decarpenterie).

PK **6.9** Motorway bridge (A7) and railway viaduct (de la Mulatière)
PK **0.0** Lyon-La Mulatière, former lock, r/b, **confluence with Rhône**

The river joins the Rhône. Just beyond the tip of land, on the right bank, there is the disused Mulatière lock used occasionally for water sports. It is has always looked empty and accessible and might make a brief or emergency mooring.

Branches off the Grande Saône

Lechâtelet arm
PK 0.0	**Junction with through route at Seurre** (PK 186)
PK 0.3	D/s tip of island, channel in l/b arm
PK 1.2	U/s tip of island (Boileau)
PK 7.2	Motorway bridge (A36)
PK 11.3	**Lechâtelet** former lock, head of navigation, moorings

River Doubs
PK 0.0	**Confluence with Saône** (PK 198)
PK 0.5	**Verdun-sur-le-Doubs**, *port de plaisance*, 22 berths, 03 85 91 85 06, night €12, water, electricity, showers €2.50, slipway, wifi, restaurants
PK 0.8	Bridge
PK 6.0	Bridge
PK 13.1	Railway bridge
PK 13.7	Navilly bridge (N73), head of navigation

The port de plaisance *and its* capitainerie *in the basin at Lyon Confluence, with the Saône in the background*

48. River Seille

THE RIVER SEILLE, ONE OF THE MOST CHARMING cruising rivers in France, extends 39km from the Saône at La Truchère (downstream of Tournus) to the head of navigation at the picturesque town of Louhans. It has four locks and weirs. The river winds peacefully past lush meadows and wooded slopes, its banks providing ample opportunity to moor overnight while tied to a tree, and the constantly changing pastoral landscape contrasts with the more slowly changing landscapes of the broad Saône valley. The river has become increasingly popular, thanks in part to the establishment of hire bases at Louhans and Branges. Excellent pontoon moorings for boats, with water and electricity, have been installed at Louhans, Cuisery and La Truchère.

There is no commercial traffic, but during the season a 30m trip boat occasionally operates between Chalon-sur-Saône or Tournus and La Truchère or Cuisery.

The river Seille was canalised in the late 18th century to provide access from the Saône to the important market town of Louhans. La Truchère lock was the only lock to be lengthened to Freycinet standards in the late 19th century.

Navigation
The Seille is an ideal cruising waterway. It has very little current and generally offers a good depth throughout its width, so there is no particular problem of navigation in the reaches. Cross-currents may present a difficulty on entering and leaving the lock-cuts in time of flood. The maximum permitted speed is 10km/h, reduced to 6km/h in the lock-cuts.

Locks
There are four locks, all situated in short lock-cuts on the left bank and overcoming a total difference in level of 7.20m. The first lock, at La Truchère, has standard barge dimensions of 38.50m by 5.20m. The other three are 31.30m long and 6.20m wide. There are no longer permanent lock-keepers at locks 2 (Brienne), 3 (Loisy) or 4 (Branges). During school holidays students may be present to assist. The locks use conventional paddle gear on the gates and chain and capstan gear for the gates. All the locks have been renovated in recent years and are easy to operate.

Draught
The maximum authorised draught is 1.30m.

Headroom
The maximum authorised air draught is 3.50m.

Authority
VNF Centre-Bourgogne
CEMI de Montceau – 9ème écluse Océan,
71300 Montceau-les-Mines
03 85 67 90 50
cemi.montceau-les-mines.dt.centrebourgogne@vnf.fr

Key dimensions (m)	
Length	31.30
Beam	5.10
Draught	1.30
Air draught*	3.50

* 3.00m under the railway bridge in Louhans

V – Southeast France

Route description

PK 0.0	Junction with Saône opposite KP 106 (just upstream of wood on left bank), enter with caution from slightly d/s and proceed slowly, awkward approach to lock
PK 0.7	Lock 1 La Truchère, bridge
PK 1.1	**La Truchère**, *base nautique* L'Embarcadère r/b (two restaurants), pontoon moorings for 15 boats, 03 85 51 70 93, night €8, water, electricity, boats for day hire

This is the ideal place to try frogs' legs. The Bresse region is famous not only for its poultry, but also for frogs.

PK 3.7	Seille bridge (D933)
PK 8.6	**Ratenelle**, bridge, restaurant, shops in village 500m r/b
PK 9.0	Railway bridge (disused)
PK 13.2	Lock 2 (Brienne), unattended out of season

Cuisery Lock PK 13. © JOHN RIDDEL, EDB

PK 13.6	Bridge (Cuisery)
PK 13.7	**Cuisery** municipal *halte*, pontoon moorings for 35 boats, 03 85 40 08 72, night €20, water and electricity included, showers, slipway, campsite r/b, village 500m
PK 17.8	**Loisy**, destroyed bridge (village 500m r/b)

Attractive hilltop village offering splendid views of the valley.

PK 18.2	Lock 3 (Loisy), unattended out of season, kiosk (arts and crafts)
PK 23.4	Port de Chevreuse, bridge, water l/b
PK 27.7	**Bantanges** l/b
PK 32.7	Auberge and restaurant r/b

Passing the Le Boat hire base on the mill stream at Branges

PK 34.8	Junction with weir stream, r/b, navigable 600m u/s to **Branges**, village with boat harbour and Le Boat hire base, 03 85 74 92 33, 16 moorings, night €20 (except weekends), water and electricity included, diesel on request, wifi, showers, slipway, restaurant

Another well-designed facility, managed for the municipality by Le Boat, but visitor moorings are available during the week.

PK 35.5	Lock 4 (Branges), bridge, unattended out of season
PK 38.7	**Louhans** quay and municipal *halte* on pontoons l/b, capacity 30 boats, 07 81 30 21 76, night €6, water and electricity (by tokens), showers, slipway, pump-out, tourist office, town centre 300m

Bustling market town with attractive arcades in the main street, and a major cattle and poultry market (Mondays). All services, and recommended visit to the old hospital and its pharmacy.

Les Canalous hire base at Louhans

PK 38.8	Confluence of Solnan l/b
PK 38.8	Railway bridge and René Cassin bridge (Louhans town centre with all services l/b)
PK 39.0	Head of navigation

49. Canal de Pont-de-Vaux

THE SHORT CANAL DE PONT-DE-VAUX gives access from the Saône at Fleurville to the market town, a distance of less than 4 km. Since it was restored to navigation, it has become firmly established as a boating destination thanks to the marina developed in two phases at the head of navigation, close to the centre of the small town.

*This short canal could have been a significant waterway if it had been continued as initially planned to Bourg-en-Bresse and the river Ain. The canal was conceded to the local intendant Louis Auguste Bertin in 1779, and engineer Léonard Racle surveyed the route. Works began in 1783, but were interrupted by the Revolution. Napoleon revived the project in 1810, but State funds were diverted to the wars. The canal was conceded to the council of Pont-de-Vaux in 1835, but it too found it impossible to fund the construction, which was finally completed by the State in 1843. The canal was conceded to the Ain **département** in 1934 for 20 years, but traffic had ceased, and the canal was officially closed when the concession ended in 1954. The author canvassed the mayor recommending restoration in 1983, and the project was eventually taken up and implemented in 1994.*

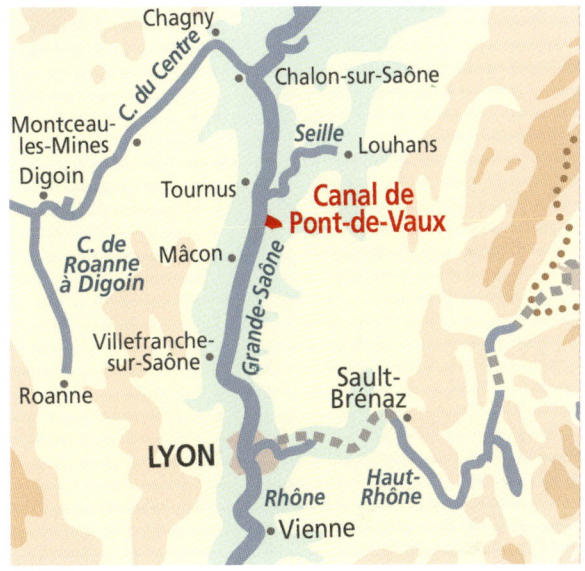

Navigation
Beware of shoals around the entrance lock from the Saône. Once in the canal navigation is straightforward, and no particular difficulties should be encountered, except when the river Reyssouze is in flood. Boats will be exposed to the river's current on entering the harbour basins at the end of the canal section. Speed is limited to 6 km/h.

Locks
The canal has one lock 38.50m by 5.00m at its entrance from the Saône. It is a semi-automatic, do-it-yourself lock.

Draught
The maximum authorised draught is 1.20m.

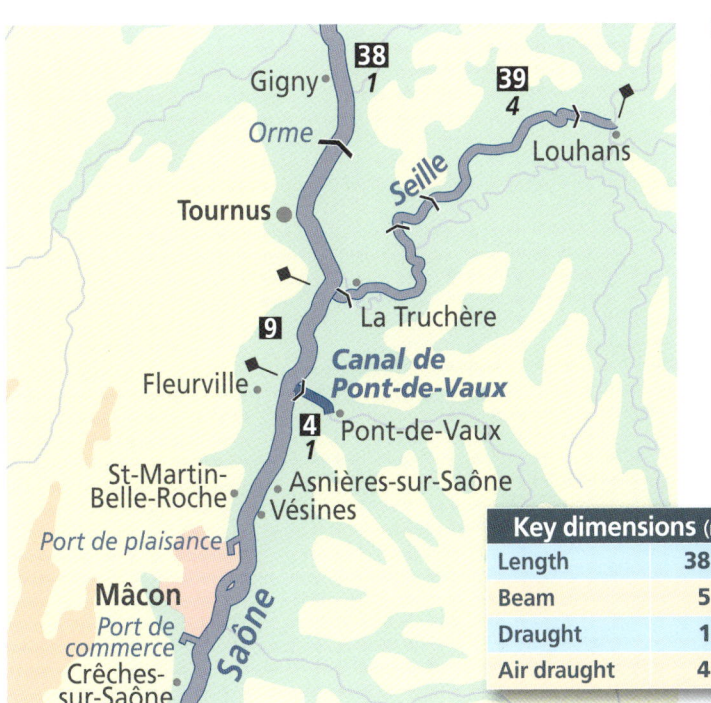

Key dimensions (m)	
Length	38.50
Beam	5.00
Draught	1.20
Air draught	4.20

The entrance lock at Fleurville. © LUDOLF

V – Southeast France

Headroom
The fixed bridges offer a minimum headroom of 4.20m above normal water level, but this is reduced when the Saône floods to higher than the canal's normal level. Navigation is not authorised when this level has been reached.

Authority
Communauté de Communes du Canton de Pont-de-Vaux – 66 rue Maréchal de Lattre de Tassigny, 01190 Pont-de-Vaux 03 85 51 45 64 *cc-pontdevaux.com*

Route description

PK 0.0	Junction with Saône	PK 267.7
PK 0.1	Lock, bridge	
PK 2.1	Bridge (La Cornate)	
PK 3.2	Canal enters river Reyssouze, bridge	
PK 3.5	**Pont-de-Vaux** footbridge, head of navigation, *port de plaisance*, Scite Plaisance, 225 berths, 03 85 30 99 10, *scite-plaisance.fr*, night €13, water €1.50, electricity (metered), showers, crane, slipway, diesel, pump-out, repairs, town 400m	

Excellent modern *port de plaisance*, highly recommended, also for over-wintering. Mooring stern-to pontoon on the right bank (town side), in season.

The marina at Pont-de-Vaux. This is the entrance to the second basin opened in a field beside the river Reyssouze. © MIVAL444

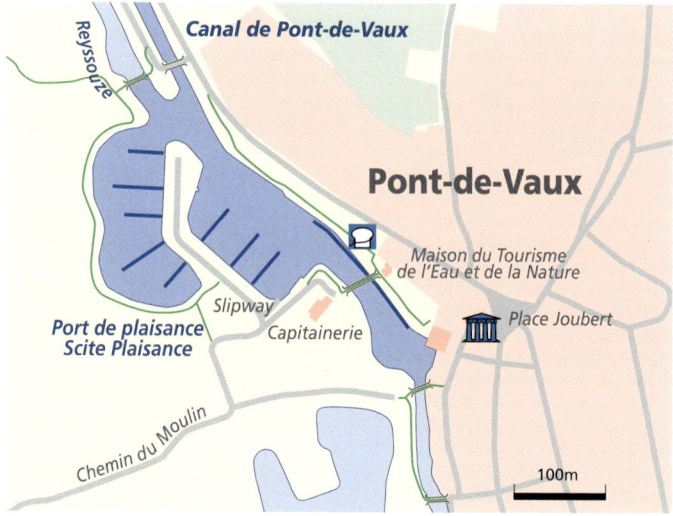

50. Rhône

The Rhône has been fully 'tamed' or engineered with dams and locks over a total distance of 310km from its confluence with the Saône at Lyon-La Mulatière to Port-Saint-Louis-du-Rhône. From here the Mediterranean is reached through a short canal, the Canal Maritime Saint-Louis. The bar formed by the river where it enters the sea, 6km further downstream, is impassable. The vast programme of works put in hand by the Compagnie Nationale du Rhône in 1933 (under an Act passed in 1921) was completed in 1980. Navigation alternates between wide deep river sections and 11 diversion canals, and bears no resemblance to that immortalised by Bernard Clavel in *Lord of the River*.

At Lyon the Rhône is joined by the Saône, which connects it with all the waterways of central and eastern France. Upstream of the confluence, the Upper Rhône route from Lyon to Lake Bourget, also now partly developed by the CNR, is covered under a separate entry.

The system of connections made by the Rhône downstream of Avignon was completely altered by the canalisation works. The Canal du Rhône à Sète is inaccessible at Beaucaire, since the entrance lock was rendered unusable by the lowering of the Rhône downstream of the Vallabrègues scheme. Instead, the Petit Rhône, formerly a semi-navigable channel of the delta, was improved for large-scale navigation (as part of the *Palier d'Arles* dredging scheme) over a distance of about 20km from Fourques, where it leaves the Rhône, to Saint-Gilles. Here a short length of canal with one lock connects with the Canal du Rhône à Sète. Similarly, on the left bank, the Canal d'Arles à Fos (formerly the Canal de Marseille au Rhône) has lost its former role as the through route to the Gulf of Fos and the Marseille region. Large commercial vessels now reach the port of Fos through the high-capacity Canal du Rhône à Fos, entered from the Rhône just upstream of Barcarin ferry, but this route is not open to private boats, which continue to use the existing link through Port-Saint-Louis-du-Rhône. This route is preferable in any case, with the numerous facilities offered by this small town.

The kilometre markers along the Rhône correspond to the original length of the river, from a point 0.7km upstream of the confluence with the Saône at Lyon to Port-Saint-Louis-du-Rhône. The route description gives these distances, since they are visible on the banks. At the end of each diversion canal we give the difference between the apparent distance and the actual kilometres covered, since the diversion canals are shorter.

Navigation

Under normal conditions, when the river is not in flood and the mistral is not blowing, the Rhône is not the daunting demon it once was. It has been tamed by the big dams and their accompanying diversion canals. The river's power is harnessed at each dam to produce hydroelectricity. The valley also has nuclear power plants and wind farms.

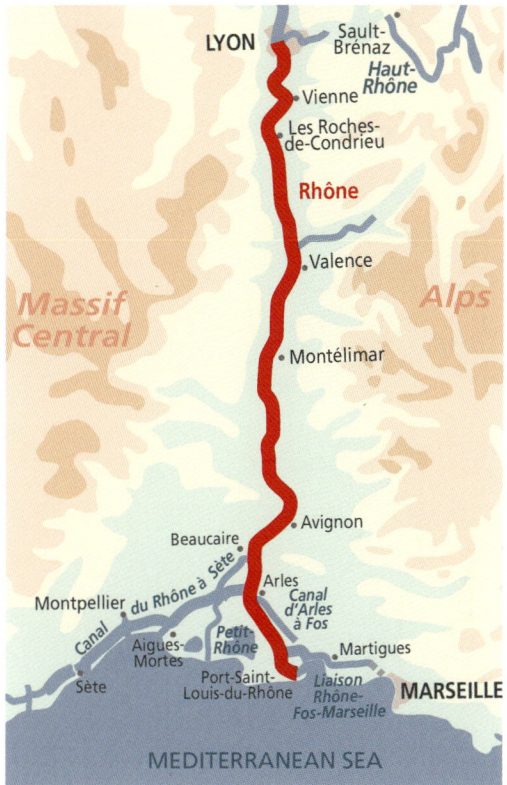

In the Roman period, the Rhône was already a key communications route already, and throughout history remained a difficult and dangerous navigation. Channel improvement works between 1885 and 1905 increased the low-water navigable draught to 1.60m, but the upstream hauls were still challenging for boatmen. The Compagnie Nationale du Rhône (CNR) was set up in 1933 to develop the river for navigation, hydropower and irrigation. The 12 hydroelectric plants and locks were built between 1964 and 1980. With a total head of 162m, they produce 13 GWh of electricity annually, or 16% of the country's total hydroelectric production (20% if the Upper Rhône schemes are added), and there have been significant benefits for agriculture throughout the Rhône valley. The landscape of the diversion canals is often bleak and austere, but efforts are being made to improve the environment of the river and its banks, especially in the main towns. The Rhône is a river of stunning contrasts, and boaters should take their time to explore the valley's many attractions.

V – Southeast France

Key dimensions (m)	
Length	185.00
Beam	12.00
Draught	3.20
Air draught	6.00

Navigation thus alternates between the bed of the Rhône, 300 to 500m wide, in which short steep waves may be generated by southerly winds, and 11 diversion canals, in which the locks are generally located towards the downstream end. The *mistral* (northerly wind) can make lock entry difficult from upstream. The current does not exceed 7km/h, but when combined with the effect of the *mistral*, it can make progress upstream laborious for low-powered boats. The channel is marked in places by red-and-white buoys or stakes on the right-bank side and (more rarely) by black-and-white markers on the left-bank side.

The maximum permitted speed is 35km/h. Lifejackets must be worn in locks – this sensible rule is rigorously enforced.

The phenomenal engineering works detract only slightly from the beauty of the valley, which runs between the foothills of the Massif Central and the Alps. On the other hand, the navigator can now take his time on the Rhône, visiting numerous towns and sites of historic interest, instead of making a non-stop dash for the Mediterranean, worrying about the dangers of the free-flowing river with its threatening groynes.

Locks

There are 12 locks built by CNR to the European waterway standards, 195 by 12m. All except Vaugris are situated on diversion canals, and are adjacent to the hydropower plants. The layout is such that the entrance is in many cases not clearly visible until the last few hundred metres. Enter only when a green light is showing. The fall varies between 6.70m (Vaugris) and 22m (Donzère-Mondragon). All locks are fitted with floating bollards. Single boats are locked through if no commercial traffic or other boat appears within 20 minutes of arrival at the lock. The sea lock at Port-Saint-Louis-du-Rhône is 160m long and 22m wide.

Draught

The minimum depth is 3.20m (guaranteed 20m from the channel marker buoys or the diversion canal banks). The minimum depth over the sill at Port-Saint-Louis-du-Rhône is 5.50m.

Headroom

The minimum air draught is 7m above the highest navigable water level, subject to variations dictated by the operating requirements of the power stations. Relatively low bridges have red and white gauges on the piers, the same indication being given by stakes situated a short distance upstream and downstream of the bridges.

Authority

VNF Rhône-Saône
Subdivision de Lyon:
– 4, rue Jonas Salk, 69007 Lyon 04 78 69 69 10 (PK 0-118)
  subdi.lyon@vnf.fr
Subdivision Grand Delta:
– 1 quai de la Gare, 13200 Arles 04 90 96 00 85 (PK 118-310)
  subdi.granddelta@vnf.fr

Rhône

Route description

PK 0.7 **Lyon-La Mulatière**, confluence with Saône (tip of peninsula, level with former lock of La Mulatière, r/b)

The *Musée des Confluences* is a massive landmark building sprawling across the neck of land at the confluence.

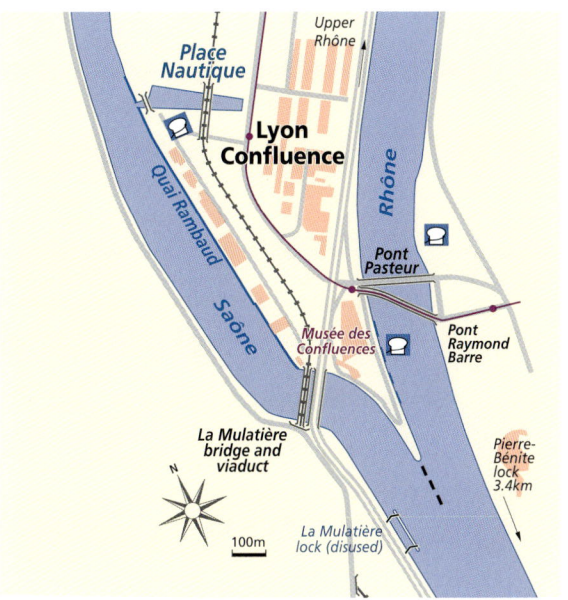

PK 3.3 Port of Lyon-Édouard Herriot basins, l/b
PK 3.9 Entrance to Pierre-Bénite diversion canal, l/b
PK 4.1 Pierre-Bénite lock (lift 9.25m) VHF 19, and power station, pontoons u/s and d/s, bridge

Coming from Lyon it can be tricky to spot where the diversion canal actually is. Keep over to the left bank or east side of the river after passing the container terminal. The diversion canal down to Givors (PK 14) is narrower than the more recent divesion canals and has a fast current. Commercial traffic and petrochemical refineries make their presence felt, and it can be a slow grind upstream.

PK 5.0 Motorway bridge (A7)
PK 7.2 Feyzin oil refinery
PK 8.1 Bridge
PK 11.0 Bridge, disused commercial quay d/s l/b
PK 15.0 End of diversion canal
PK 17.2 Arboras railway viaduct
PK 17.9 Motorway bridge (A47), oil terminal u/s
PK 18.3 Confluence of Giers, r/b
PK 18.4 **Givors** *port de plaisance* pontoons r/b, up to 12 boats, free (maximum 4 days), water, electricity, slipway

Halte on the west bank between the two bridges.

PK 18.9 Suspension bridge (Chasse)
PK 19.7 Fertiliser factory, l/b
PK 21.0 Water intake for power station, r/b
PK 22.0 Basin r/b for Loire-sur-Rhône power station (disused)
PK 26.4 Motorway bridge (A7)
PK 26.5 *Port de plaisance* in backwater r/b, 04 74 78 38 80, 3 berths, water, electricity, slipway opposite, mooring free (limited depth), restaurant

PK 28.6 **Vienne** bridge (de Lattre de Tassigny)

There are various pontoons and quays between the two bridges in Vienne. The photo shows a new pontoon on the west bank, just downstream of the footbridge, opposite Vienne, with a history dating back 2000 years, and a world-famous jazz festival in the Roman amphitheatre in the first half of July.

Pontoon mooring in Vienne, PK 29.

PK 29.0 Suspension bridge (Sainte Colombe)
PK 29.3 Mooring l/b to pontoon, trip boat mooring
PK 32.7 Motorway bridge (A7)
PK 34.0 Vaugris lock (lift 6.70m), bridge, VHF 22, and power station
PK 35.4 Château d'Arenc, r/b
PK 35.6 **Ampuis** pontoon moorings r/b

Good long pontoon, close to Vaugris lock, but the facility appears to be abandoned. It may be possible to moor on the inside (but depth not checked). Passenger boats may occupy the outside. Charming village. The main line railway is on the opposite bank.

PK 39.5 Meander cut-off (former channel dammed, l/b)
PK 40.7 **Les Roches-de-Condrieu** *port de plaisance* l/b, in a sheltered backwater l/b, 207 berths, 14 visitor moorings, 06 64 47 76 58, night €19.70, fuel, water, electricity, showers, pump-out, crane on request, slipway, restaurant

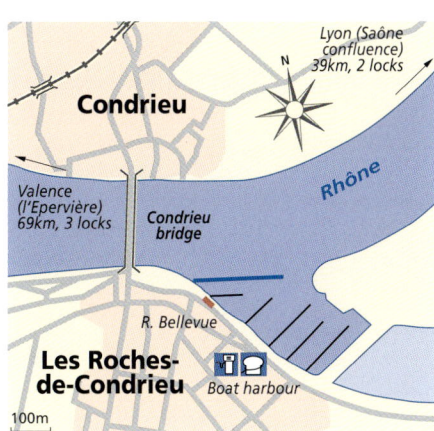

This port is neatly tucked into an enclosed backwater on the river's former route. There are plans to extend the marina further into the branch. It is already extensive and well used, but shows signs of wear and tear. The outside pontoons (along the river) have few electricity or water points that

103

V – Southeast France

work, possibly because they are very vulnerable to boats colliding with them, carried by wind and current. These are significant factors to take into account when berthing or entering the marina, and there are back eddies to the left of the entrance, when coming in. The *capitainerie* is very friendly and there are good showers, fuel and a repair yard. The village has a small supermarket, a *boulangerie* and a post office.

PK 40.7	Condrieu suspension bridge
PK 42.9	Saint-Clair-du-Rhône industrial complex, potash unloading quay, l/b
PK 46.5	**Chavanay**, r/b, pontoon mooring beside former bridge abutment

A new pontoon by the old suspension bridge support. An idyllic spot.

PK 47.1	Chavanay bridge
PK 47.7	Saint-Alban nuclear power station, l/b
PK 50.0	Entrance to Le Péage-de-Roussillon diversion canal, l/b
PK 55.5	Bridge and public quay, l/b (**Serrières**, 2 km)
PK 58.5	Bridge (D1082)
PK 59.5	Sablons lock (lift 14.50m), bridge, VHF 20, and power station
PK 60.1	Railway viaduct (Peyraud)
PK 63.3	End of diversion canal

Below Sablons the river can have a strong current and there are short breakwaters that project out from the banks – below the waterline – at frequent intervals to slow the flow. Keep to the marked channel.

PK 64.5	Champagne, r/b, former ferry, dangerous groyne
PK 68.8	Suspension bridge (Andance), **Andance** r/b, **Andancette** l/b, quay d/s r/b, slipway, pontoon mooring u/s l/b, water, electricity

A small pontoon at Andancette (left bank) by the bridge over to the very pretty village of Andance.

PK 60.8	Sarrasinière tower (ruin, r/b)
PK 73.1	Confluence of Cance, r/b
PK 74.8	Confluence of Ay, r/b
PK 75.5	**Saint-Vallier** bridge, town l/b

New pontoon on piles above the bridge, east bank. Choice of several *boulangeries* within walking distance, and a big Intermarché supermarket, if you turn left off the pontoon and walk for about 1 kilometre. A variety of shops. Convenient mooring, perhaps a little exposed for mooring overnight.

PK 76.3	Confluence of Galaure, l/b
PK 78.1	Quay (Olanet) l/b, slipway
PK 81.9	Serves castle, l/b, and Arras tower, r/b
PK 82.7	Entrance to Saint-Vallier diversion canal, l/b
PK 86.1	Gervans lock (lift 10.75m), bridge, VHF 19, and power station
PK 86.5	End of diversion canal
PK 89.1	Table du Roy rock in mid-channel (pass r/b side)
PK 90.1	Confluence of Doux, r/b
PK 90.8	**Tournon-sur-Rhône** *port de plaisance* r/b, 06 85 40 04 00, 20 boats, 14 visitor moorings, depth 1.50m, night €21, water, and electricity included, showers, slipway, pump-out

Tournon and Tain l'Hermitage (on the left bank) are interesting towns, well worth visiting. The harbour on the Tournon side of the river just above the suspension footbridge is quite restricted and shallow, and features concrete jetties. Larger and deeper craft may not get in, nor exit easily. It is also subject to wash from the commercial vessels that pass by, since the harbour wall is not a solid barrier. It is quite feasible to moor alongside the quay behind the wall and not venture in as far as the jetties. Depths must be watched.

PK 91.0	Tournon suspension footbridge (Marc Séguin), **Tain-l'Hermitage** l/b
PK 88.8	Tournon suspension bridge (Gustave Toursier)
PK 95.6	Auberge de Frais Matin, quay for clients, l/b
PK 98.2	Entrance to Bourg-lès-Valence diversion canal, l/b, moorings (**La Roche de Glun**) in bypassed Rhône, l/b

Pontoon located in the wide expanse of water at the entrance to the diversion canal, where there is plenty of depth. A very peaceful spot, by the village park and with the village of La Roche de Glun itself nearby. A few shops and *boulangerie*. The immediately neighbouring hamlet of Glun (15-20mins walk across the barrage) is highly picturesque. This once active place, the haunt of 14th century river pirates, has now been sent to sleep, bypassed by the modern waterway.

PK 98.9	Bridge
PK 101.9	Canal enters river Isère
PK 103.0	Canal leaves river Isère (outlet weir, r/b)
PK 105.6	Bourg-lès-Valence lock (lift 11.70m), bridge, VHF 22, and power station
PK 107.8	End of diversion canal (difference = 1.5 km)
PK 109.2	Bassin de Joutes l/b
PK 109.8	Valence bridge (Frédéric Mistral)
PK 110.0	**Valence** public quay l/b, below autoroute

It is feasible to moor at the town quay but it is noisy (beside the motorway).

Port de plaisance at Valence-l'Épervière, PK 112. © J-L PIALLAT

PK **111.9 Valence l'Éperviére** marina, l/b, 04 75 81 18 93, VHF 9, 06 87 59 87 43, 427 berths, 30 visitor berths, , night €20, fuel, water and electricity included, showers, crane 30t (max 18m), slipway, pump-out, repairs, restaurant, supermarket 500m *portplaisance@drome.cci.fr*

The fully equipped 420-berth *port de plaisance* has a boatyard with travel-lift, fuel, etc. The port is surrounded by parkland south of Valence. Shops, supermarkets and bricos within a fairly short walk from the marina, although along a busy road. The route into the marina from the river is marked with buoys.

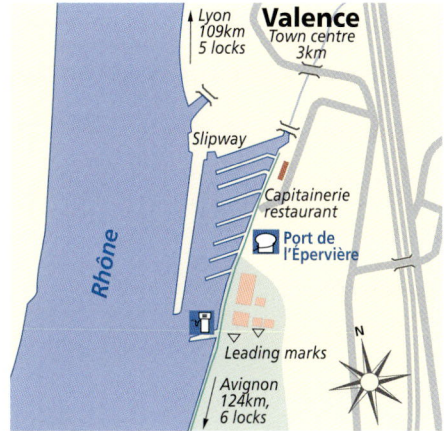

PK **112.6** Main road bridge (D96/D534n)
PK **114.8 Soyons**, r/b, leaning tower (ruin)
PK **116.3** Portes-lès-Valence quay (commercial) and VNF office, l/b
PK **119.5 Charmes** r/b, entrance to Beauchastel diversion canal, r/b, bridge (D11)
PK **119.7** Boat club moorings, r/b
PK **123.8** Beauchastel lock (lift 12.65m), bridge, VHF 20, power station, village 500m r/b
PK **125.4** End of diversion canal (difference = 0.7km, 2.2km total from Lyon)
PK **126.4** Confluence of Eyrieux, r/b
PK **128.0 La Voulte** suspension bridge, mooring and town centre r/b

Sloping quay with bollards. Large fenders necessary.

Hotel barge Napoleon *moored to the sloping quay wall at La Voulte*

PK **128.7** La Voulte railway viaduct
PK **131.6** Confluence of Drôme, l/b
PK **133.2 Le Pouzin** bridge, village r/b, commercial quay u/s r/b (very high, not recommended)
PK **133.5** Confluence of Ouvèze, r/b
PK **135.3** Entrance to Baix-Le-Logis-Neuf diversion canal, l/b
PK **142.6** Logis-Neuf lock (lift 13.00m), bridge, VHF 19, power station
PK **144.0** End of diversion canal
PK **144.9 Cruas**, quay, r/b, *port de plaisance*, 06 79 17 92 18, 70 berths, 7 visitor moorings, night €12, water and electricity included, shower, slipway, village 500m

The recently established *port de plaisance* gets good reports but is somewhat isolated. It is important to follow the marked entrance channel – there are rocks and shallows elsewhere. Welcoming *Capitainerie*. The town is prosperous thanks to the EDF nuclear power station and Lafarge quarries. Both have contributed significantly to the amenities and upkeep of the town, with its lavish sports ground and playing fields. The town is inland of the railway line. Cruas also has an SNCF station. The church dates back to 804 AD. The oldest part of the town is on the hillside and is being rebuilt; one or two houses are already in occupation. In short; a good port for a welcome break with marina power, water and town facilities including a small *supermarché*.

The port de plaisance at Cruas, in sight of the nuclear power station cooling towers. ©F-W

PK **148.0** Cruas-Meysse nuclear power station, r/b
PK **148.0** Island, main channel on r/b side, boatyard on l/b side (access from d/s)

Opposite the power station is a *péniche* repair yard, almost hidden by several islets.

PK **152.6** Entrance to Montélimar diversion canal, l/b
PK **154.0 Ancône** mooring to dolphins l/b, used by commercial craft, exposed to wind, village 400m
PK **154.8** Bridge (D11)
PK **157.2** Bridge (N102)
PK **157.7** Crossing of river Roubion
PK **159.4** Gournier suspension bridge (D237)

V – Southeast France

PK 159.5 Montélimar harbour (inconvenient mooring), piled quay 175m long

Mooring along this commercial quay is a possibility, but the boat should certainly not be left unattended, in case a barge or a ship needs to use the facility.

PK 163.0 Châteauneuf lock, lift 18.5m, bridge, VHF 22, pontoons u/s and d/s, power station (village 2 km)

The CNR staff in the control room at this lock now monitor traffic and remotely operate all 12 locks on the Rhône from Lyon to the Mediterranean.

PK 165.8 End of diversion canal (Rhône navigable 4km u/s to Lafarge cement works) (difference = 0.2km, 2.4km total from Lyon), **Viviers** municipal *port de plaisance*, 400m upstream on Rhône r/b, 06 33 40 84 16, 16 berths, night €16, water, electricity (16A), showers, wifi (at the guinguette)

Viviers is one of France's hidden gems: an unspoilt walled medieval hilltop town with France's smallest cathedral at the top (Gobelin tapestries), nNarrow twisty streets, little courtyards, Provence-style tiled roofs, gargoyles, sculpted façades and faded painted signs. The general character of the village beyond the walls is also charming, with the plane trees, the renaissance bishop's residence… Walking out of Viviers heading north-west (turn right at the tourist office), you will come to a river bed (it joins the Rhone just above the *port de plaisance*) upstream of which is a completely intact Roman bridge. Viviers is magic. The *port de plaisance* has been dredged and reopened. It is possible to cruise for a 4km distance along the by-passed river upstream from Viviers but this leads to the enormous and very dusty cement lime quarry, at Lafarge.

PK 166.8 Viviers suspension bridge, entrance to Donzère gorge

The spectacular *défilé de Donzère* is the narrowest natural gorge on the Rhône downstream of Lyon.

PK 169.5 Donzère bridge (Pont du Robinet)

Pont du Robinet near the entrance to Donzère gorge © HUGGY 26

PK 170.7 Entrance to Donzère-Mondragon diversion canal, l/b
PK 170.8 Bridge with flood gate, quay r/b

Private boats enter the diversion canal through the left bank pass.

PK 174.2 Railway viaduct (through route Lyon-Marseille)
PK 174.3 Bridge (N7)
PK 178.4 Bridge (D358)
PK 179.2 Skew railway bridge (TGV Méditerrannée), l/b abutment
PK 180.3 Bridge (D59)
PK 182.8 Pierrelatte atomic energy centre r/b
PK 184.3 Tricastin nuclear power station r/b
PK 185.0 Bridge (D204)
PK 186.1 Lock approach channel, l/b, commercial quay r/b
PK 187.1 Bollène lock (22.00m) VHF 20, pontoons u/s and d/s, André Blondel power station, bridge

Was the deepest lock in Europe, possibly the world's best known. Amazingly big to be inside at the bottom, like a concrete cathedral with the roof off. Very smooth and very easy. Quite an experience for a small boat.

PK 189.4 Bridge (D994), **Bollène** 1 km l/b
PK 192.5 Railway viaduct (through route Lyon-Marseille)
PK 193.2 Bridge (N7)
PK 194.4 Bridge (D44), Mondragon 500m
PK 197.6 End of diversion canal (difference = 2.9km, 5.1km total)

Where the river rejoins on the right bank there is a commercial (sand and gravel) quay at the tip and a new TGV bowstring span rail bridge. Opposite the quay, toward the flat bridge span, there is a small inlet that looks like a good anchoring spot (check depths).

PK 202.2 Railway bridge (TGV Méditerrannée)
PK 203.5 Saint-Étienne-des-Sorts *halte* on pontoon r/b, 06 37 59 11 34, 4 boats, free, water, electricity, slipway, former boatman's village

A pretty, wine-oriented, village. Quayside (high) with mooring rings, but also a recently installed pontoon, with room for no more than two boats.

Small pontoon halte at Saint-Étienne-des-Sorts. © F-W

PK 208.2 Marcoule nuclear power station, r/b
PK 212.5 Entrance to Caderousse diversion canal, l/b
PK 215.0 Caderousse lock (9.00m) VHF 19, pontoons u/s and d/s, bridge, power plant

Rhône

PK **217.3** End of diversion canal Rhône navigable 5km upstream to **L'Ardoise** *port de plaisance*, 40 berths, 5 to 8 visitor berths in season, 06 77 08 11 10, night €18, fuel on request (minimum 600 litres), water €2, electricity €1.50, showers €2, wifi, crane 10t on request, pump-out, repairs, *port-rhone-provence.com*

This port may not suit all *plaisanciers*, but it has all basic services and is secure and safe. It is peaceful, despite background noise from the cement plant nearby. Well suited for a night's stay, a month or for long-term berthing. A mixture of industry and rurality, and good walks. Small supermarket and *boulangerie* in the village, about 10-15mins walk. Buses to Avignon and Pont-Saint-Esprit, which has an exceptional long ancient river bridge.

The marina at L'Ardoise is nestled into the tree-lined bank of the Rhône. © F-W

PK **221.0** Montfaucon castle, r/b
PK **221.7** Railway bridge (TGV Méditerrannée)
PK **221.9** Motorway bridge (A9)
PK **222.0** Suspension bridge (D976)
PK **225.0** **Roquemaure** quay r/b, exposed to wind, castle, Tour de l'Hers tower l/b

This is a piles-and-platform combination, for *péniches* and cruise ships, but there is also a separate small pontoon – or possibly, the village quayside. Opposite the romantic Château de l'Hers, a ruined castle built on a rocky outcrop.

PK **230.2** Entrance to Villeneuve-les-Avignon diversion canal
PK **232.3** Villeneuve dam, r/b, and bridge
PK **233.2** Crossing of former Villeneuve arm of Rhône
PK **234.5** Avignon lock (10.50m) VHF 22, bridge, power plant
PK **235.1** End of diversion canal, (difference = 4.6km, 14.1km total from Lyon)
PK **242.2** **Villeneuve-lès-Avignon** bridge (Pont du Royaume)
PK **243.1** Express road bridge (N100, Pont de l'Europe)
PK **243.7** Overhead power line
PK **244.0** Railway bridge, *junction with Avignon arm*

Turn into the arm from below the railway bridge.

Reception barge for the halte at Avignon. Moorings are now on the Quai de la Ligne

V – Southeast France

The Saint-Bénézet bridge in Avignon © CLAUDE ROUSSEL-DUPRÉ

Avignon arm

Enter the Avignon arm from downstream of the railway bridge for the highlight of the cruise on the Rhône. Pass the big, long, river cruise ships and the remains of Pont Saint-Bénézet. Just beyond the famous bridge is the *capitainerie* barge. This is where the *port de plaisance* once was, until it was swept away during the winter of 2002/3. Even in summer the strong downstream current here has to be respected. Moor to the public quayside (Quai de la Ligne). It can get crowded and it may feel unsafe.

The bridge once had many more arches, and reached one kilometre from Avignon to the Philippe le Bel tower at what is now Villeneuve. Only a few arches are left. The song is about dancing on the isthmus island across the river from Avignon, under (*sous*) the bridge not on (*sur*) *le pont*. Also at Villeneuve, Saint-André is an outstanding example of medieval fortification. The Pope was obliged to flee Rome in 1309 and established his relocated court and palace at Avignon; the result is a soaring architectural masterpiece. Besides the palace, the town itself shelters a maze of streets behind massive defensive walls. Villeneuve was the location for 15 cardinals' palaces. It all lasted 70 years, then the Pope went back to Rome, although a series of quasi-Popes then continued to operate from Avignon.

PK **244.0** Railway bridge *entrance to the arm from main river*
PK **242.8** Road bridge (N100, Pont de l'Europe)
PK **242.1** Villeneuve bridge (pont Édouard Daladier)
PK **241.6** Saint-Bénézet bridge (the famous 'Pont d'Avignon')
PK **241.0** **Avignon** *halte* near town centre, harbourmaster's office and reception barge, 450m-long quai de la Ligne l/b, 04 90 85 65 54, night €23, fuel, water and electricity (6A) included, showers, crane on request, slipway, VHF call on channels 9/16, restaurants
PK **236.0** Le Pontet, quay, l/b
PK **234.9** Overhead power line
PK **234.3** Limit of navigation, turning basin

Navigation continues on river Rhône

PK **246.1** Railway viaducts (Les Angles), TGV Méditerranée
PK **247.8** Confluence of Durance l/b, not navigable
PK **252.3** Aramon bridge
PK **254.5** **Aramon** *relais fluvial* 'Les Estères' r/b, for 30 boats up to 15m, 06 66 59 02 17, water and electricity (16 A), fuel with 48 hours' notice, pump-out, wifi *air-et-o-nautique.com*

The pontoon moorings were opened here in 2014. Do not pass between the marker buoys outside, which identify a submerged training wall; enter from upstream or downstream. The depth on the bank side of the pontoon drops to 1.50m. Barges may be accommodated by breasting up outside. The mooring is secure, with the port capitain living on site. *Capitainerie* with facilities and bikes for hire. Aramon village is 350m away, has shops, is charming and has several restaurants and two bars. Buses to Avignon, Uzès and the Pont du Gard.

The pontoon at the relais fluvial in Aramon, PK 254. © F-W

PK **256.4** Aramon solar power station, r/b, former tanker quay
PK **261.0** **Vallabrègues** *port de plaisance* l/b, 06 70 56 81 71, 17 berths, night €32, water, electricity, slipway, village with restaurant 1 km

This facility is managed by the capitainerie at Beaucaire. All normal services, pontoons on the river. The village was a well-known centre of basket-making. *port@beaucaire.fr*

PK **262.4** Entrance to Vallabrègues diversion canal, l/b
PK **265.0** Beaucaire lock (12.15m) VHF 20, pontoons u/s and d/s, 04 66 59 58 43, bridge, power plant
PK **267.4** **Tarascon** bridge, town l/b but no moorings (**Beaucaire** r/b)

Rhône

The famous château built by King René in Tarascon, PK 267 © F-W.

PK **267.8** Railway viaduct
PK **269.1** End of diversion canal (Rhône not navigable, entrance to Canal du Rhône à Sète closed, connection made via Petit Rhône d/s)
PK **269.2** Commercial port of Beaucaire, r/b, high quay wall
PK **269.4** New bridge (Beaucaire and Tarascon bypass)
PK **277.3** Intake of Philippe Lamour irrigation canal, r/b
PK **279.1** Junction with Petit Rhône r/b, and turning basin
PK **281.9** Commercial quay r/b, built as a RO-RO terminal, cruise ship moorings l/b
PK **282.2** **Arles** pontoon moorings (35m long) r/b

It has always been a problem to know where best to moor in Arles. This pontoon is ideally situated, but occupied by local boat owners.

PK **282.5** Trinquetaille bridge, VNF office d/s r/b, mooring possible on quay

Works to consolidate the quay in the centre of Arles, in 2016. Cruise ships moor to dolphins upstream of the sweeping bend of the Rhône.

PK **283.0** Main road bridge (N113/N572)
PK **283.6** Junction with Canal d'Arles à Fos, l/b

See under that canal. Advance notice to be given to use the lock to access the canal basin and boatyard in Arles.

PK **293.2** Terrin shoals, fast current
PK **316.4** Junction with Canal du Rhône à Fos, l/b

This route east to the port of Fos is forbidden to *plaisanciers*.

PK **316.7** Barcarin car ferry
PK **317.3** Private rail ferry serving Salin de Giraud salt marshes
PK **319.1** Port de l'Esquineau, quay, r/b
PK **322.2** Small sheltered basin l/b (no services)
PK **323.2** Junction with Canal maritime Saint-Louis, end of navigation in the Rhône

Canal maritime Saint-Louis

PK **0.0** Junction with Rhône u/s of lock, mooring pontoon
PK **0.3** Lock (Port Saint-Louis-du-Rhône), VHF 12
PK **0.4** **Port-Saint-Louis-du-Rhône** *port de plaisance*, 04 42 86 39 11, 340 berths, 25 visitor berths, night €26, fuel (on request), water and electricity included, showers, wifi free for 2 hous, small town and restaurants
PK **3.1** Les Tellines commercial quay north bank
PK **4.3** Outlet in Gulf of Fos (navigation extended into the gulf by a dredged channel protected by a breakwater over a further length of 2 km).

The Port Napoléon is another large *port de plaisance*, reached by heading out into the Gulf of Fos then turning right and back into a dead-end channel running parallel to the Canal maritime.

V – Southeast France

51. Petit Rhône and Canal de Saint-Gilles

THE PETIT RHÔNE MAKES A GRAND FINALE to the cruise south to the Mediterranean, leaving the mighty river just north of Arles. It is a narrow and relatively shallow arm of the Rhône delta, but has always been navigable. Its winding course through an often Amazonian landscape is no less than 58 km from the Rhône to the Mediterranean at Grau d'Orgon. The channel was deepened in the 1970s for high-capacity barges over a distance of 20 km from its entrance at Fourques to Saint-Gilles, where a new cut with a massive lock connects with the Canal du Rhône à Sète. Down to this point the river thus forms the first section of the route across southern France towards Toulouse and eventually the Atlantic Ocean. This first section is 20 km in length. Beyond the entrance to the canal at Saint-Gilles the river is a picturesque navigation winding through the Camargue national park down to the Mediterranean at Grau d'Orgon, a distance of 38 km. There are no channel markings, and boats should proceed with caution, keeping to the middle of the channel. The route description gives the kilometre distances continuing those of the main river, which will be seen on stakes on the banks.

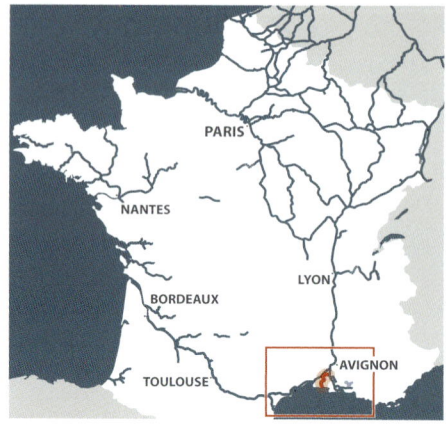

As a natural distributary of the Rhône, the 'Petit Rhône' has always been navigable, and was the main route inland until the Roman period. It was left in that (shallow) state until the CNR adapted it in 1970 as the new route to Sète, using a novel technique of bottom panels to ensure the required depth of 2.50 m.

Navigation
The channel on the through route is well marked by stakes. Below the Saint-Gilles link canal there are no markings but the twisting river is easy to follow. It is bounded by high, thick foliage, offering a dramatic contrast with the wide, open Rhône. Encounters with other craft will be rare, but the possibility of meeting a large vessel making its way between the Rhône and the port of Sète should be allowed for down to the lock at Saint-Gilles. The channel is marked by poles.

Locks
None on the river itself. The lock on the Canal de Saint-Gilles, of Rhône dimensions (195 by 12 m, with a sill depth of 4.50 m), gives access to the Canal du Rhône à Sète.

Key dimensions (m)	
Length	–
Beam	–
Draught	1.00
Air draught	3.00

Petit-Rhône and Canal de Saint-Gilles

Draught
The depth of the 30m-wide channel on the main route is maintained at 2.20m at low water level. Outside the channel depths are variable, there are sandbanks and more particularly there are sections bounded by submerged iron stake 'fences'. On the unmaintained waterway beyond Saint-Gilles there are also plenty of fallen trees and branches at the river edges. These lower reaches of the Petit-Rhône are not suited for boats drawing more than 1.00m.

Headroom
There are five bridges on the main route. The lowest is the railway bridge at PK 294.7, offering a minimum headroom of 4.75m. On the unregulated Petit-Rhône, there is only one bridge, at Sylveréal, but the lowest obstruction is the cable at the Sauvage ferry, limiting the air draught to 3.00m.

Authority
VNF Rhône-Saône
Subdivision Grand Delta:
– 1 quai de la Gare, 13200 Arles 04 90 96 00 85 (PK 118-310)
   subdi.granddelta@vnf.fr

A commercial barge passes through the girder bridge at Fourques (PK 282) © F-W

Route description

PK 279.6 **Junction with Rhône at Fourques**
PK 281.1 **Fourques** suspension bridge, possible mooring to two piles d/s l/b, village

A useful, albeit very basic, mooring.

PK 281.8 Fourques girder bridge (D6113/D113)
PK 288.3 Motorway bridge (A54)
PK 294.5 Railway bridge (Cavalès)
PK 297.3 Bridge (Saint-Gilles), D6572
PK 299.6 **Entrance to Canal de Saint-Gilles**, r/b

Beginning of navigation in the unregulated river.

PK 301.8 Pontoon r/b
PK 305.0 Mas Marignan, r/b
PK 307.1 La Motte, r/b
PK 316.6 **Château d'Avignon**, pontoon mooring l/b
PK 318.3 Junction with Canal des Capettes, r/b (abandoned navigation)
PK 321.9 **Sylveréal** girder bridge, village r/b

PK 322.0 Junction with Canal du Peccais à Sylveréal, r/b (abandoned navigation)
PK 326.0 **Mas des Baumelles**, pontoon mooring l/b, water, restaurant
PK 331.0 **Sauvage** ferry, village (Le Petit Sauvage) r/b

Hire boats are not allowed to continue downstream from here.

PK 335.1 Port Dromar harbour (private) in small basin l/b
PK 335.5 La Fouque harbour (private) in basin l/b
PK 335.8 L'Amarée harbour (private) in basin l/b
PK 337.9 **Grau d'Orgon** outfall in Mediterranean

Canal de Saint-Gilles

PK 299.6 **Entrance from river Rhône**
PK 300.1 Lock (Saint-Gilles), bridge, VHF 18
PK 302.0 **Junction with Canal du Rhône à Sète** (PK 29)

Navigation continues on the Canal du Rhône à Sète.

Aspects of the Camargue near the mouth of the Petit Rhône, revealed by the passenger boat Tiki III. The boat operates from its base at the Sauvage ferry (PK 331).

V – Southeast France

52. Haut Rhône

THE UPPER RHÔNE IS THEORETICALLY navigable from Lyon to the dam at Seyssel. In practice, the river is made up of isolated sections, and the two big gaps in the location map right are likely to remain indefinitely. The situation in 2016 is as follows: navigation is possible from the confluence with the Saône at Lyon to La Feyssine lock in Villeurbanne, a distance of 9.6km. This lock built in the 1980s cannot be operated, and will only be of interest if the upstream Canal de Jonage is restored from PK 11 to PK 30. The canal is conceded to Électricité de France, with locks to be built inside the enormous existing chambers. There is no date yet for these works. From PK 30 to PK 66 (Sault-Brénaz), the Upper Rhône will remain a free-flow navigation offering variable depths. The project designed in 1999 involved local improvements to increase the available depth, and the provision of buoyage to mark the channel, but navigation is at present incompatible with ecological conservation in the area of the confluence of the river Ain. The waterway of interest to boaters thus begins upstream of the dam at Sault-Brénaz, at a point defined here as PK 0. It extends 81 km to Seyssel. At PK 62 there is a link through the picturesque Canal de Savières into Lake Bourget, the biggest natural lake in France, with the important tourist and spa resort of Aix-les-Bains on its eastern shore. This link from Chanaz to Viviers-du-Lac, a few kilometres north of Chambéry, adds 23km, so the total navigable length of the Upper Rhône/Lake Bourget system is 104 km.

The Upper Rhône was historically navigated up to Le Parc, at the entrance to a narrow gorge with rapids. To develop combined passenger and freight steamer services from Lyon to Aix-les-Bains, a large lock was built at Sault-Brénaz in the 1880s, to bypass the rapids here. Then in 1897 a private concessionary opened the Canal de Jonage with two hydropower dams and locks (a double staircase at Cusset). Génissiat dam (70m high), was completed in 1948, with Seyssel dam a few kilometres downstream to create a compensating reservoir. In the 1980s the CNR built a series of hydropower schemes, which brought significant changes and created a virtually navigable waterway through most of the length of the Upper Rhône, using the diversion canals. These are now being linked up with 38m locks, but the final objective of through navigation from Lyon is only a remote prospect.

This section has four diversion canals and hydropower plants built by the CNR (Compagnie Nationale du Rhône) in the 1980s. Boat elevators bypassing each power plant were provided, but were never much used, hence the project started in 2000, after a study by the author, which involves building a short bypass with one or two locks at each of the four hydropower plants. The works started at the upstream end, and bypasses with two locks each were built at the Chautagne and Brens (Belley) power plants. A single lock is to be built at Brégnier-Cordon, starting in 2021, for a cost of €22 milllion. The works are entirely funded by CNR. The fourth modern dam at Sault-Brénaz is expected to keep its ramps and boat elevator, since the Rhône rapidly becomes unnavigable downstream of the village.

The two locks and intermediate basin at the Brens hydropower plant (just out of the picture to the left).
© CNR

Owners of trailed boats are strongly encouraged to make use of one of the numerous *ports de plaisance* indicated in the route description to explore this navigable section.

Navigation

The cruise up the river, with its dramatic alpine landscapes, and through the charming Canal de Savières to Lake Bourget is a unique experience on the French waterways. Few boaters have undertaken this cruise to date, because the waterway is isolated from the main system. When the navigable length is increased to just over 100km by around 2024, it should become feasible to transport hire boats here and develop the traffic, possibly even a longer-distance passenger vessel. The CNR distributes an excellent brochure in French, English and German setting out all the navigation rules and instructions for using the locks.

Locks

There are 7 structures overcoming a difference in level of 78m between Lyon and Seyssel (not taking into account the 12m rise in the 36km free-flow section between Jons and Sault-Brénaz). The first is the lock built at La Feyssine (Villeurbanne) as part of a major ring road in Lyon. The following two locks were built by EDF under the Jonage hydroelectric scheme. These locks, of substantial dimensions (114 by 16m), were rarely operated and became disused after the last paddle steamer plied the route from Lyon to Aix-les-Bains (post World War II). Proposed reinstatement involves building new open walls, gate abutments and gates within the existing chambers. The other four structures are the hydropower dams completed during the 1980s. Two of these, Chautagne and Brens (Belley) have substantial locks 40m by 5.25m, one above and one below each power plant, with intermediate basins. These locks are operated by remote control following the instructions on the control panels. A technician can be called in case of difficulty.

At Brégnier-Cordon, a mobile elevator is operated on request (giving 24 hours notice), between ramps in the bank above and below the power plant. The elevator can handle boats up to 5 tonnes, with a maximum length of 9.50m and maximum beam 3.40m. The telephone number of the local mechanic to be called for operation of the elevator is posted at each ramp. A single lock is to be built here, starting in 2022, to replace this cumbersome and little-used facility.

There is a conventional do-it-yourself mechanised lock at Savières, with navigable dimensions of 18m by 5.25m. The lock is operated simply by selecting the direction of passage and pushing a button on the control cabinet by the lock side. The cycle is automatic.

Draught

There is no draught limitation in the regulations for navigation on the Upper Rhône. The sill depth of Savières lock is 2.50m and a depth of 2.00m is available throughout the navigable length of the river and the Canal de Savières.

Headroom

The lowest bridge is at Portout, on the Canal de Savières, offering a minimum headroom of 3.50m. On the Rhône itself, the minimum headroom is 6.00m.

Towpath

There is no towpath.

Authority

VNF Rhône-Saône
– 4, rue Jonas Salk, 69007 Lyon, 04 78 69 69 10
CNR - 2 rue André Bonin, 69316 Lyon Cedex 04,
04 72 00 69 69 *cnr.tm.fr*

Key dimensions (m)	
Length	38.50
[C. Savières	18.00]
Beam	5.25
Draught	2.00
Air draught	6.00
[C. Savières	3.50]

V – Southeast France

Route description

Upstream from Saône confluence in Lyon

PK 0.0	Confluence with Saône at La Mulatière/Gerland
PK 0.5	Bridge (Raymond Barre), tramway line T1
PK 0.6	Bridge (Pasteur)
PK 2.2	Railway bridge (Perrache)
PK 2.5	Bridge (Galliéni), tramway lines T1 & T2
PK 3.0	Bridge (Université)
PK 3.5	Bridge (Guillotière)
PK 3.9	Bridge (Wilson)
PK 4.3	Bridge (Lafayette)
PK 4.5	Footbridge (Collège), residential moorings l/b
PK 4.9	Bridge (Morand), metro, **Lyon** (Place des Terreaux, Hôtel de Ville and Opera) 400m r/b
PK 5.3	Bridge (De Lattre de Tassigny)
PK 6.0	Bridge (Winston Churchill)
PK 7.9	Railway bridge, strong current, dangerous
PK 8.0	Road bridge (Raymond Poincaré)
PK 9.6	Lock (La Feyssine) in short cut, l/b, rise 2.50m, not in operation

Continuously navigable section from Sault-Brénaz to Seyssel

PK 0.0	**Sault-Brénaz** u/s elevator ramp, future lock entrance, current d/s limit of navigation on Haut Rhône (after completion of Brégnier-Cordon lock)

Sault-Brénaz is 67 km from the confluence of the Saône in Lyon.

Boat portage ramp leading out of the old lock chamber at Sault-Brénaz to the upper reach, which is several metres higher than the lock's upper level. A lock could take the place of the ramp, but there is little demand, since the Rhône becomes unnavigable immediately downstream.

PK 0.8	Dam (Villebois) r/b, end of diversion canal
PK 4.5	**Montalieu-Vercieu** port de plaisance and water park (La Vallée Bleue) l/b in widening, with sheltered basin, 04 74 88 49 23, 90 berths, 2 visitor moorings, night €10 to €35 depending on position, water, electricity, showers at campsite, slipway

In the absence of the projected lock upstream at Brégnier-Cordon (PK 31), the *port de plaisance* is essentially used by day boats and water sports.

PK 5.5	Island l/b, camp site and restaurant r/b
PK 8.1	Overhead power lines
PK 10.0	Bridge (D52/D119a, Pont de Briord)
PK 10.6	**Briord** port de plaisance (Loisirs Nautiques), pontoon moorings r/b, 06 08 25 10 28, 38 berths, 2 visitor moorings, free (maximum 2 hours), water and electricity only on long-term moorings, slipway, restaurant

Interesting archeological museum in the village.

PK 13.1	Creys-Malville nuclear power station (disused), private mooring l/b
PK 15.5	River enters narrow gorge (Défilé de Malarage)
PK 16.5	End of gorge, river widens, small island r/b
PK 16.8	Castle (Mérieu) l/b
PK 21.6	**Le Port de Groslée** suspension bridge (D60), pontoon moorings u/s r/b, no services, restaurant, village 500m r/b
PK 23.4	River divides, take middle channel, keeping towards l/b side
PK 24.7	U/s tip of La Sauge island, navigation in l/b arm
PK 25.4	**La Sauge** r/b
PK 27.6	**Évieu** bridge, village 200m r/b
PK 28.0	Navigation enters Brégnier-Cordon diversion canal r/b
PK 30.7	Brégnier-Cordon lock (projected, level with the power plant), rise 13.70m

Works could begin on this lock in 2023, after the renewal of the State's concession to the Compagnie Nationale du Rhône. A solution with a single lock was preferred to the solutions adopted upstream, with two separate locks and an intermediate basin. In the meantime, passage by boat elevator is possible using the upstream and downstream ramps.

PK 33.3	**Brégnier-Cordon** bridge (La Bruyère), *Maison du Rhône* environmental interpretation and visitor centre u/s r/b, village 1200m r/b
PK 34.9	Bridge (D992)
PK 35.2	**Murs-et-Gélignieux** boat moorings at camp site r/b, 04 79 87 23 84, 80 berths, water, electricity, slipway, no overnight mooring, opposite water sports area in canal widening, l/b
PK 35.9	Brégnier-Cordon dam l/b, end of diversion canal
PK 45.2	D/s tip of Chantemerle island, keep to l/b arm
PK 45.6	U/s tip of island, heading d/s keep to l/b arm
PK 47.2	Navigation enters Brens-Belley diversion canal, r/b (canoes and other portable boats continue right on bypassed Rhône, weirs with portage paths)
PK 47.7	Bridge (Brens-Virignin), D31a
PK 48.7	Belley downstream lock, rise 7.30m
PK 48.8	**Virignin** port de plaisance in the basin between the two locks, 120 berths, 30 visitor berths, night €5, water and electricity included, showers, slipway

Good mooring for Belley, while the village of Virignin is 2.5 km away.

PK 49.0	Belley upstream lock, rise 10.00m
PK 50.3	Bridge (La Combe), small basin, boat club u/s l/b
PK 52.2	**Belley** bridge (D1504, landing stage u/s r/b for trip boats only), town centre 2 km
PK 53.6	Belley-Magnieu pontoon moorings r/b (Belley 3200m)
PK 55.9	Canal enters narrow gorge

Haut-Rhône

PK 56.4	Bridge (Lit au Roi) at end of gorge
PK 56.5	Canal widens into Lac du Lit au Roi
PK 56.9	**Massignieu-de-Rives** municipal *port de plaisance* l/b, 04 79 42 10 03, 132 berths, water, electricity, showers, slipway, visitors contact *mairie@massignieu.fr*
PK 57.1	Île aux Oiseaux island in middle of lake
PK 57.9	End of lake, beach l/b
PK 58.6	Bridge (Cressin-Rochefort)
PK 61.9	Dam (Lavours) l/b, end of diversion canal
PK 62.3	*Junction with link to Lac du Bourget via Canal de Savières*, entrance lock l/b
PK 62.7	Moorings at Auberge de la Paillère, r/b
PK 64.7	Railway bridge (Vions), Aix-Culoz line
PK 66.9	Bridge (Pont de la Loi, D904), Culoz 1800m r/b
PK 67.2	Navigation enters Chautagne diversion canal, r/b
PK 70.1	Chautagne downstream lock, lift 7.30m
PK 70.3	Intermediate basin level with hydropower plant, mooring l/b (*halte nautique*)
PK 70.6	Chautagne upstream lock, rise 10.00m
PK 72.6	Overhead power lines
PK 75.8	End of diversion canal, Motz dam l/b
PK 77.7	Confluence of the river Fier, l/b
PK 78.3	Entrance to bay r/b (water sports area)
PK 79.3	New bridge (Seyssel), d/s tip of island
PK 79.6	U/s tip of island
PK 79.8	**Seyssel** municipal *port de plaisance* (Port Galatin) l/b, 24 pontoon berths, 04 50 56 15 30, free, water, electricity, slipway, wifi at *capitainerie*

Port Galatin, a bold investment by the local council, completed more than 10 years in advance of the current restoration project.

PK 80.0	Suspension bridge (Pont Vieux), Seyssel (Haute-Savoie) l/b, Seyssel (Ain) r/b
PK 81.0	Seyssel dam, upstream limit of navigation 200m below dam

Canal de Savières and Lac du Bourget

PK 0.0	*Junction with Rhône* (PK 129), Savières lock, lift 4.25m, do-it-yourself, push-button operation, bridge
PK 0.2	*Port de plaisance* l/b, 04 79 54 59 58, 124 berths, 4 visitor berths, night €25, water, electricity, shower at campsite, village 500m *mkeller@chanaz.fr*
PK 0.5	Turn north from Rhône into Canal de Savières
PK 0.7	Footbridge, entrance to small basin north bank
PK 0.9	**Chanaz** boat moorings (timber boardwalk) south bank, village with hotels, restaurants

This site is a little-known gem of the French waterways, nestled into the hillside. The village, boardwalk and high-arched pedestrian bridge form an enchanting landscape.

PK 1.2	Bridge (Chanaz)
PK 2.5	Private mooring north bank
PK 2.7	Private mooring north bank
PK 4.2	Portout bridge and pontoons for trip boats, restaurant
PK 4.4	**Portout** marina r/b, 04 79 35 00 51, 60 berths, night €17, water, electricity
PK 5.0	Stake marking entrance to Canal de Savières, navigation enters Lake Bourget

Straight line distances across lake to each point indicated, from the canal entrance heading south to the *port de plaisance* entrance channel (Port des Quatre Chemins).

PK 6.0	**La Châtière** *port de plaisance* west shore, 150 berths, 04 79 54 25 40, night €17, water, electricity, shower, slipway, Conjux 700m south
PK 6.7	Châtillon harbour beneath castle, north-east shore, 04 79 35 00 51, 150 berths, night €17, water, electricity, shower, attractive picnic area, restaurant
PK 8.5	Saint-Gilles private harbour west shore
PK 10.5	*Port de plaisance* west shore (for visit to abbey)
PK 10.8	**Hautecombe** royal abbey, west shore, burial place of princes and princesses of Savoy
PK 12.0	Brison harbour east shore beside railway halt, 04 79 35 00 51, 58 berths, small village
PK 13.4	Grésine *port de plaisance*, east shore, 131 berths
PK 15.1	Pointe de l'Ardre headland, east shore
PK 16.8	**Aix-les-Bains** Le Grand Port east shore, 04 79 61 28 29, 2900 berths including Le Petit Port, night €20, water, electricity (not at all moorings), showers, crane, slipway, town centre 3km *capitainerieaix@grand-lac.fr*
PK 18.2	Le Petit Port, east shore, managed by *capitainerie*, town centre 2.5km
PK 19.0	**Bourdeau** *port de plaisance*, west shore, 34 berths, château and village 70m above lake on west shore
PK 21.3	**Charpignat** *port de plaisance* west shore, 440 berths, 04 79 25 93 90, night €17, water, electricity, shower, slipway
PK 21.4	**Le Bourget-du-Lac** 2km south, small town, *port de plaisance* (Bras Mort de la Leysse), 94 berths
PK 22.5	Outer mole of breakwater marking channel entrance
PK 22.9	*Port de plaisance* (Terre-Nue), east shore, 28 berths
PK 23.0	*Port de plaisance* (Quatre Chemins) at southern end of lake, 04 79 35 00 51, 187 berths, night €17, water, electricity, shower, Chambéry 10km

53a. Canal d'Arles à Fos

This canal parallels the Rhône over a distance of 31km from the town of Arles on the left bank to the point where its course is joined by the new Canal du Rhône à Fos. It is virtually disused. It was closed as a through route in the 1970s when a salt barrier was built at the junction with the new cut, and it now serves mainly as a storm water drain for the land lying south-east of Arles. The canal is entered through the large entrance lock from the Rhône at Arles, giving access to the canal basin and moorings for barges as well as a boat club. From here on, the canal is under the jurisdiction of the Grand port maritime de Marseille. Navigation ends at Le Relai, where the salt marshes used to load salt for shipment up the Rhône. Although the canal is theoretically navigable down to Le Relai, the effective limit of navigation is now the canal basin in Arles, as the lack of maintenance excludes navigation through to the village of Mas-Thibert (PK 18.5).

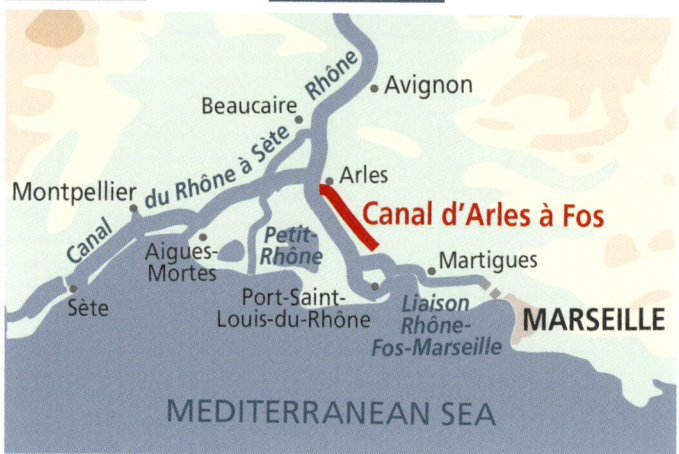

> The Canal d'Arles à Bouc was built on the line of an early Gallo-Roman canal. Works started in 1804, and the canal was opened in 1834. Part of the original canal, south of the salt barrier, has been enlarged and incorporated in the Liaison Rhône-Fos-Bouc. It is famous for the Pont de Langlois, the lift bridge painted by Van Gogh. It is potentially of interest for cruising, even as a dead end, offering views over the unspoilt landscape of La Crau, but no development is currently envisaged.

Navigation

The canal is today used only as moorings for barges, some waiting for service and repairs at the Chantiers Navals Barriol just outside the entrance lock. Navigation is not formally forbidden beyond the basin in Arles, but the lack of basic maintenance makes it virtually impracticable.

Locks

The entrance lock at Arles, replacing the original lock, which was filled in as part of the Rhône development works, was built to large dimensions, 165 by 12m. VNF needs to be given 48 hours notice for passage through the lock. A lock-keeper has to travel from Saint-Gilles lock (see Petit-Rhône) to operate the lock, 04 66 87 75 30. There are two other locks at Montcalde (PK 2.5) and L'Étourneau (PK 21), both permanently open, their gates having been removed. The width of the chambers is 8.00m.

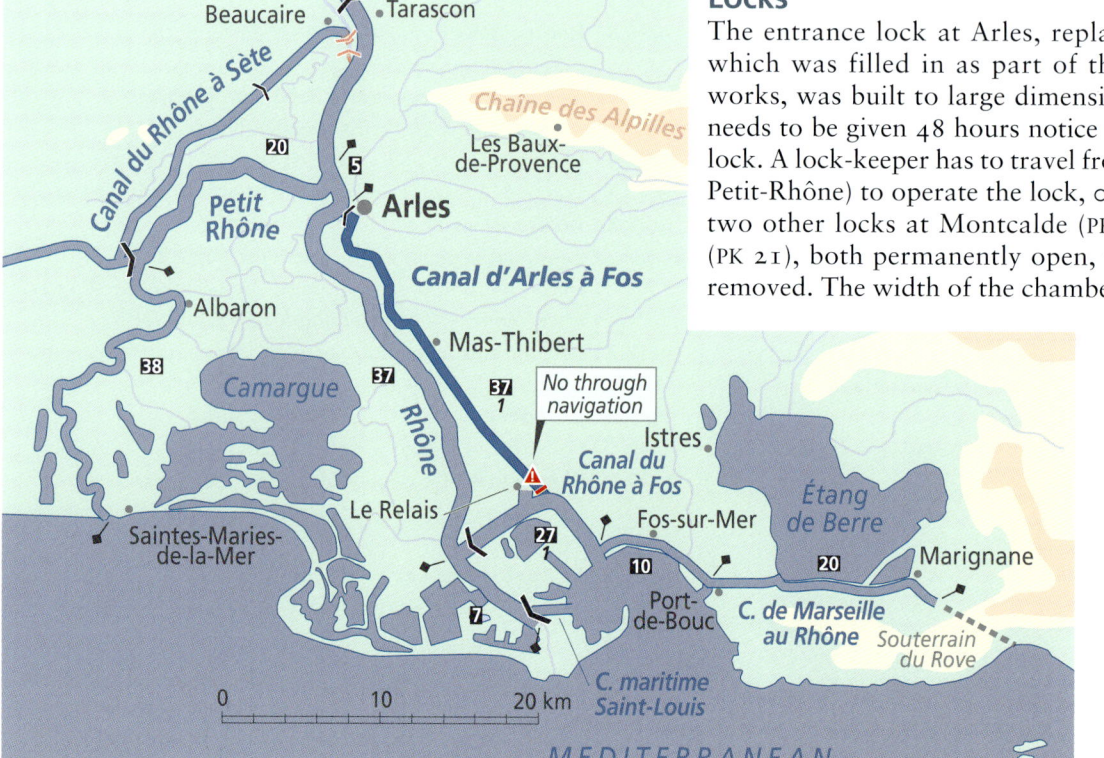

Key dimensions*	
(m)	
Length	165.00
Beam	12.00
Draught	2.50
Air draught	—

* Dimensions apply only to the entrance lock and the basin in Arles

Canal d'Arles à Fos

Draught
The maximum authorised draught is 1.20m, but this depth cannot be guaranteed and care is required, for there are local obstacles such as wrecked cars and domestic appliances.

Headroom
The maximum authorised air draught is 3.50m.

Authority
VNF Rhône-Saône
Subdivision Grand Delta:
– 1 quai de la Gare, 13200 Arles 04 90 96 00 85
  subdi.granddelta@vnf.fr

Route description

PK 0.0	**Junction with Rhône** on l/b d/s of Arles
PK 0.2	Entrance lock
PK 0.4	**Arles** canal basin, town centre 500m, water, electricity

As indicated above, 48 hours' notice must be given to VNF to pass through the lock into or out of the basin. There are no staff on site.

PK 0.5	Bridge (Réginet), boatyard d/s r/b
PK 0.9	Railway bridge
PK 1.2	**Arles** turning basin, *base nautique* moorings r/b managed by an association of *plaisanciers*, 07 81 74 18 67, 13 berths (all occupied by members), water, electricity
PK 2.5	Former lock (Montcalde), bridge, gates removed, and 'Van Gogh' lift bridge (Pont de Langlois)

Van Gogh's Pont de Langlois looking south. © WOLFGANG LAMPE

PK 4.5	Bridge (Allen)
PK 7.0	Bridge (Mas de la Ville)
PK 9.1	Bridge (Mollégès)
PK 14.5	Bridge (Beyne)
PK 18.5	**Mas-Thibert** bridge, moorings, small village l/b

A charming, sleepy little village set between the arid heathland of La Crau to the east and the lush Camargue to the west, worth exploring by bike from boat moorings in Arles or Port-Saint-Louis-du-Rhône.

PK 21.0	Former lock (Étourneau), gates removed
PK 31.0	**Le Relai** salt marshes r/b, effective limit of navigation
PK 31.3	Salt barrier just before junction with the Rhône-Fos canal (no through navigation)

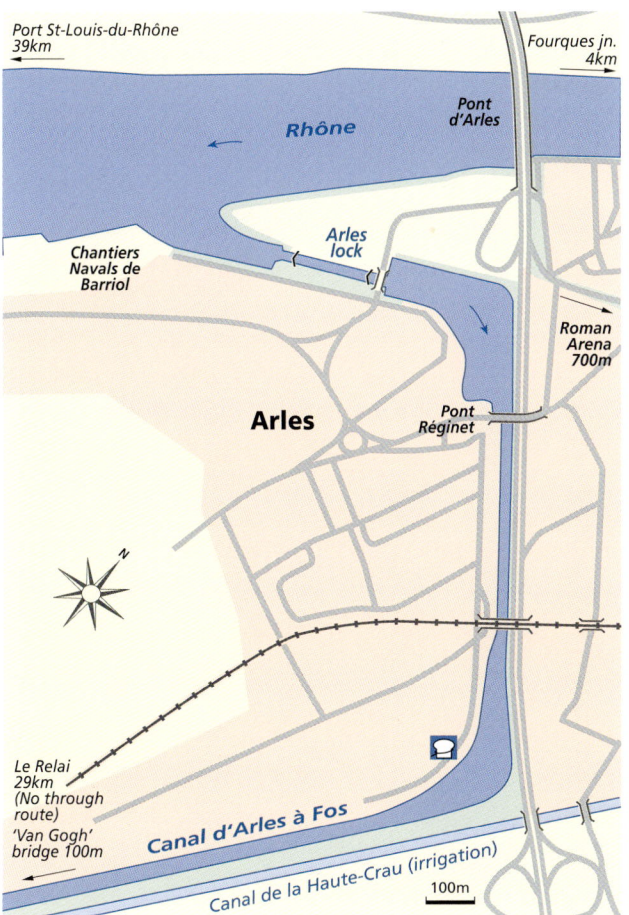

V – Southeast France

53b. Liaison Rhône-Fos-Marseille

THIS NAME COVERS A SERIES OF CANALS connecting Marseille to the Rhône, which have seen many changes over the years. The former Canal de Marseille au Rhône was closed as a through route after failure of a section of the 7km long Rove tunnel. Although the canal remained open to navigation it carried very little traffic, since the 38.50m barges for which it was designed were unable to navigate on the Rhône. The Canal maritime Saint-Louis (see under Rhône) was the obligatory route for commercial barges and the preferred route for boats. However, with completion of canalisation works on the Rhône in 1980, it became necessary to provide a safe link between the river and Fos (and Port-de-Bouc) for large push-tows, which had to split to negotiate the lock at Port-Saint-Louis, and were often delayed by rough water conditions in the Gulf of Fos. Enlargement of the existing Canal d'Arles à Fos would have been too costly, so a new canal was opened from the Rhône at PK 303 to Darse 1 at Fos. The canal uses the last 2km of the canal d'Arles à Fos, for which purpose the anti-salt lock had to be demolished. The replacement structure on the canal upstream of the junction with the new cut is an anti-salt barrier, which obstructs navigation. The Canal d'Arles à Fos is therefore closed as a through route. The Rhône-Fos link is not open to boats, which must continue to use the canal maritime Saint-Louis. The waterway described here is divided into several sections: the **Rhône-Fos junction canal** (PK 0-11), including the branch to be built to provide a direct link to the container terminal (shown on the map below), the basins of the **port of Fos** (PK 11-18), the **Fos-Bouc junction canal** (PK 18-27), finally the **Canal de Marseille au Rhône** (PK 27-47), including the Caronte Canal.

Navigation

The first section is open only to commercial traffic, and is given here for reference only. Boats will enter the waterway at Fos-sur-Mer, where the canal wraps round the edge of the Gulf of Fos to Port-de-Bouc.

Key dimensions*	
	(m)
Length	195.00
Beam	12.00
Draught	3.20
Air draught	–

This waterway is made up of several canals built at different times. The Canal d'Arles à Bouc was built under concession by a private company and opened in 1834. It provided sheltered access to the port of Bouc. The extension east to Marignane and Marseille, including the Canal de Caronte and the Rove tunnel, was built in 1911-1927, and the 22m wide tunnel was big enough for coastal shipping. It collapsed in 1963 and has remained closed since then. Restoration for various functions is regularly envisaged. In 1970, development of the port of Fos resulted in closure of part of the canal. A new anti-salt lock was built to give access from the canal to one of the basins (Darse 1) of the port of Fos, and the canal changed its name to Canal d'Arles à Fos. In 1982 the new high-capacity canal was built from the Rhône to Darse 1, and the anti-salt lock was demolished. The only route from Fos to Arles was then through the new canal. A new link for inland water transport is to be built between the canal and the container terminal (Darse 2).

Liaison Rhône-Fos-Marseille

The waterway is open to push-tows of international dimensions throughout, but the last section will remain a dead end unless the Rove tunnel is reopened. It should be noted that traffic through the narrow cutting in Port-de-Bouc is one-way only, controlled by lights. Navigation is sheltered and easy, although the canal narrows through the deep cutting approaching Port-de-Bouc, and traffic of all sorts of craft can be quite dense. The Caronte channel is effectively a ship canal. The effective limit of navigation is the small town of Marignane, since the approach to the Rove tunnel is silted up and may have extensive weed growth.

Locks
There is just one lock on the waterway, near the entrance from the Rhône at Barcarin. It has the same dimensions as the locks on the Rhône, 195 by 12m, and overcomes a difference in level ranging between a few centimetres and 2.30m when the Rhône is in flood. It is open to commercial traffic only.

Draught
The maximum authorised draught is 3.20m between the Rhône and Port-de-Bouc. The available depth in the last section to Marignane is approximately 2.00m.

Authority
Grand port maritime de Marseille:
– 23 place de la Joliette, BP 1965, 13226 Marseille cedex 02
04 91 39 40 00

Route description

PK 0.0	**Junction with Rhône** (PK 316)
PK 1.9	Lock (Barcarin), VHF 12, bridge
PK 4.7	Future junction with high-capacity link to Darse 2 container terminal
PK 9.0	Anti-salt barrier l/b
PK 9.7	Bridge (D268)
PK 9.8	Railway bridge
PK 11.3	Navigation enters Darse 1 of port of Fos (end of Rhône-Fos junction canal)
PK 16.0	Navigation enters Darse Sud of port of Fos
PK 18.3	Limit of Darse Sud, navigation enters Fos-Port-de-Bouc junction canal

This marks the start of the route available to *plaisanciers*.

PK 20.1	Turning basin (Carrefour des Joncs)
PK 21.6	**Fos-sur-Mer** bridge, village 700m
PK 24.5	Moorings south bank (for vessels waiting to proceed through one-way cutting)
PK 25.2	Railway bridge
PK 25.9	Bridge
PK 26.7	**Port-de-Bouc** railway and road bridges
PK 27.1	End of one-way cutting, basin (Port-de-Bouc)
PK 28.1	Entrance to Canal de Caronte
PK 30.3	Railway viaduct (Caronte)
PK 31.7	Motorway bridge (A55)
PK 32.2	Access to *port de plaisance* (Port de Ferrières) in north arm, 06 88 05 26 50, 180 berths, maximum 13m, night €22.50, water and electricity included, showers, wifi, pump-out, repairs *port-maritima@semovim-martigues.com*
PK 32.9	**Martigues** lift bridge (Jonquières), navigation enters Étang de Berre
PK 33.2	*Port de plaisance* (Port Sainte-Anne), 06 24 25 43 52, 180 berths, night €15, water, electricity, showers, crane, pump-out

Martigues is a delightful town, with its canal Saint-Sébastien lined by colourful boats and houses.

The Canal Saint-Sébastien in Martigues. © GILLES HARS

PK 38.1	Cutting (La Mède)
PK 38.2	**La Mède** quay, access to Étang de Berre opposite, village 700m
PK 39.8	Bridge (Jai)
PK 44.6	Basin (Bolmon)
PK 45.5	**Marignane** basin, village 1200m north, entrance to Gignac cutting
PK 45.8	Road and railway bridges (Floride)
PK 46.6	Bridge (Toës)
PK 47.4	Entrance to Rove tunnel (navigation interrupted)

What a fabulous project it would be, to fully restore the 7120m long tunnel and allow inland vessels to trade and carry passengers into Marseille. The canal could potentially accommodate cruise ships up to 11.50m in beam and with an air draught of 5.50m.

PK 54.5	Southern entrance to Rove tunnel at L'Estaque
PK 60.4	The original PK 0 of the Canal de Marseille au Rhône, at the Marseille cruise ship terminal (and dry docks)

Index

Waterway names in bold (excepting historic names and disused waterways)
Topics (historic or current, including personalities) in italics

Abergement-la-Ronce 85
Aisne, river 30
l'Aisne, Canal latéral à 30, 33
Aix-les-Bains 112, 115
Albigny 94
Allenjoie 80-81
d'Alsace, Grand Canal 66, 69, 76, 78
Ambly-Fleury 32
Ambly-sur-Meuse 29
Ampuis 103
Anchamps 26
Ancône 105
Ancy-sur-Moselle 37
Andance 104
Andancette 104
Apach 18, 34, 35
Aproport (Pagny) 88
Aramon 108
Arc-lès-Gray 64
Arciat 93
Ardennes, Canal des 4, 23, 27, 30-33
L'Ardoise 107
Arles 87, 101, 109, 116-18
d'Arles à Bouc, Canal 116, 118
d'Arles à Fos, Canal 87, 101, 109, 116-18
Ars-sur-Moselle 37
Arzviller 23, 40, 50
Asnières-sur-Saône 93
Attigny 32
Aubencheul-au-Bac 7
Aubrives 26
Aulne, river 6
Autet 63
authorities 21
  see also start of each waterway
automated locks 14-16
Auxonne 65
Avanne-Aveney 83
Aveyron 5
Avignon 101, 107, 108
Avignon Arm (Rhône) 107-8

Bacarin, Canal de 87
Bains-les-Bains 57
Balham 33
Bantanges 98
Bar-le-Duc 40, 43
Barcarin 119
The Barge Association (DBA) 4, 10, 19
Basle 23, 66, 67
Basse-Guénange 35
Basse-Ham 35
Baulay 62
Baume-les-Dames 82
Bauzemont 48
Bayon 56

Beaucaire 101, 108-9
Beinheim 68
Belfort 23, 85
Belfort Branch (Canal du Rhône au Rhin) 76, 78, 80, 85
Belgium 18, 23, 24
Belleville-sur-Saône 94
Belley 6, 112, 114
Berg-sur-Moselle 35
Besançon 23, 76, 82-3
Besançon Loop 78, 83
Biermes 32
Biesheim 69, 75
Bignicourt-sur-Saulx 42
Bischheim 51
Bisset-Harskirchen 53
Blavet, river 6
blue flag rule 13
Blue Links project 5
boat hire 11-12
boat licences (péage plaisance) 10-11
Bogny-sur-Meuse 26
bollards at locks 14
Bollène 106
Boofzheim 51, 74
books 18-20
Botans 76, 78, 85
Bouc (Port-de-Bouc) 116, 118, 119
Bouc, Canal d'Arles à 116, 118
Bourdeau 115
Bourget, Lake (Lac du) 101, 112, 113, 115
Le Bourget-du-Lac 115
Bourgogne, Canal de 60, 88, 90
Bourgogne, Canal entre Champagne et 60
Bourogne 80
Branges 97, 98
Branne 81
Bras-sur-Meuse 28
Braux 26
Bray 8
Brebotte 80
Brégnier-Cordon 6, 112, 114
Brest, Canal de Nantes à 6
bridge signs 15
Briord 114
Brittany Canals 5-6
Brumath 51

Caderousse Diversion Canal 106-7
Camargue 110
Caronte, Canal de 118, 119
Cassine 31
Cattenom 35
Cendrecourt 62
Centre, Canal du 87, 88
certificates of competence 9-10
CEVNI rules 9, 10
Chalampé 69
Chalon-sur-Saône 87, 88, 91-2
Chambéry 112

Champagne et Bourgogne, Canal entre 60
Champigneulles 47
Chanaz 6, 112, 115
Chantagne 6
Chantes 63
Charentenay 63
Charleville-Mézières 26-7
Charmes 56, 105
Charpignat 115
Château-d'Avignon 111
Château-Porcien 33
Château-Regnault 26
La Châtière 115
Chaumousey 57
Chavanay 104
Chavelot 57
Chazelles 91
Chémery-sur-Bar 31
Cher, river 6
Le Chesne 23, 31-2
Clerval 81
Coblence 34
Collonges 94
Colmar 5, 69, 71, 75
Colmar Branch (Canal du Rhône au Rhin) 69, 71, 74, 75, 76
Colombier-Fontaine 81
COLREGS 10
Commercy 29
Compiègne 7, 8
Condrieu 87, 103
Conflandey 62
Consenvoye 28
Constance 66
Contrisson 42
Contz-les-Bains 35
Corny-sur-Moselle 37
Corre 23, 55, 58, 60, 62
COVID-19 3-4
Crèches-sur-Saône 93
Crévechamps 56
Crévic 48
Cruas 105
cruise planning 1, 9-20, 21
Cruising Association 19-20
Cubry-lès-Soing 63
Cuisery 97, 98
Custines 34

Dannemarie 80
DBA (The Barge Association) 4, 10, 19
Deluz 82
Demange-aux-Eaux 44
Demangevelle 58
depths 13
  see also start of each waterway
Dettwiler 50
Deville 26
Diane-Capelle 53
Dieue-sur-Meuse 29
Dieulouard 37
dimensions, navigable 13
  see also start of each waterway
DIY locks 17
documentation 9
Dole 76, 84

Dombasle 48
Donchery 27
Donzère-Mondragon Diversion Canal 106
Douai 6
Doubs, river 18, 23, 76, 81-4, 87, 91, 96
draught 13
  see also start of each waterway
Drusenheim 68
Dun-sur-Meuse 28

Eckwersheim 51
Ecuelles 91
Editions du Breil 19
Eglingen 79
Einville-au-Jard 48
Épinal 55, 57, 59
Épinal Branch (Canal des Vosges) 55, 57, 59
Erstein 74
Erstein-Krafft 74
Escaut, river 6, 8
Eschau 74
l'Est, Canal de 24, 39, 55, 60
L'Estaque 119
Étang de Berre 119
EU 5-10
European Boating Association 10
Euville 29
Evieu 114

Fains-Véel 43
Fareins 94
Faux Remparts, Canal des 51, 71, 72, 73
Fesches 80, 81
flags 9, 13-14
Flavigny 56
Fleurville 92, 99
Fléville-devant-Nancy 59
Flize 27
Fluviacarte 19
Fontaines-sur-Saône 94
Fontenoy-le-Château 57-8
Les Forges 57
formalities 9-11
Fort-Louis 68
Fos (port & town) 87, 101, 109, 118, 119
Fos, Canal d'Arles à 87, 101, 109, 116, 117, 118
Fos, Canal du Rhône à 109, 116, 117
Fos, Gulf of 18, 101, 109, 118, 119
Fos-Port-de-Bouc Junction Canal 118, 119
Fos-Rhône *see* Liaison Rhône-Fos-Marseille; Rhône-Fos Junction Canal
Fouchécourt 62
Foug 44-5
Fourques 101, 110, 111
Franche-Comté, Canal de 77
Freycinet (standard class) waterways 13, 14-16

121

Index

Friesenheim 74
Friesenheim-Rhinau link canal 74
Froidefontaine 80
Frouard 37, 38, 40, 46-7
Frouard Branch (Canal de la Marne au Rhin) 37, 38, 46
Fumay 26
Fumel 4

Genay 94
Génicourt-sur-Meuse 29
Gergy 91
Germany 18, 23, 34, 40, 52, 76
Gerstheim 74
Gigny-sur-Saône 92
Girancourt 57
Givet 4, 18, 24-5
Givors 103
Givry 32
Gondrexange 40, 49, 52, 53
grand gabarit (high-capacity) waterways 13, 14
Grande Saône, river 85, 87, 88-96, 101
Grau d'Orgon 110, 111
Gray 60, 64
Greffern 68
Gripport 56
Groslée, Le Port de 114
Güdingen 52
Guerlédan 6
guides (publications) 18-20

Hagenbach 79
Hagondange Branch (Moselle) 36
Ham 7, 25-6
Hannogne-Saint-Martin 31
Harskirchen 53
Hauconcourt 36
Haut (Upper) Rhône, river 6, 101, 112-15
Haute-Saône, Canal de Montbéliard à la 23, 81
Hautecombe 115
Haybes 26
headroom & heights 13
  see also start of each waterway
Heidwiller 79
Héming 49
Herbitzheim 54
Hesse 49
Heuilley-sur-Saône 64-5
hire boats 11-12
Hochfelden 51
Hoenheim 51
Houdelaincourt 46
Houdelaincourt Branch (Canal de la Marne au Rhin) 40, 46
Houillères de la Sarre, Canal des 52
Houillon, Port du 49, 53
hours of navigation 18
Huningue 69
Huningue Branch (Canal du Rhône au Rhin) 69, 78

Iffezheim 66-7, 68
Ile Napoléon 79

Ill, river 70-73
Illfurth 79
Illkirch-Graffenstaden 74
Imray publications 19, 20
Inland Waterways International 4
Inor 28
insurance 9
l'Isle-sur-le-Doubs 76, 81

Jarville-la-Malgrange 48
Jassans-Riottier 94
Joigny-sur-Meuse 26
Jonage, Canal de 112
Jouy à Metz, Canal de 34, 37, 39
Juliana Canal 24
Jussey 62

Kehl 68, 69
Kembs 66, 69, 76, 78
Kœnigsmacker 34, 35
Kunheim 75

La Châtière 115
La Mède 119
La Roche de Glun 104
La Sauge 114
La Truchère 97, 98
La Voulte 105
Lacroix-sur-Meuse 29
Lagarde 48
Laifour 26
Lake (Lac du) Bourget 101, 112, 113, 115
Lallaing 6
Lamarche-sur-Saône 65
Laneuveville-devant-Nancy 40, 48, 59
L'Ardoise 107
Lauterbourg 66, 67, 68
Le Bourget-du-Lac 115
Le Chesne 23, 31-2
Le Port de Groslée 114
Le Pouzin 105
Le Relai 116, 117
Lechâtelet Arm (Grande Saône) 96
Lérouville 29
Les Forges 57
Les Roches de Condrieu 87, 103
L'Estaque 119
Liaison Dunkerque-Escaut 8
Liaison Rhône-Fos-Marseille 116, 118-19
licences 9-11
lights 15, 16
Ligny-en-Barrois 43
Liny-devant-Dun 28
Liverdun 37, 46
locks & lock-keepers 14-17
  see also start of each waterway
Loisy 98
Longeaux 44
Longeville-lès-Metz 37
Losne 65, 90
Lot 4-5
Louhans 87, 97, 98
Lumes 27
Lupstein 50

Lutzelbourg 50
Luxembourg 23, 34
Lyon 18, 87, 88, 95-6, 112, 114
Lyon-Confluence (Lyon-La Mulatière) 87, 95-6, 101, 103, 114

Mâcon 88, 93
Maizey 29
Maizières-lès-Metz 36
Malling 35
Malroy 36
Malzéville 47
Mangonville 56
Mantoche 64
maps 18-20
Marbache 37
Marignane 118, 119
Maron 38
Marne au Rhin, Canal de la 23, 24, 34, 40-51, 70
Marseille 87, 101, 116, 118, 119
Marseille au Rhône, Canal de 118, 119
Martigues 87, 119
Mas de Baumelles 111
Mas-Thibert 116, 117
Massignieu-de-Rives 115
mast manoeuvres 18
La Mède 119
Mediterranean (*routes*) 18, 76, 87, 101
Méloménil 57
Messein 55, 56
Metz 34, 36-7, 39
Metz, Canal de Jouy à 34, 37, 39
Meuse, river 18, 23, 24
Meuse, Canal de la 23, 24-9, 30, 31, 44
Midi, Canal du 18, 87
Millery, 37
Mines de Fer de la Moselle, Canal des 34, 36
Mittersheim 53
Mondelange 36
Montalieu-Verceu 114
Montbéliard 23, 81
Montbéliard à la Haute-Saône, Canal de 8
Montélimar 106
Montélimar Diversion Canal 105-6
Montgon 32
Monthermé 26
Montigny Arm (Moselle) 36-7
Montigny-lès-Metz 39
Montmerle-sur-Saône 94
Montreux-Château 80
Montreux-Vieux 80
Montureaux-lès-Baulay 62
mooring 11, 17, 21
Moselle, river 8, 18, 23, 34-9, 40, 46, 52, 55
Moselle, Canal des Mines de Fer de la 34, 36
Moulins-lès-Metz 37
Mouzay 28

Mouzon 27-8
Mulhouse 8, 23, 70, 76, 78-9
Munchhausen 68
Muntzenheim 75
Murs-et-Géligneux 114

Nancy 23, 40, 47
Nancy Branch (Canal des Vosges) 40, 48, 55, 59
Nancy-Frouard 34, 38, 46
Nantes à Brest, Canal de 6
Nanteuil-sur-Aisne 33
Napoléon, Canal de 77
navigable dimensions 13
  see also start of each waterway
navigation, hours of 18
navigation signs & signals 14, 15
Netherlands 18, 24
Neuf-Brisach 69, 70, 71, 75, 76
Neuves-Maisons 34, 38, 55
Neuville-Day 4, 32
Neuville-sur-Ornain 43
Neuville-sur-Saône 94
Niderviller-Neubruch 49
Niffer 66, 69, 76, 77, 78-9
Niffer Branch (Canal du Rhône au Rhin) 69, 76
Nogent 8
Nord, Canal du 7
North Sea-Mediterranean Link 8
Nouzonville 26

Obenheim 74
Offendorf 68
Oise, river 4, 7, 8
l'Oise, Canal de la Sambre à 4
Omicourt 31
Orchamps 84
Orléans, Canal d' 6
Ormoy 62
Ostwald 70
Ougney-la-Roche 82
overtaking 13-14

Pagny (Grande Saône) 87, 88
Pagny-sur-Meuse 44
Pagny-sur-Moselle 37
Parcieux 94
Pargny-sur-Saulx 42
Parroy 48
Passavant-la-Rochère 58
Petit Rhône, river 18, 87, 101, 109, 110-111
Petite Saône, river 23, 60-65, 76, 88
Pierre-la-Treiche 38
planning a cruise 1, 9-20, 21
Plichancourt 42
Plobsheim 69, 74
Pompey 37, 38, 46, 47
Pont-à-Bar 27, 30, 31
Pont-du-Bois 58
Pont-à-Mousson 37
Pont-de-Vaux 87, 99-100
Pont-de-Vaux, Canal de 99-100
Pontailler-sur-Saône 65

Index

Ponthion 42
Port d'Atelier 62
Le Port de Groslée 114
Port du Houillon 49, 53
Port Napoléon 109
Port-de-Bouc 116, 118, 119
Port-Saint-Louis-du-Rhône 18, 87, 101, 109, 118
Port-Sainte-Marie 49
Port-sur-Saône 62, 78
Portout 115
Pouilly 28
Le Pouzin 105
priority rules & etiquette 13
publications 18-20
Puy-l'Evêque 5
Quitteur 63
radio telephone ship licence 9
Ranchot 84
Rans 84
Ratenelle 98
Ray-sur-Saône 63
Recologne 63
registration documents 9
Reichstett 51
Le Relai 116, 117
Remelfing 54
Remilly 27
Rethel 33
Rettel 35
Revigny 42
Revin 26
Reyssouze 99, 100
Rhin (Rhine), river 6, 8, 23, 34, 66-9
Rhin, Canal de la Marne au 23, 24, 34, 40-51, 70
Rhin, Canal du Rhône au 23, 60, 76-85
Rhin, Canal du Rhône au (Northern Branch) 5, 18, 23, 70-75
Rhinau 69, 74
Rhine-Rhône waterway 6, 8
Rhône, river 6, 8, 18, 87, 96, 101-9, 118,
  see also Haut (Upper) Rhône; Petit Rhône
Rhône, Canal de Marseille au 118, 119
Rhône à Fos, Canal du 109, 116, 117
Rhône au Rhin, Canal du 23, 60, 76-85
Rhône au Rhin, Canal du (Northern Branch) 5, 18, 23, 70-75
Rhône à Sète, Canal du 8, 18, 101, 110, 111
Rhône-Fos Junction Canal 118, 119
Rhône-Fos-Marseille, Liaison 116, 118-19
Richardménil 56
Rigny 64
Rilly-sur-Aisne 31, 32
La Roche de Glun 104
Rochefort-sur-Nenon 84
Les Roches de Condrieu 87, 103
Roquemaure 107
Roubaix Canal 5

routes (through routes) 18
  see also Mediterranean
Rouvrois 29
Rove Tunnel 87, 118, 119
Royal Yachting Association 9, 10, 11
rules & regulations 9-11
rules of the road 13-14
Rupt-sur-Saône 63

Saarbrücken 52
Saint-Aignan 31
Saint-Amand-sur-Ornain 44
Saint-Armand-les-Eaux 6
Saint-Bernard 94
Saint-Etienne-des-Sorts 106
Saint-Germain-au-Mont d'Or 94
Saint-Gilles 101, 110, 111
Saint-Gilles, Canal de 110, 111
Saint-Jean-de-Losne 23, 60, 65, 87, 88, 90
Saint-Joire 44
Saint-Laurent 93
Saint-Louis, Canal Maritime 101, 109, 118
Saint-Martin-Belle-Roche 93
Saint-Mihiel 29
Saint-Roman-des-Îles 93
Saint-Symphorien 76, 85, 88
Saint-Vallier 104
Saint-Vit (Canal du Rhône au Rhin) 84
Saint-Vite (Lot) 4
Sambre à l'Oise, Canal de la 4
Sampigny 29
Sanchey 57
Saône, river 8, 23, 55, 76, 85, 101, see also Grande Saône; Petite Saône
Sarralbe 54
Sarre 23, 52, 54
Sarre, Canal de la 23, 40, 49, 52-4
Sarreguemines 52, 54
Sarreinsming 54
La Sauge 114
Sault-Brénaz 112, 114
Sauvage 111
Sauville 31
Sauvoy 44
Saverne 40, 50
Savières, Canal de 6, 112, 113, 115
Savoyeux 63
Scarpe inférieure, river 6
Scey-sur-Saône 62-3
Schiltigheim 51
Schwindratzheim 51
Scy-Chazelles 37
seasons 18
Sedan 4, 24, 27
Seille, river 87, 92, 97-8
Seine, 8, 16
Seine-Nord Europe Canal 7-8
Selles 58
Seltz 68
Semuy 30, 32, 33
Sermaize-les-Bains 42
Serrières 104
Sète 8

Sète, Canal du Rhône à 8, 18, 101, 110, 111
Seurre 87, 88, 90, 96
Seveux 63
Seyssel 112, 115
ship's radio licence 9
Sierck-les-Bains 35
signs & signals 14, 15
Sivry-sur-Meuse 28
Small Ships Register 9
Soing 63
Somerville, Robert 17
Somme, Upper Canal de la 7
Souffelweyersheim 51
sound signals 15
Soyons 105
speed limits 14
Steinbourg 50
Stenay 28
Strasbourg 18, 23, 40, 51, 66, 68-9, 70-73
Switzerland 6, 23, 66-7, 76
Sylvéréal 111

Tain-l'Hermitage 104
Tannay 31
Tannois 43
Tarascon 108
Tavaux-Cité 85
taxes 9
Thaon-les-Vosges 57
Thiélouze 57
Thionville 35
Thoissey 93
Thoraise 84
Thugny-Trugny 32
time of day 18
time of year 18
tipping 16
Toul 34, 38, 40, 41, 45-6
Toulouse 110
Tournon-sur-Rhône 104
Tournus 92, 97
towpaths see start of each waterway
trailer-sailing 11
Traves 63
Trévenans 85
Tréveray 44
Trévoux 94
Trier 52
Tronville 43
Troussey 24, 29, 40, 55
La Truchère 97, 98
turning 14

Uchizy 92
Uckange 35
Uzemain 57

Vacherauville 28
Valdieu 80
Valence 104
Valence l'Epervière 87, 104-5
Vallabrègues 87, 101, 108
Vallabrègues Diversion Canal 108-9
Vandières 37
Varangéville 48
VAT documentation 9
Velaines 43
Vendenheim 51

Verdun (Meuse) 24, 28-9
Verdun-sur-le-Doubs 87, 91, 96
Vertuzey 29
Vésines 93
Vienne 103
Vieux-lès-Asfeld 30, 33
vignettes 10-11
Villefranche-sur-Saône 94
Villeneuve-lès-Avignon 107
Villeurbanne 112
Vilosne 28
Vincey 56
Vireux-Wallerand 26
Viriginin 114
Vitry-le-François 40, 42
Viviers 87, 106
Viviers-du-Lac 112
VNF (Voies Navigables de France) 1, 3-11, 21
Void 44
Voncq 33
Vosges, Canal des 18, 23, 34, 55-9, 60
La Voulte 105
Vouziers 30, 33
Vouziers Branch (Canal des Ardennes) 31, 33
Vrizy 33

Waltenheim 51
waterway classes 13
weather 18
websites 9, 19-21
Welferding 54
Wickerschwihr 75
Wittring 54

Xouaxange 49
Xures 48

Yonne, river 16

Zetting 54
Zillisheim 79

123